THE MEDICINE OF MEMORY

The Medicine of Memory

A MEXICA CLAN IN CALIFORNIA

by Alejandro Murguía

 UNIVERSITY OF TEXAS PRESS, AUSTIN

Requests for permission to reproduce material from this work
should be sent to Permissions, University of Texas Press,
P.O. Box 7819, Austin, TX 78713-7819.

♾ The paper used in this book meets the minimum requirements of
ANSI/NISO Z39.48-1992 (R1997) (Permanence of Paper).

Library of Congress Cataloging-in-Publication Data

Murguía, Alejandro, 1949–
    The medicine of memory : a Mexican clan in California / by
Alejandro Murguía. — 1st ed.
        p.   cm.
    Includes bibliographical references and index.
    ISBN 0-292-75265-2 (alk. paper) — ISBN 0-292-75267-9 (pbk. : alk. paper)
    1. Mexican Americans—California—Biography.   2. Mexican Americans—
California—History.   3. Mexican American families—California—History.
4. Aztecs—First contact with Europeans—California—History.   5. Lugo family.
6. Olivas family.   7. Murguía family.   8. Murguía, Alejandro, 1949– .   9. Mexican
Americans—California—San Francisco—Biography.   10. San Francisco (Calif.)—
Biography.   I. Title.
    F870.M5M87   2002
    929'.2'0973—dc21   2002010187

Frontispiece: Mission Dolores, 1856, watercolor, José Clemente Orozco Farías.
    Front cover photos: Soledad Lugo, c. 1944; the Murguías (standing, left to right) Arturo,
Alvar, Enrique, Luis, (sitting, left to right) Petra and Margarita, and two unidentified
children, Mexico City, c. 1940; (background) Mission Dolores, 1856, watercolor, José
Clemente Orozco Farías.
    Back cover: (left to right) Ygnacio Lugo, Ramona Nájera Olivas Lugo, and Antonio
Lugo, Colonia Horcasitas, San Fernando Valley, 1936. Photo courtesy of Roberto Olivas.

To Soledad Lugo and Enrique García Murguía,
whose memory is my medicine,
and for Marisol Mineya Murguía,
so she will always remember

CONTENTS

PREFACE

Maize for the Metate

Memory is history, but history is not always memory. By that I mean that memory is not always included in the history of this country. Take my memory of California as an example. My California is different from the histories I had to endure as a young man, the ones that left me out of the picture while rugged white pioneers conquered the West. In that history I am merely a passive figure, useful only as a foil for actions taken by others. This sort of history I do not accept, not because I'm stubborn (which I am), but because it's a simplistic view and at its core untrue.

The Medicine of Memory argues that without historical memory, I am a displaced person, severed from the land, nothing and no one. My assertion is that we all have historical memory. You don't have to be a scholar to discover your historical memory, you just have to be curious. Go explore history for yourself, in public libraries or archives, in state parks and historical sites, even in petroglyph caves; interpret it your way, demystify it, strip it of its privileged, elitist, inaccessible stance, as if it were pure and you were going to spoil it with your dark soiled hands.

Every writer will tell you that stories are healing, liberating. But only if we write ourselves into history, expropriate it in a sense, redefine it, rewrite it even, can it be liberating, a means of breaking down oppression and confusion. If I appear in history, then I have a chance to understand myself. And I am a complex person, a twenty-first-century mestizo, and even that concept needs some fine-tuning, a reevaluation, and a new definition. I must also warn you that some wounds just won't heal, no matter how we write them. Some insist on festering, making closure elusive, perhaps not achievable until another generation comes along to better understand our past: how we were killed and massacred and how the evidence was buried in archives or deep within our memory.

The approach to writing history has changed a lot since I was a young man. The new Chicano historians are much more inclusive, are more conscious of different viewpoints, and are gradually recovering our history.[1] But when I think of California, I still find many incidents whose place in history leaves me unsatisfied. To insist on taking another look at history implies a challenge to the belief that history is certain. And the most certain truth about California history is that it is uncertain. The past is far too complex to have just one fixed version. The past is like a *trensa*, a braid of many different strands twined together, and each historian picks one strand to follow, reject, recover, or rewrite.

It is clear to me that history depends on the writer's subjective arrangement of details and events. Whenever you look at the past, whether through the lens of memory or the opaqueness of text, the view is distorted by the viewer's own subjective place in the present. Objectivity is a myth. Historians who claim objectivity are fooling themselves and their audience.

Since history is subjective, there is no zero degree of bias. Take, for example, Hubert Howe Bancroft's massive multivolume history of California, based on his impressive collection of manuscripts and documents. In the final analysis, his California is mostly his subjective interpretation (and the subjective interpretation of those he employed to write sections of it), with all his biases (and his writers' biases) on race, ethnicity, class, and gender, which are obvious to any careful reader.[2] With a stroke of the pen, for instance, he dismisses a central event of Mariano Guadalupe Vallejo's narrative as "purely imaginary."[3]

So here's my first confession: I am not objective; this is not an objective story. I'll be the first to admit that my California is subjective; there is no objective wall between the subject and myself. I am not writing history per se; instead I am unraveling the strands of time/space/memory that define my presence here. I propose a history based not on "objective" Western methodologies, which are not "objective" anyway, but on intuition, memory, and landscape; not on linear chronological time, but on circling the events till they become understandable to me.

Historians are trained to find patterns;[4] I have looked for the pattern of names—the Lugos, Olivas, and Murguías—that appear in history and have tried to make sense of the whole through their individual experiences. In a way I have engendered my own line back through history. But it is not exclusively family names that I relate to; I also use the Nahuatl concept of *calpulli* (clans), the shared characteristics and experiences, as a template of my landscape. Besides researching the usual sources, I also researched my imagination. I looked at the landscape as a guide to what I needed to tell. I wrote about those places that hurt and tried to figure out why they hurt. What atavistic memory drove me to the site of the lynching of a Mexican woman, or to the Modoc Lava Beds? All I can say is that I was compelled to understand these events from my own perspective. Now as I look back, most everything in this book circles around resistance and survival—resistance to annihilation; survival because we were not annihilated.

So who am I? *Yo soy* Californio, Latino, Mexica, Xicano, or whatever you call me. I am one of those faceless millions who seem to have popped up overnight and you now see everywhere. If you spot me on the street, my historical connection to the land you call California, and I call Califas, is hardly obvious. But believe me, it is here and it is deep. I am a native son; my placenta is buried in the backyard of my mother's house in the barrio of Horcasitas, where her family, the Lugos, are a vast clan that settled in and helped populate Southern California. So I have never considered myself a newcomer here. The first diaries of overland exploration cite the name Murguía on the topography of the Bay Area—Punto Murguía is located just beyond present-day Point Reyes—yet our name has long been erased from all current maps.

Now comes the question of language. I am bilingual and I love it. To me, being bilingual is natural, no big deal. My father always insisted that we master Spanish and English. His advice was that in knowing two languages we would be able to communicate with twice as many people and also serve as a bridge between Mexico and the United States. My father, with his sixth-grade education, has more sense and wisdom than recent governors of this state do. How hard can it be to handle both languages? Néstor García Canclini, in *Hybrid Cultures*, tells of meeting a Zapotec Indian who handled three languages and cultures (Zapotec, Spanish, and English) and switched instantly back and forth without missing a beat, or losing his Zapotec identity.[5] If we don't move in the sphere of bilingual, trilingual, multilingual, or even interlingual worlds, we'll get left further behind by the day.

The attacks on the Spanish language have been constant and continuous since 1846. Just in my lifetime I've survived two waves of anti-Spanish furor, one in the sixties and one in the nineties. So for me to be bilingual, to be a part of the Spanish-speaking world, is a right worth fighting for. I love the sense of expansion that I get from knowing more than one language; I love how English takes me one place and Spanish a different place. English gives me a sense of precision, and because it is so flexible, it allows me to borrow from other languages. *Español* allows me to look at the world with a different lens, to save the language and culture, to keep the world from being homogenized; with Spanish I can describe things, concepts, and relationships that don't exist in Anglo-Saxon culture—piñata, *mestizaje*, *compadre*. With Spanish I can love in the most romantic language; English allows me to argue with my opponents or to curse them in their own tongue so they understand precisely that they are bastards, sons of bitches. Spanish makes me part of Cervantes and García Márquez; English gives me Donne and Ondaatje. Why should I give up one for the other, when I can have my cake and eat it twice?

Spanish also puts me in touch with a part of California that English can't. Through Spanish, I'm part of the first diarists who came through here and jotted down their impressions of this land; I see the landscape through their eyes, feel it through their words. I am part of California in a way I could never be if I was monolingual. To me, being monolingual is madness, ignorance, and a sign of being culturally challenged. Whoever has traveled in other parts of the world knows that people speak more than one language. It is a shame that in California, a truly multiethnic land, the cause célèbre is monolingualism. The public school system in particular lacks bilingual teachers, not to mention texts. Imagine how innovative our schools would be with a more bilingual-bicultural curriculum. If we lose our Spanish, whether through politics or acculturation, we'll be cut off from the continent we belong to, the source of our culture and power; we'll be relegated to isolated islands of thought, able to understand our bosses' commands but unable to express who we really are.

But we Latinos need to express ourselves, otherwise we're just figures in the background making wild gestures like actors in a silent movie. We need to place ourselves on center stage, to rid ourselves of complexes as immigrants. To do that we must destroy the belief that we don't belong here, that we just arrived and therefore haven't contributed to this society, or that our language is foreign to this landscape. These are terribly false assumptions. We have not just arrived. We have not always been poor and landless and powerless. Before we can write history, we must first know language, and for us, language is a two-headed beast. At one time, Spanish was the language of California, and that is important to remember because it shows how deep our roots go. Just look around you. Can you pronounce the Spanish place-names in your city, town, or neighborhood? If you can name the ground you stand on, if you know where the bones are buried, the land is yours. And since 50 percent or more of the population of California now speaks Spanish, that language is as important to us as English. I only wish I knew more languages—Japanese, for instance, or a little Russian besides *Nasrovia*. Being bilingual-bicultural brings me closer to California's past and future. Spanish is the future language of California, just as it was the past language of California. English, of course, is the present, so this book is in English, though I consider it the bastard tongue.

• • •

People who live in California deny the past. In this land, what matters is keeping up with the current trends, fads, or latest computer gizmo. And as the present moment fades, our memories of it are discarded like yesterday's newspaper. We go through our daily lives—raise kids, shop at the mall, eat at our favorite *taquería* or Thai restaurant—without the time, energy, or desire to reflect on what happened last week, much less what happened ten years ago, or a hundred. We also pretend ours is a perfect state, a sort of nirvana on earth, with wealth and pleasure enough for everyone, and we delude ourselves that we live blessed by God and flag, and that is how it's always been. But if you want to raise the hackles of those who live in comfort and delusion, just take a look at our collective past. If you look at the number of lynchings that occurred during the Gold Rush, suddenly the romanticism associated with this event goes right out the window. Our pretensions about a "Golden State" with a romantic past don't stand up to scrutiny. The past is the prime enemy of California's own vision of itself.

I suspect we also turn our back on the past because we simply don't want to know that California history is filled with vicious and violent incidents. It is also filled with contradictions that are difficult to reconcile, since we have few heroes and many villains. The difference for me is that I want to know what my place here is. What is it that draws me and keeps me here? Intuitively, I've always felt this land was mine. Now, through writing this book, I've come to understand why this is so. Not only is this land mine, but I will not be removed, deported, or relocated from it. I am here permanently; this is my space I'm telling you about.

I am interested in history, but I'm not a historian. I'm not a journalist either. (I've been accused of being a poet, but that's another issue.) In writing about California, I let myself be guided by my own interests, by the stories that piqued me: mostly stories excluded from the official histories and anthologies or, if they are included, given little importance. I'm writing somewhat like José del Carmen Lugo or Mariano Guadalupe Vallejo, the dispossessed Californios who wrote about their lives in the 1870s; at least that's been my approach. Although I do not have Vallejo's prestige or influence, I fuse my own story with the political and cultural history of my time. In the words of Señor Vallejo written back in 1875: "It is my story, not yours, I propose to tell. . . . If I give my story it must be worthy of the cause and of me."[6]

I have approached these stories with the lay reader in mind, as opposed to the specialist or the professor. I call them stories because of a sentence in Tomás Eloy Martínez's book on Eva Perón: "If history—as appears to be the case—is just another literary genre, why take away from it the imagination, the foolishness, the indiscretion, the exaggeration, and the defeat that are the raw materials without which literature is inconceivable?"[7]

My approach is that history is not static, it's not something cast in stone. I'm concerned with living history; I have deliberately inserted myself into the story. The past in this case is also the present. In the process of writing this book, I used what came my way, just as a Huichol shaman crossing the desert picks only the peyote buds that appear along his path. I wanted chance to intercede as it does in life. The texts I found, and the quirky things that happened in my life on a day-to-day basis—all of it was maize for the metate. To give just one example: for weeks I searched in libraries for an account of the battle of San Pasqual. I found it one bleak Sunday at a friend's house in an old magazine that he'd kept for years, not knowing the reason was so he could show it to me and I could insert it into this story.

Academics and purists will criticize my methods, but every native son has the right to tell his roots. I don't know if being born here gives me the right to take this approach, but what of it? I did not ask anyone's permission to live here, and I won't ask it for what I'm going to say. I'm not even sure this is history as much as it is a retelling and re-imagining of selected events that I believe have shaped this land and have shaped me. This is my California history, my memories, richly subjective and atavistic, though I stay as accurate as I can to what Gore Vidal calls "the agreed-upon facts."[8] Whether you accept my story or not, I list my sources.

• • •

History—as the saying goes—is written by the victors, never by the vanquished. I am neither of the victors nor the vanquished. If anything, I am of the survivors—the curious survivors who have brooded on the past and wondered about the future. What is my history of California? I know for sure that it has many facets, each angle reflecting a particular light. I consider indigenous creation myths as important as scientific geological studies. The California in this book exists in my memory and in my subjective perceptions; this book is as much about this *pequeño país* as it is about myself—if and where these two roads cross is something for the reader to decide.

In the end, though, I stand with Oscar Wilde when he says, "The only duty we have toward history is to rewrite it."[9]

THE MEDICINE OF MEMORY

Mission Dolores, 1856.
Photo courtesy of San Francisco History Center, San Francisco Public Library.

Colonia Horcasitas, 1936.
Ygnacio Lugo, Ramona Nájera Olivas Lugo, Antonio Lugo

"La Sally," Soledad Lugo, circa 1944.

"El Catrín," Enrique García Murguía, in Mexico City, 1943.

Enrique García Murguía (fourth from left, with hat brim backwards) as foreman for Sunkist, 1957.

Sixteenth and Valencia Street in San Francisco's Mission District at the time of the influx of Central American immigrants, October 1958. The five-story building is the Gartland Apartments, which became the first victim of gentrification when an arson fire burned it to the foundation in 1982. Twelve people died in the fire. Photo courtesy of San Francisco History Center, San Francisco Public Library.

Roberto Vargas (left) and the author, marching down Mission Street during the first Nicaraguan solidarity rally, December 1974. Photo by Alejandro Stuart; author's collection.

The poster of the first demonstration for the FSLN, 1975. Printed by La Raza Silk Screen Center. Courtesy of Mission Gráfica Archives.

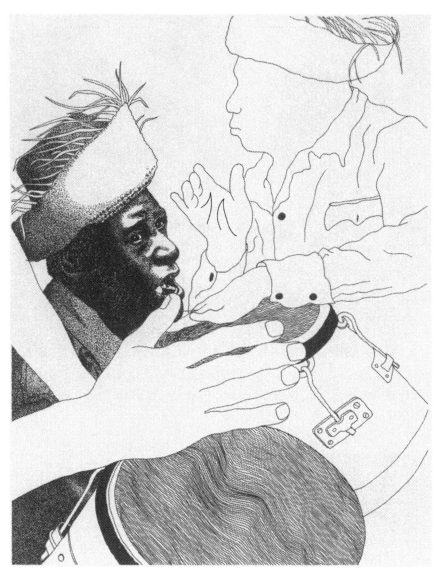

Inside front cover of *Tin-Tan* magazine, No. 2, 1975. Copyright © Juan R. Fuentes. Used by permission.

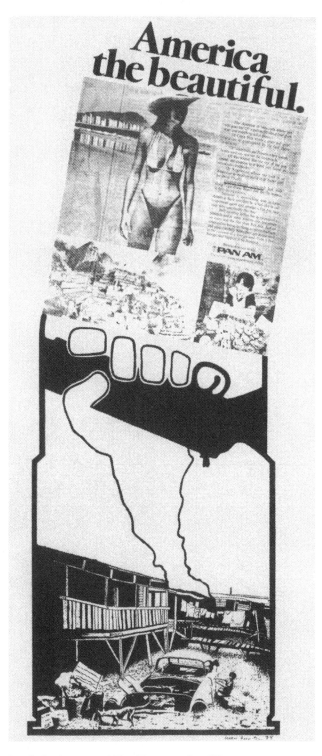

Inside back cover of *Tin-Tan* magazine, No. 2, 1975.
Copyright © Juan R. Fuentes. Used by permission.

The poster with the dual portrait of Allende and Neruda for the San Francisco reading to express outrage over the U.S.-sponsored military coup in Chile, September 11, 1973. Artist: Rupert García; author's collection.

Halloween dance poster, October 1978, at the height of the tropicalization of La Mission, a year before the Final Offensive against Somoza. Artist: Juan R. Fuentes; author's collection.

María Xabela, Ariel, and Dr. Concha Saucedo at the Azteca-Mexica wedding, 1998. Copyright © Francisco Domínguez. Used by permission.

The women's altar at the Azteca-Mexica wedding. Copyright © Francisco Domínguez. Used by permission.

The groom thanks the musicians. Copyright © Eric Norberg. Used by permission.

Ariel and María Xabela after the wedding. Copyright © Eric Norberg. Used by permission.

The destroyed *Lilly Ann* mural. Copyright © Andrés Campusano and Sandra Camacho. Photo by Tim Drescher. Used by permission.

PHANTOMS IN THE MIRROR

History, then, can clarify the origins of many of our
phantoms, but it cannot dissipate them. We must confront
them ourselves.

—Octavio Paz

My curse is memory. I remember the car accident
that changed my life when I was barely eighteen months old. I remember
my childhood with exacting clarity—the day, for instance, when I was six
and spoke my first words of English, and I can tell you exactly how those
words made me feel: filled with pride but also with insecurity. You can see
how I've learned to use this bastard tongue to my advantage. I have come
a long way with my hoard of memories, and the road has not been straight,
but rather a zigzag that at times seemed to lack any particular direction. Be
patient: I speak from the Indian side of myself, the nonlinear, non-Western
side, and the story eventually circles back to the starting point. You see, my
curse is also my salvation: I remember not just *my* story, but the stories of
my family and of my clan. I am of the Lugos, and the Olivas, and the Murguías, and we have been here for centuries, in this place called California.

Back in 1773, Francisco Palóu, the right-hand man of Father Junípero
Serra, led a group of Franciscan missionaries on foot from Baja California
to Alta California, and there was a Murguía with him every step of the
way. José Antonio Murguía was the cofounder and builder of Mission Santa
Clara, located a few miles north of present-day San Jose. A dedicated and
hardworking friar, he raised a magnificent church from the swamps, which
he achieved through the forced labor of the Tares Indians.[1] In 1776, when
Juan Bautista de Anza marched into Alta California from Sonora with
250 settlers, my name is already part of the topography and is recorded
in the diary of Pedro Font, the friar of the expedition. How the Murguía
name preceded the first *pobladores* to the Bay Area I do not know.

While José Antonio Murguía builds the mission at Santa Clara, another one of my clan, Seferino Lugo, a Mexican soldier, is a founder of the first civilian settlement established in California, San José de Guadalupe. In 1781, when Nuestra Señora la Reina de Los Angeles is founded on the banks of the Porciúncula River, one of the soldiers in the expedition is Manuel Ygnacio Lugo and another is Juan Matías Olivas. And like most of the *pobladores* of early California, they were dark, *indios* or mestizos, not light-skinned Spanish criollos.[2] Wherever you go in California, a Lugo or an Olivas or a Murguía has probably already stood there, going back at least 225 years.

My clan prospered as Californios, benefiting from all the contradictions of the newly established government of Mexico—we owned ranchos that stretched from the coast to the sierras, and we fought Indians without qualms or quarter. We were, if not a privileged class, certainly a group that prided ourselves on our skill with horses and guitars, and we welcomed all strangers to our houses, asking nothing in return for feeding them but their company. When the United States invaded California, José del Carmen Lugo took up arms and left his ranch to serve his *pequeño país*. Although untrained in war, he whipped the invaders at a desert outpost near Chino in a battle for independence as passionate as any in this hemisphere. But after 1846 and the U.S. occupation, like so many other Californios, Lugo lost everything he had, slowly slipping into historical shadows, vanquished and nearly vanished from memory.

Then, just when it seemed that my clan would disappear from California, another generation of the Lugos is among the first to settle in the San Fernando Valley, when mostly citrus orchards and vegetable farms dotted the landscape.

Twice in this century members of my family went to war for this country: my uncle Agustín in the Pacific in World War II and my older brother, Raymond, in Viet Nam. And as a reward for two hundred some years of nurturing this land with our sweat and blood, ignorant governors and racist psychopaths shout at us to go back to where we came from, and even the most well intentioned liberal believes we are foreigners here. But as I write this, I am standing where I was born; this *is* where I am from. And now in the name of the Lugos and the Olivas and the Murguías and our memory of California, I claim this land is ours as much as it is yours—whoever you may be.

But things haven't always been so clear to me. When I was growing up in Southern California in the 1950s and 1960s, the history of my clan had been forgotten. I was invisible, ignored, not even a footnote in history. I remember in the seventh grade in the library at George K. Porter Junior High, a friend showing me in a Hammond Atlas the city of England that carried his name—Sheffield—and I wondered where my name was on the map. And for a long time I have wondered about my place here—do I really belong? It is only now, as I write the story of my clan, that I realize I have never left, I was never gone, never disappeared. I have always been here and I am not ever leaving. This is what I remember. I am the keeper of the fire. I know the story.

•　•　•

The sun is at its zenith as I start out. Since the story is circular, it begins somewhere near the middle.

In February 1519, Hernán Cortés sails out of Havana, Cuba, leading an expedition of eleven ships manned by a hundred sailors and carrying 508 soldiers, 32 of them armed with crossbows and 13 with arquebuses. Aboard the ships are sixteen horses, some bronze cannons, and plenty of cannonballs, gunpowder, armor, and swords. It is the most powerful force in the hemisphere at that time, and its true intentions are known only to Cortés.[3] Although historians lump the men together as Spaniards, the army represents many nationalities from southern Europe: Portuguese, Biscayans, Andalusians, Extremadurans, Asturians, Italians, Venetians, Sicilians, Montenegrins, and Greeks.[4]

Aboard one of the ships is twenty-year-old Francisco de Lugo, who sometimes serves as captain, and whose relative Bernal Díaz del Castillo will write a first-person memoir of this expedition. There's a province in Spain named Lugo, and the capital of that province has the same name, and since *de* in Spanish means "from," his origin is most likely from that region. But that doesn't matter in this story. What's important is that Francisco de Lugo is that unique sort of military man who feels and thinks as well as acts.

As the expedition explores the coast of Yucatán, Francisco de Lugo can see on the leeward side the mangroves and the Mayan villages with their temples rising like stone mountains above the green canopy. The brown-skinned natives wave at him from the shore. When Cortés loses one of the ships, the squadron backtracks until the lost ship is found anchored in a small bay. Cortés sends Francisco de Lugo, as well as the pilot of one ship, in two small boats to reconnoiter the land. The first Lugo comes ashore on March 6, 1519, and finds the Indians cultivating maize and harvesting salt. He also discovers four of their temples, which the Indians call *cues*. The idols therein are mostly tall female figures. It is his discovery of the temples with the female figures that gives this place its present name, Punta de las Mujeres,[5] across from the now popular tourist spot Isla de Mujeres.

A week later, at a site known as Champotón, in the present state of Campeche, Francisco de Lugo has his first taste of battle. At the head of a hundred soldiers, including a dozen crossbowmen and musketeers, he explores inland for some three miles until he is met by an Indian war party armed with lances and shields, waving their war standards, and pounding drums. The Indians attack, crying "Al calacheoni! Al calacheoni!" meaning "Death to the captain." A flurry of fire-toughened darts and stones fall like rain on de Lugo and his men. When the Indian warriors are close enough to the Spaniards, they swing their fearsome *macanas*, two-sided clubs edged with obsidian blades. Realizing that he cannot stop this attack, de Lugo retreats toward the main camp, holding off the Indians by having his crossbowmen and musketeers fire in alternating sequence, so each group can have time to reload. As they are retreating, de Lugo sends a runner, an Indian from Cuba, to Cortés with a plea for help. It is this Indian, most likely a Taino, who saves de Lugo's life and that of his men.

As soon as Cortés receives the message that de Lugo is in danger, he sets out with another detachment of soldiers. The two groups meet about a mile and a half from the main camp, and thus de Lugo is rescued. Safely back in camp, de Lugo and his men bandage their wounds and take stock of the battle. Two Spaniards were killed and eight wounded. On the Indian side, fifteen were killed and three were taken captive.[6] In terms of casualties, this is a mere drop in the bloodbath that will soon flood Mexico.

Off the coast of Cozumel the expedition rescues a shipwrecked Spaniard, Jerónimo de Aguilar, who during his time as a captive of the Mayans has learned their language. His knowledge of Mayan, combined with that of an Indian woman named Ce Malinalli Tenepal (One Grass of Penance), who speaks Nahuatl and Mayan (Chontal, from the Putún region), will prove invaluable to the success of the military campaign that lies ahead. Cortés will speak to Aguilar, who will then translate the message into Mayan; Malinalli will translate the Mayan to Nahuatl, the language of the Mexicas—whom the Spaniards call Aztecs. Malinalli will quickly learn Spanish and thus supplant Aguilar. She will serve both as translator and advisor to Cortés, guiding him through the intricacies of Mexica culture and politics. To call her "Malinche" is a complete misnomer. Rather, in the Mexicas' view, Malinalli and Cortés are so closely twined together that they refer to Cortés by *her* name, "Malinalli's Captain," which is shortened to Malinche.[7] In this first encounter between two very different worlds, the key to success is language—and the one who wields the key is a woman.

•   •   •

On his war stallion, Captain Francisco de Lugo rides into the heartland of Mexico, armed with his lance and his double-handed sword, and running ahead of him is the huge greyhound he'd brought to attack and terrorize the Indians. In the campaign that takes the Spaniards through the steamy jungles of Vera Cruz, the dry plains of Tlaxcala, and into the fertile lands of Cholula, de Lugo fights with all the cunning and savagery that the Spaniards had learned in their eight-hundred-year war against the Moors. To the Spaniards, this is total war against infidels, and either the Indian towns submit to Cortés, or they are razed. At first, the Tlaxcalans fight fiercely, but once defeated they become the Spaniards' closest allies. Next comes the city of Cholula, with its sacred circular temple that covers an area bigger than Cheop's pyramid in Egypt. Here, in the city where Quetzalcóatl, the Feathered-Serpent God, rules, Cortés unleashes a slaughter so horrific that, to this day, Cholula is synonymous with the massacre of Indians.

It would be easy to say that all the Spaniards were bloody butchers, but Francisco de Lugo also shows a humane side. Perhaps he remembered the Taino who saved his life at Champotón. When Cortés tries to force the rulers of Tlaxcala to convert immediately to Christianity, de Lugo, speaking for several captains, counsels patience: "The priest is quite right. You have fulfilled your duty by doing what you have done. Don't refer to the matter again when speaking to these Caciques."[8]

The Spaniards, victorious over the Cholulans and fortified with their Tlaxcalan allies, cross through the pass of Popocatepetl and into the Valley of Mexico. From the crest of a hill called Ahualco, de Lugo, along with the other Spaniards, sees for the first time the grand valley covered with forests, plains, and lakes that stretches out before them like a fantastic dream. And in the center of the largest lake, the great city of Tenochtitlan rises like an apparition, its white temples shimmering in that rarefied air of the valley that made the buildings shine like rare jewels. The two huge lakes of the valley are bordered with forests of sycamore, oak, and cedar, interspersed with fields of maize and maguey, orchards, and floating gardens. De Lugo can see the royal hill of Chapultepec, the residence of Moctezuma, crowned with gigantic cypresses, and way in the distance, like a glimmering speck, the rival city of Texcoco.[9]

Bernal Díaz del Castillo, de Lugo's comrade in arms, recounts this view in his narrative *The Conquest of New Spain*, and he claims that soldiers who'd seen Constantinople had not seen anything as marvelous as this. Fifty years later, Díaz del Castillo would write about their first view of the city, the image still vivid in his mind: "And when we saw all those cities and villages built in the water, and other great towns on dry land, and that straight and level causeway leading to Mexico, we were astounded. These great towns and *cues* and buildings rising from the water, all made of stone, seemed like an enchanted vision from the tale of Amadis. Indeed, some of our soldiers asked whether it was not all a dream."[10]

On the causeway of Iztapalapa, the Mexica ruler, Moctezuma, appears to welcome his guests. His official title is Tlatoani, the Speaker, and he is borne on a royal litter extravagantly decorated with quetzal feathers, gold, silver, pearls, and *chalchiuites* (turquoise). The emperor is richly clad and wears sandals, the soles of which are made of gold and the tops decorated with precious stones. He descends from the royal litter supported by four lords; no one is allowed to even glance up at him. As he approaches the Spaniards, other lords sweep the ground before him and throw down cloaks so that his feet do not touch the ground.[11]

Moctezuma greets Cortés and his entourage of captains, translators, and soldiers. As part of the entourage, Francisco de Lugo is present when Cortés, through his interpreters Aguilar and Malinalli, exchanges the first words with Moctezuma. The moment marks the dividing line between indigenous Mexico and what will be its mestizo future. It is November 8, 1519, and within two years Moctezuma will be dead and Tenochtitlan, the grand city on the lake, will be a charred ruin.

Let me here say something about Malinalli and Moctezuma. Mexicans consider Malinalli a traitor, but since the concept of Mexico did not exist at that time, she could hardly have betrayed it. From Bernal Díaz's description of her, Malinalli is intelligent and quick witted, knows several languages, and is as brave as any soldier. She is astute politically, and to top it off—she's beautiful. And she's barely eighteen years old when she becomes the eyes, ears, and mouth of Cortés. But she is not an aberration in regards to pre-Cortesian Indian women, in the sense that, within the culture, women exercised professions equal to their abilities and hence were astute in the ways of business and trading and were also priestesses and even heads of government. So our understanding of the role of women in pre-Cortesian society has not yet been fully explored. For instance, lineage was often traced through the women, and in the case of Huitzilopochtli, the main Mexica deity, he has no father, but is born from only one parent, Coatlicue, the Mother of the Gods. And early in the Mexicas' rise, their legitimacy comes through marriage with Acolhua royalty, the princess Ilancueitl, who by some accounts is the actual ruler and her husband, Acamapichtli, just the royal consort.[12] So although Malinalli is quite young, she is acting well within women's roles for those times.

For me, Moctezuma is the passive figure. Although he was a seasoned general, a leader of three major military campaigns as well as a priest who practiced the rituals of self-sacrifice, he fails to act. During the six months or so that he lived with the Spaniards, Moctezuma got to know all of Cortés's soldiers by name and rank and distributed gifts accordingly, but he never understood the true mission of Cortés—the complete and total subjugation of the Mexica world. Moctezuma turns over his own nephew, Cacamatzin, the ruler of neighboring Texcoco, to Cortés, who has him chained by the neck. It should be noted that Cacamatzin had gathered an army to expel the Spaniards, which is why Moctezuma betrays him.[13] That Moctezuma was a fawning, obeisant host is also true. He hands over his kingdom, not even for a horse, and condemns his people to three centuries of slavery.

Francisco de Lugo had firsthand experience with Moctezuma, as did many other soldiers. He witnessed the everyday events of the royal court: Moctezuma swimming in his pool or settling in for a meal featuring dishes of quail, venison, wild boar, pigeons, and many other delicacies, including fresh fish from the Gulf Coast. To wash down the meal Moctezuma would drink a bit of foamy chocolate served in a solid gold cup. Dinner was followed by entertainment supplied by clowns or dwarf jesters, perhaps a little music or joke telling, and then Moctezuma would smoke a pipe of herb-scented tobacco and fall asleep.[14]

But when, a few weeks after their arrival, some Spaniards are killed on the coast, Cortés orders the arrest of Moctezuma. For this dangerous mission, Cortés brings his most trusted captains to the emperor's palace: Pedro de Alvarado, Gonzalo de Sandoval, Juan Velásquez de León, Alonso de Avila, and Francisco de Lugo. The heavily armed group surprises Moctezuma, and as Cortés delicately puts it: "If you don't come with us, my captains will kill you immediately."[15]

As the months pass, Moctezuma loses his royal prestige and influence, and the relations between the Indians and the Spaniards worsen. When Cortés rushes to Vera Cruz to deal with Pánfilo de Narváez, who has come to arrest him, Pedro de Alvarado massacres the Mexica nobility as they celebrate the feast of Toxcatl in the Great Temple. This unprovoked attack further heightens the tension in Tenochtitlan. Even Moctezuma cannot save the Spaniards now, and the Mexica emperor is stoned by an enraged mob that demands war against the foreigners. Cortés, trapped in the Mexica capital, opts to flee under cover of darkness, and his soldiers load up on gold, jewels, and anything else they can haul off, including concubines and cotton mantels. The Spaniards leave their fortress in the middle of the night, with Cortés in the vanguard, Alvarado in the rear guard, and Sandoval and de Lugo each leading a company of shock troops to cover the gaps. But the Indians surprise the Spaniards in the unlit avenues of the city, and they fall on them with a vengeance, hurling stones from rooftops, calling them cowards, and attacking them with a fury that stuns the Spaniards. The Spaniards are routed and nearly destroyed, driven from the city with heavy losses of men and materiel. De Lugo is one of the few who fights his way out through the causeways of the city, and then he, Cortés, and the other survivors retreat to Tlaxcala to heal their wounds.[16] This Mexica victory is referred to by the Spaniards as "La Noche Triste," but it is not a sad night to me.

It takes Cortés months to regroup his forces, and when the reinforced Spaniards again attack the Mexica capital, de Lugo is still with them. The Spaniards advance along the shore of the lake, burning all the villages, destroying everything in their path. Unknown to them, their greatest ally has already ravaged the Mexica capital. The plague of smallpox has struck the Mexicas before the Spaniards return to lay siege to the city. The Mexicas have no immunity against this disease, and sores erupt all over their bodies, covering them from head to toe. Some are so ill they cannot leave their *petates* to search for food and thus they starve to death. The disease, in one form or another, strikes nearly everyone; some are even left blind.[17] And to compound their woes, the Mexicas are decimated by famine.

When the Spaniards approach with over a hundred thousand Indian allies, they fight their way into the city, destroying it house by house, brick by brick, filling in the causeways with rubble so as to tighten the noose around the Mexicas. In this final assault, de Lugo is under the command of Cristóbal de Olid. He is in the column that attacks from Coyoacán. After this column meets its objective, securing the causeway that leads to Tenochtitlan, de Lugo is sent by Cortés to rescue Díaz del Castillo and others who are trapped in Tacuba. In vicious hand-to-hand combat, de Lugo rescues the surrounded Spanish force.[18]

The twenty-five-year-old Cuauhtémoc, the new emperor of the Mexicas, leads the resistance against the Spaniards. The Mexicas learn to avoid the line of fire of the Spanish muskets and cannons by throwing themselves on the ground or running in zigzag patterns. Or they cut holes in the houses so they can escape the charging horses.[19] The great Otomí warrior Tzilacatzín scorns his enemies and charges into battle sometimes dressed as a chief, with lip plug and gold earrings; other times with only his cotton armor and a kerchief wrapped around his head; and still other times in the full regalia of a high priest, with gleaming gold bracelets on his arms and ankles.[20]

The Mexicas fight on for months, sometimes pushing the Spaniards back, but day by day they lose ground. After ninety-three days of warfare, the Mexica capital is in ruins, clouds of smoke rising from all its quarters. The two armies are so exhausted that they stop fighting from pure weariness on both sides. The Spaniards have already taken the heart of Tenochtitlan, its great Zócalo, and now only Tlatelolco, the smaller of the twin cities, is in Mexica hands.

By now the city is a mere ghost of what the Spaniards had seen two years before. Two out of every three persons have either fled the city or have died of war or disease. The survivors are reduced to drinking stagnant water or brine from the lake. They eat lizards and whatever birds they can catch. Some, the old and the sick, are eating grass and weeds.[21] The stench of death permeates the pores of everyone, Indian and Spaniard alike. The once fabulous city is now devastated, the streets empty, the *mercados* destroyed, the temples bombed and burned; the whole island appears as if the five horsemen of the apocalypse had swooped upon it with a vengeance.

It's then that the news comes to the Spanish camp that Cuauhtémoc, the young Mexica emperor, has been captured on the lake, trying to flee in a pirogue. A Spanish brigantine is bringing him to Cortés. The surrender of Cuauhtémoc takes place in Tlatelolco, in the burning ruins of the great marketplace that had once fed 300,000 people. The young emperor, realizing his fate, tells Cortés to take his knife and kill him and be done with it. But Cortés will bide his time: first he will torture Cuauhtémoc by burning his feet, then he will drag him in chains to Guatemala, before finally having him hung.

To celebrate the capture of the city, Cortés holds a banquet at Coyoacán, where the Spaniards feast on wine and pigs brought from Spain. To join him in celebration, Cortés invites the most worthy of his captains and soldiers—Pedro de Alvarado, Gonzalo de Sandoval, Bernal Díaz del Castillo —as well as Malinalli, who is now his lover, and there among all the others is Francisco de Lugo, survivor of the siege of Tenochtitlan.

It is only now that I can tell you of Francisco de Lugo with neither pride nor shame. Only now can I look him in the eye, not as the white god come to save us, but merely man to man. And only now can I claim him as part of me, for we are, after all, of the same clan; our name and our memories unite us, survivors both of us. He brought death to me in Tenochtitlan, but I have been reborn in him. And now it is I who control his story. Francisco de Lugo lives because I have rescued him from oblivion. I am his father, I have raised him from the dead. And if I trust you with this confidence—is it a weakness? Does it mean I'm selling out, *un vendido?* It doesn't matter to me anymore; it's enough that I admit that part of me is not Indian. I may be dark as coffee, but my feet are milky white, incongruous with the rest of me.

It's not that my memory begins with the encounter of these two worlds, indigenous and European, and then grows like a ceiba tree, as strong above ground as below the earth. My memory does not begin with Francisco de Lugo. My memory is much deeper than 1519. But I had to explain this encounter with the other that lives inside me so you would understand how someone like me, who has no European features, can have a Spanish last name.

Now to return one last time to Francisco de Lugo. From Mexico City, the Spaniards will spread northward toward Tarascan territory and southward toward Guatemala and Nicaragua. These were the old territories of the Mexicas, and the Spaniards didn't merely replace them and their system, they advanced the concept of tribute and subjugation. Within a year of occupying Tenochtitlan, perhaps the very night of the celebration in Coyoacán, Cortés starts planning a sea exploration in hopes of finding a passage to China; instead, what he will find is California.

It is at the victory feast in Coyoacán that Francisco de Lugo realizes that they are not the victors they pretend to be. For all the hardship and warfare that de Lugo had endured over nearly two years, for all the wounds on his body, Cortés would offer de Lugo a mere 80 pesos as payment.[22] The celebration leaves a bitter taste in de Lugo's mouth, and from that day forward he is drawn inexorably toward the interior of Mexico, and with each step he leaves behind his Spanish sensibilities and becomes more and more Indian. Nearly five centuries later, searching through the *Diccionario autobiográfico de los conquistadores y pobladores de Nueva España*, I will discover that de Lugo's name is conspicuously missing from the claims for payment or land.[23] Sometime after that August day in 1521, de Lugo relinquished his Spanish privilege and vanished into the landscape he had come to conquer.

•   •   •

Now that I've told you about Francisco de Lugo, let me say this: I take his memory and I question it. Like the other Spaniards, de Lugo betrayed his host, Moctezuma, and the generosity that was offered him. He discovers Moctezuma's sealed chamber and, like a common thief, helps break down the wall and is one of the first Spaniards to glimpse the immense wealth that the Mexica emperor possessed.[24] After the holocaust of Tenochtitlan, I'm sure de Lugo took his share of slaves branded on the face as prisoners of war, and fathered children with Indian women who became part of the new mestizo nation.

But my sympathy is with the Indian side of the story I just told you. When I was in college in the late 1960s, I belonged to a student organization that had as its motto Por la Raza Hablará el Espíritu. We weren't exactly sure what that meant, The Spirit Will Speak for the Race, but it sounded good. What spirit were we talking about? And what was the spirit going to say? This slogan comes from José Vasconcelos, who, as Minister of Education in Mexico during the 1920s, did much to promote murals and popular access to schools. He also wrote the book that for many Chicanos was the paradigm for how we looked at ourselves: *The Cosmic Race: La raza cósmica*.

The button on the front of the army fatigue jacket I wore in those days had the well-known image of a three-sided face: a left- and right-side view, meant to represent the Indian and the European, and then another, a whole face looking straight ahead, meant to represent the mestizo, the two cultures blending into one, or the "Cosmic Race." But all we ever claimed was the Indian or mestizo side of our blood. There wasn't one among us who would dare claim, or even wanted to claim, any link to the Spaniards, the hated *gachupines*, the white-skinned demons who destroyed beautiful Tenochtitlan. But that is what Vasconcelos argues in his book—that only by an infusion of Christianity, a blending of races, can the Indian be saved, be civilized.[25] Today, the ideas in *La raza cósmica* appear terribly dated, more like intellectual posturing than penetrating perceptions. Although Vasconcelos praises mestizos for their creative lifestyle, and he wants an aesthetic movement of art, peace, and happiness to sweep the continent, the language and tone of the work are purely European. Vasconcelos, for instance, doesn't use one word of Nahuatl or any Mexicanisms in his writing. Only once or twice does he look at history from an indigenous point of view, and when he does mention Cuauhtémoc and Atahualpa, the Inca, a few paragraphs later, he extols Cortés, Pizarro, and Alvarado as "great captains that joined destructive impetus to creative genius. Immediately after victory, they traced the plans of new cities and wrote the statutes of their foundation."[26] Give me a break. The Mexica city of Tenochtitlan was better built and better conceptualized than whatever mess the Spaniards made of it.

In hindsight, I don't know why Vasconcelos was my hero. I recently reread his prologue to *Breve historia de México* (A Brief History of Mexico) and found it so virulently anti-Indian I had to stop reading it.[27] I suspect that Vasconcelos's writing speaks to the criollos or Europeans who believe they can save the natives. But he doesn't really speak to me, or for me, anymore.

In my college days, I was not mature enough to accept that who I am is not a simple either/or matter. I remember one day coming home from college to visit and confronting my father with my Chicano militant attitude and my little tri-faced button. My father, still sweaty from his job as a laborer, had just stepped into the house—he barely tanned in the scorching Southern California summers—and he rolled up his shirtsleeves and showed me his forearms, pale as any European's. And I hurled the centuries-old epithet for Spaniard at him—*gachupín*—and stormed out, not to return for many months. It was a cruel thing to say, as if I was denying my own blood.

And now just as I claim my Spanish side, I also claim my Indian, indigenous side. I understand this commingling as the natural order of life. The biggest myth in our continent is the purity of blood. When de Lugo arrived here, he was not pure-blooded anything. Bernal Díaz del Castillo calls him *"un hijo natural,"* a polite way of saying he was a bastard. In some ways, even though de Lugo came from another continent, he too was *un hijo de la chingada*. He was already dark, a mixture of Arab, Spaniard, maybe Goth, maybe Sephardi, perhaps Basque, and who knows what else. Even later, a Mexican could buy a certificate claiming "pure Spanish blood," which is utter nonsense. A Spanish *dicho* over five hundred years old says it best: "Scratch a Spaniard, bleed a Moor." And the Mexicas were not pure-blooded either. They had arrived quite recently in the Valley of Mexico, a mere two hundred years before, as a clan of semibarbarians that had wandered for generations from their ancestral home in the north. To establish themselves in the Valley of Mexico, the Mexicas had sought alliances with the more powerful clans and had mixed their lineage with the Acolhua and the Tepenac.[28] I see no contradiction between my past and my present heritage. I refuse the either/or dichotomy—I am more than two, I am a whole range of subtleties, but I also know my heart is red, has always been red. The important thing is that I know who I am, therefore I am complete and indivisible.

Octavio Paz offers an interesting perspective on how this commingling of races and cultures is incorporated into the Mexican psyche and language when he probes the word *"chingar"* in *The Labyrinth of Solitude*.[29] All those who claim to be Mexican, and by extension Chicano or Mexica, are in some way *hijos de la chingada*, born of violence, of a woman defiled.

But I have my own metaphor for the synthesis of *mestizaje*, something perhaps less reliant on the father who rapes or the mother who is raped. I accept neither of those concepts; instead I propose as a model the god Huitzilopochtli, who is born of his own will to survive. I too am born of the will to survive. Let me explain: Huitzilopochtli, born without a father to Coatlicue, the Mother of the Gods, is symbolized by the hummingbird. As Arnold Carlos Vento puts it in his book *The Mestizo*, Huitzilopochtli symbolizes "the will to conquer oneself spiritually . . . a force, a symbol of proper will to overcome changes and subsequent fears, from a spiritual level."[30] The metaphor came to me one morning as I watched a hummingbird darting in between the needles of a cactus so it could suck nectar from a red cactus flower. In my metaphor for *mestizaje*—the hummingbird in the cactus flower—the hummingbird (the will) flies around the cactus needles that sting (the antithesis of the will), and the cactus flower that provides nutrients for the hummingbird is the synthesis of the two. The hummingbird, the cactus needle, and the cactus flower are one image, not to be separated but to be kept whole in the mind. I am one, but of multiple shadings: the good, the bad, the compassionate, the cruel, the sweet, and the bitter, and I need multiple languages—Nahuatl, *español*, and English—to express my subtleties. I've taken what each world offers, with apologies to none.

So let me tell you that my darkness is beautiful. It has always been beautiful. And this other side, my Indian side, has been here forever. And that's a long time. Even when I was younger I felt the darkness in me; it spoke to me through the hummingbirds, the *nopal*, the obsidian. I speak Spanish and English, in some ways twice oppressed by language, but I also know the codices, the Nahua prayers to the Goddess of Corn, and the poems of Nezahualcoyotl, the poet-prince of ancient Texcoco, and that knowledge saves me. When I look in the mirror, I see the toasted skin, prominent cheekbones, mouth, and eyes that are *puro indio*—so I know what it's like to be on the pointed end of the sword.

The shock of conception is permanent—phantoms are lurking in the mist, ancient clan lines appear when I least expect them. I see the question in the eyes of strangers as they pass, whether they be mestizo or Indian or European: there's a quick glance, as if asking, Are you one of us or one of them? Paz also says, "He [the Mexican] is afraid of others' looks and therefore he withdraws, contracts, becomes a shadow, a phantasm, an echo."[31] But being a Xicano, someone who looks at the world through indigenous eyes, I do not withdraw, I do not become a shadow; instead, I challenge you to accept me just as I am, however I look.

And that's the difference between being Mexican and being Xicano. In Mexico, despite its lengthy pre-Cortesian history, to be Indian is still a negative condition, and the language of Mexico describes it so: "*indio patarajada*," "*indio salvaje*," "*no seas indio.*" Just flip through the channels of Mexican television; you won't see any Indian-looking faces reading the news, advertising toothpaste, or dancing on kiddy shows. But I accept being *indio* and love it, not in the abstract but in the concrete. I am happy in my own skin. My diet is Indian: I do not eat cow or pig for environmental and health reasons. My protein comes from the nearly perfect combination of tortillas and beans.[32] I stick mostly to native food: corn, chiles, *nopalitos*, vegetables with seeds, some fish and small game, turkey, duck, rabbit. I love quail—in chipotle sauce and grilled over mesquite. I sacrifice the best orchids in my garden; I burn copal and sage: and I plant salvias to feed hummingbirds and butterflies. Except for once or twice during the year, I stay away from alcohol. When I do drink, I drink 100 percent agave. I keep the holy days of the indigenous calendar. My concept of justice and honor is based on what happens to indigenous people. After five centuries, I know how to love myself, all of myself. And now I reclaim and re-create our reality; let the word *india* or *indio* signify the best that we are: "*Bella como india*," "*Hecho y derecho como indio*," "*Sabio como indio.*"

Yet I also fully embrace the conflict that has forged me. Every morning before the mirror, I trim my mustache, my centuries-old inheritance from Francisco de Lugo. At the same time, I cannot deny that my psyche is affected by the violence waged by my ancestor against my ancestor, as a Viet Nam veteran might be affected by post-traumatic stress syndrome. And this shock, this emotion, for me is concentrated in the Zócalo of Mexico City, the center of the universe, the place of death and rebirth. I feel it when I go through there, riding late at night in the back seat of a taxi on the way to my hotel or to my aunt's house in San Angel. It's there when I walk through the stone porticos at noon, with the wind blowing and clouds gathering on the peaks of Popocatepetl, and as I watch the street fires of the *ambulantes* smoldering beneath the arches of the cathedral, sinking into the mud of the once-upon-a-time lake. The burning of Tenochtitlan is seared into my historical memory, like a red-hot brand on the face of an Indian slave.

But the Zócalo is not just a place of destruction; it is also a site of resurrection. When I stand before the ruins of the Templo Mayor, the Mexica *teocalli* that seems to be slowly rising again in the heart of the modern city, I feel the power of the ancient gods prodding me forward, daring me to stare into the holy fire of my past. Here in the Zócalo, century by century, the old gods have risen from the rubble of Tenochtitlan to claim their place in the cosmos: Quetzalcóatl, the Feathered Serpent; Coatlicue, the Mother of the Gods; Huitzilopochtli, the Hummingbird of the South; and Coyolxuahqui, the Moon Goddess.

These are the gods of my world. If you don't know this, you don't really know me—you only think you do. With a righteous thunderbolt in my hand, I baptize myself in the twenty-first century as the dark son of Coatlicue, born of my own volition.

THE "GOOD OLD MISSION DAYS" NEVER EXISTED

If you were raised in Fresno, Bakersfield, or Sacramento, you don't have a connection to the California missions. Yes, you recognize the oxidized iron bells along the highway marking their relative location, but you don't give them much attention. When you visit a mission, as everyone in California does sooner or later, it is merely an ethnic curiosity left over from two centuries ago that has nothing to do with you or your growing up in Sacramento or wherever. To you the missions are relics of a romantic past lit by the sunset's rosy glow and, like all relics, they are not a part of your life. But if you grew up in a mission town, near any of the twenty-one California missions, they leave a definite impression—you wonder about their history, you try to make them fit into the historical landscape of your memory, and you are not impartial to them.

I grew up a hop and a skip from Mission San Fernando, so I have my own sense of the "mission days." From the age of ten till I leave my father's house at eighteen, I am within the sphere of the mission, its myth, and its history. I also had as a neighbor the respected archaeologist Dr. Mark R. Harrington, curator emeritus of the Southwest Museum of Natural History, who played an important role in the restoration of Mission San Fernando in the 1930s and 1940s. On Saturdays, I often worked for him, earning a few dollars by cleaning up the thick wall of opuntia in his front yard or splitting oak for his fireplace. He loved to talk about his work, which had taken him all over North America, including Cuba. With his thick bifocals, a weathered hat, and a hobble caused by one leg being several inches shorter than the other due to polio, Harrington was my original source on mission as well as California history. Through him, I learned firsthand about the process of building the missions, their ruin, and their restoration; I also received a top-notch guide to the Indian communities that existed before the missions and the rancheros and ranches that followed. These two quirks of fate, the proximity of Mission San Fernando and my interaction with Dr. Harrington (plus a dash of curiosity), instilled in me an intimacy with California missions that had nothing to do with schoolbooks or classroom lectures or tourist maps.

As a young man, I often wondered what my place in the mission system would have been. I don't fit into the racial category of light-skinned *gente de razón*, the Spaniards who were the creators and supporters of the missions. Instead, I despise the concept that Spaniards were people of reason, people who could think, whereas Indians were considered savage, nonthinking beings, children incapable of critical thought. Since I am dark, I'm not *gente de razón*, which doesn't bother me; I'd rather be a wild, crazy Indian, free to bare my ass on Hollywood Boulevard if I want.

Now, had I lived during the mission days—say in the same locale I actually grew up in—I would have been a mission Indian. And my short life would have been a tight regimen of work, work, work, and in between work periods, religion, with the threat of a whipping or lashing if I stepped out of line at work or church. Some life.

I must confess I have never cared for religion or for the doctrine of the Catholic Church. To begin with, our working-class household wasn't all that concerned with the sins of the flesh. The way my father saw it, we weren't supposed to sin, period; so religion wasn't essential, it was more of a cultural remnant he clung to as a reminder of Mexico. He seldom attended mass, though our house was a gallery of saints' photos in the living room and bedrooms. But neither the concept nor the practice of religion moved me. To be honest, religion scared me. I was deathly afraid of it—the fiery torments of hell seemed to have been created for boys with vivid imaginations, just like me. Even heaven scared me; I couldn't conceptualize eternity at the side of God back then, and I can't conceive of it now. I think the idea of eternity in heaven, more than the fear of hell, caused me to break with Catholicism.

In general, I just seemed to be a bad candidate for sainthood. I flunked out of catechism and never made my first communion, as my older brother did; his communion photo, proudly displayed in our living room, shows him in a white shirt, with his hair slicked back, holding a taper candle. And in the fourth grade, I committed one of the worst sins of all time. My father still had hope for me, so he enrolled me in after-school catechism. But my heart wasn't in it, so I mostly skipped the class. Then when Easter came around, I failed to qualify. Instead of coming clean with my father, I decided

to make up a tall tale. I told him that there wasn't going to be any big ceremony, just me taking the host along with everyone else that Sunday. He
seemed a bit suspicious of that, and I can't blame him. After all, the ritual
of the first Holy Communion plays a big role in our culture, especially for
boys, since we have no ritual of manhood, unlike young girls, who have
their *quinceañeras*. I guess we're expected to be men from birth.

Unfortunately for me, my father had big plans for my communion.
He'd bought a camera, had even bought me a new white shirt and a pair
of slacks. With all this pressure, it became harder and harder to tell him
about the nuns' decision, and postponing the dreaded moment only made it
worse. On Good Friday, my conscience got the best of me, and I couldn't
go through with it. I didn't even know the Act of Contrition that I'd have
to say to the priest. And I was not willing to take communion without confession. I may not have been a good Catholic, but I knew that much. So
that night I hauled my own cross to my father and told him there would
be no communion, that, in other words, I had been bullshitting him. Let
me tell you, my father's belt sang a bloody *corrido*—and for days after, I
could contemplate the bruises on my butt as a small reminder of what Jesus
must've felt.

I guess you could say I've always had a love-hate relationship with the
California missions. About once a month, sometimes less frequently, I'd
walk from our house, cross Brand Boulevard, go through Memory Gardens
to Mission San Fernando, and there I was in another world. If I came to
Sunday mass at all, it was because the mission grounds had a peacefulness
that attracted me. I liked walking through the gardens lush with bougainvil-
lea and citrus trees, especially after it had rained and the richly scented
earth seemed alive. Inside the church I felt in touch with a part of myself
that was Latin American; the polychrome statues of the saints on the main
altar reminded me then, as they do now, of every church in Mexico I've ever
stepped into. The liturgies were still sung in Latin during my youth, and
although I didn't understand it, I knew that Spanish was derived from it.
After mass I'd walk in the cemetery out back and read the Spanish names on
the gravestones. All this made me romanticize the mission days, a nostalgia
that was more myth than reality.

•   •   •

In front of Mission San Fernando stands Brand Park, built in the 1920s by
a real estate developer on what had been part of the mission orchards. Some
of the original mission olive trees still line the main walk that cuts through
the center of the park. On the west end of Brand Park is Memory Gardens,
shaded by aged lemon trees and dotted with palms. In the Gardens, two

fountains, originally built in the 1820s, create a contemplative mood, making this the most beautiful spot in the San Fernando Valley. But in spite of the beauty and the elegiac mood of Memory Gardens, it was here where one day I sensed another facet of mission life.

In the center of Brand Park sits a small mound with a rectangular stone structure on top. These are the tallow pits of the old mission, where cow fat was boiled for use as candles. The Indians, as usual, did all the work, and one Saturday as I played there, I imagined myself working in the tallow pits, stirring the cow fat with wooden poles, filling the leather *botas*, and the stench I imagined made me sick. Another day, while horsing around in the Gardens, I jumped onto the bigger-than-life bronze statue of Junípero Serra that stands next to one of the fountains. Junípero Serra has a staff in one hand, and his other hand rests on the shoulder of an Indian youth, as if walking him to the Promised Land. I pretended to be that Indian youth, the hands of the good padre on my shoulder. I wanted to see the world from the eyes of the Native American boy, who in this case is supposedly Juan Evangelista, one of Serra's first converts. (Only through a miracle could Serra have converted anyone at San Fernando, since he'd been dead for thirteen years when this mission was founded.) But the imaginative leap did not happen. Life as a pious Indian neophyte seemed phony to me. I jumped down from the statue feeling unsatisfied and rebellious.

Eventually I realized, little by little, one small insight at a time, that as nostalgic and romantic as the images of the missions are, they are not historical memories that I cherish. I tend to see the missions and the missionaries as oppressors, even if in their own eyes they were benevolent. For the Indians, the missions meant a virtual turning over of their lives to the friars, who then controlled their time with work and prayers. In my imagination, had I lived two hundred years ago as a young Indian trapped in the mission, I would have run away, chancing the soldiers' whips, because only in the *cañones* would I have been free. But that's just me. Some of my friends in the same barrio saw themselves as priests baptizing the pagans.

I have other memories of Brand Park. As a teenager, my friends and I came to the park on Saturday afternoons to wash our cars or to smoke *yesca*, Mexican pot that we bought for ten dollars an ounce; or on Sundays, to cruise around and around in our lowriders playing oldies music. Sometimes a girl would come with us at night, and we'd scare her with stories of the headless woman who supposedly haunted the Gardens. If the moon was full, rising up between the palms and the olives trees, or if the girl we were with got scared by our ghost story, or if we were lucky, the girl would snuggle up to us, and we'd make out, practicing our sloppy kisses.

For a while—just after I'd moved away—most of Brand Park was heavily tagged by the *vatos* of San Fernando. All the benches, the fountains, the walls, were scrawled with spray-painted graffiti more important to us than whatever history was implied in the mission and Brand Park. The stone sundial in the center of the Gardens was vandalized, and its bronze face removed. It was as if history didn't matter to the new generation of Chicanos, as if we didn't care what the mission represented. I understand that feeling.

Still, Mission San Fernando left an impression on me. Even now, in every mission town from Sonoma to San Diego, I find my bearings according to where the mission is located. Eventually, I discovered that the mission system created in California had previously existed in Mexico, in Querétaro, Sinaloa, and all the way up Baja California. So, for me, the California missions are intimately linked with that whole colonial period of the continent. By extension, then, I consider the missions to be part of the Latin American experience. That's the good thing about the missions: they make the Latin American roots of California familiar to me; I see them in Mexico, and I understand the concept of being both oppressor and oppressed.

●   ●   ●

In 1769, Junípero Serra leads a military-religious force to establish the first permanent outpost of Spanish imperialism in what was then known as Alta California. This expedition sets out from La Paz, Baja California, with a three-pronged purpose: to spread the dominion of Spanish rule, to establish presidios for the political subjugation of the land, and to build missions for the "Spiritual conquest" of the natives.[1] Serra believes the missionaries are bringing the Paradise of Heaven to the heathens, but California is already an earthly Eden, where nature provides everything and in abundance, and the natives are healthy, fat, and go about dressed not much different than Adam and Eve in the biblical paradise. Instead of creating a paradise, Serra sets in motion the hellish destruction of the native communities he'd come to save.

The Franciscans are different from the Jesuits. who, at the time, had recently been expelled from Mexico and Baja California. The Jesuits are teachers and scholars; the Franciscans, missionaries and colonizers. Whereas the Jesuits oppose enslavement of the Indians, the Franciscans are enemies of the flesh and firm believers in punishment. Serra, in particular, is fanatical and often wears a hair shirt or flagellates himself during sermons; at other times, he beats his chest with a stone or burns his hand with a candle to impress upon the neophytes what awaits them in hell.[2] He also keeps a logbook with a running tab of how many Indians he has converted, how many souls he's added to the kingdom of God, as if souls were widgets and this tally, proof of his spirituality and good work.

Among the missionaries chosen by Junípero Serra to partake in the spiritual and physical conquest of California is a Murguía. A native of Domayguia, Alava, Spain, José Antonio Murguía came to Mexico as a layman at the age of twenty. Later, following a spiritual conversion, he entered San Fernando College in Mexico City and was ordained a priest in 1744. As a Franciscan missionary, he worked in the Pame Indian communities of the Sierra Gorda near Querétaro, where he first came under the influence of Junípero Serra, whom he had preceded in Mexico by fourteen years. Murguía ministered under Serra at Miguel de Concá, and erected the stone-and-mortar church, the first in the region, that still stands today.[3] Because of Murguía's exemplary work, skill, and dedication, Serra named him to be one of the missionaries to take over the ex-Jesuit missions in Baja California. He sailed with Serra and Francisco Palóu to Loreto, Baja California, arriving April 1, 1767, aboard the packet *Concepción*. For the next year, Murguía worked at Santiago de las Coras among the native communities near San José del Cabo, many of whose inhabitants were suffering from *gálico* (syphilis) and whose numbers were very reduced.[4]

Serra assigned Murguía to be chaplain to the first expedition bound for Alta California. Murguía is set to sail on the packet *San José* in May 1769, when a severe pestilence breaks out at San José del Cabo, and he rushes to attend the sick at the mission. Although he survived the pestilence, he too became ill; when he recovers, Palóu sends him to Loreto, where he stays until May 1770. In a weird twist of fate, because he risked death by helping out with the pestilence, Murguía missed the trip to California aboard the *San José*, which was lost at sea and never heard from again.[5]

In the meantime, one arm of the Spanish expedition sails up the Pacific Coast searching for San Diego Bay while another, composed of priests, soldiers, muleteers, and Indians, travels fifty-two days by land, during which the Indian porters abandon them. In truth, though the military aspect of the expedition lacked tenacity, the religious goals were implemented with fanatical fervor. Hardly anyone remembers anymore the military leader of the expedition, Captain Gaspar de Portolá, but everyone in California knows the name of Junípero Serra. The land and sea forces eventually connect near the site of a Kumeyaay Indian village called Cosoy (present-day San Diego), where the expedition, by now a sorry bunch of sick, hungry, and scurvy-ridden men, huddles together. Meanwhile, the Indians they meet are described by Serra in a letter to his associate Father Francisco Palóu: "There are immense numbers of the native pagans and all those of this coast (on the Pacific), among whom we have come, beginning with those of la Ensenada of Todos Santos, as it is called on the maps and charts, live very well provided for, with their different crops and with the fishery which they carry on in their rush canoes, with which they go far out to sea. They are very affable, and all the men, large and small, go about naked; the women and girls are modestly dressed, as are even the babies."[6]

It is ironic that the Spaniards, sick and starving as they camped on the beach, and who were ready to abandon the expedition and stayed only at Serra's insistence, believed they were bringing a better life to the Indians. This is like bringing coconuts to Colima or coals to Newcastle.

The natives don't necessarily want Serra's version of paradise. On August 15, three months after the Spaniards have established camp and barely a month after Serra raises the first cross on a sand dune, the Indians attack. In the skirmish that ensues, two Spaniards are killed, several are wounded, and three Indians go down.[7] This battle begins the modern history of California, a history that has never been resolved: the clash of opposing cultures, religions, and ways of life.

As the mission project expands, San Diego will be the site of fierce fighting between natives and colonizers. The Indians launch another attack on November 4, 1775, in which they burn the barracks down, loot the sacristy, and destroy sacred vessels and books. They also kill a priest and five other Spaniards. When Serra, who is at San Carlos in Monterey, hears the news, he exclaims, "Thanks be to God that the land is irrigated with the blood of martyrs!"[8] In 1778 another revolt rocks San Diego. This time four Indian leaders are captured, Aachil, Aalcuirin, Aaaran, and Taguagui; they are brought back to the mission, tried, and executed by a firing squad. This is the first time that a public execution occurs in California.[9]

By 1773, Serra and the other missionaries have established five missions in Alta California, and Serra calls for reinforcements to spread the work. A second expedition is organized under the religious leadership of Friar Francisco Palóu, who will eventually write the account of Serra's life. Palóu, like Serra, is a Franciscan who spent many years in the Sierra Gorda of Mexico as a missionary before coming to Baja California.

Friar Murguía joins Palóu in Loreto, and in August they start for San Diego on foot, a distance of nearly fifteen hundred miles through harsh desert landscape, pushed along by their faith. The column of missionaries, soldiers, and Indian porters herding mules loaded with supplies and religious objects, beads, cloth, crosses, and vestments eventually reaches San Diego on August 30, 1773.[10] After stopping at Mission San Diego, Murguía continues northward, to San Luis Obispo, then to San Antonio, where he hooks up again with Serra, who'd just returned from Mexico City. From

San Antonio the two priests travel together to Mission San Carlos, the mission at Carmel in Monterey Bay. While at San Carlos, Murguía witnessed the arrival of the Anza expedition that was on its way to establish the presidio at San Francisco.[11] Perhaps it is here that he meets Pedro Font, the diarist of the Anza expedition, who later cites a landmark across from Point Reyes that carries Murguía's name.

A few years later, in 1777, the Spaniards propose a new mission on the banks of a river they name Nuestra Señora de Guadalupe. This new mission is the only one named after a female saint, Santa Clara de Asís. Once the site is picked out, Murguía is sent from Carmel with the supplies and religious artifacts required by all the missions, and he arrives January 21, 1777, nine days after the initial founding.

Although I have little sympathy for missionaries, having seen the destruction left in their wake all over Mexico and Latin America, I have a grudging admiration for Friar Murguía. He is one of the few missionaries in California who actually tried to understand the Indian communities; he learned several California native tongues, which is one reason he is sent to Santa Clara. And, unlike other missionaries, he doesn't just force the Indians to build and work with Western tools and materials; he actually gets his own hands dirty, just like any other laborer. Murguía lived with the *indios*, worked with them, suffered from fleas as they did, and all the rest. He wore away his gray monk's habit, never washing it; perhaps he didn't bathe much either. His tenure was filled with loneliness, solitude, and work. This is what he had asked for and what he had selected for his life. With his skin darkened under the sun, he might have looked much like the Other he had come to save.

Still, at Santa Clara, just like at the other missions, the initial encounter with the Native American is violent. Shortly after the Spaniards' arrival, Indians make off with some of their mules, and soldiers are sent after them. When the Indian camp is discovered, they are roasting the mules, and the soldiers unleash an attack that kills three Indians, while others are captured, taken to the mission, and flogged.[12] The attitude of the Spaniards, in all their contacts with Native Americans, is the arrogant presumption that Spanish laws are applicable to societies that have no understanding or knowledge of them.

From the start, Mission Santa Clara is beset by calamities. Within months, an epidemic strikes the Indian communities that abounded in the region, causing the death of many infants. Palóu doesn't find this disturbing; instead he writes joyfully in his account of Serra's life that "they [the missionaries] succeeded in sending a great many children (which died almost as soon as they were baptized) to Heaven as the first fruits that they might ask of God the conversion of their relatives and tribesmen."[13] Then the original mission structure, made of upright logs chinked with clay and a flat roof covered with earth, is washed away when the Guadalupe River floods during the winter storms of 1779. One of the two priests at the mission flees to higher ground, but Murguía, stubborn as the mules he's brought—a trait still common to our clan—stays on at the risk of his life, guarding the supplies till the waters recede. Interestingly enough, the *pobladores* at San José refuse to lift a finger to help the missionaries during this flood.[14]

With the original structure destroyed, the two missionaries at Santa Clara occupy a temporary church built of upright logs with a roof of tules and brush. Murguía, with his building skills acquired in Mexico, starts planning a more permanent structure of adobe. On November 19, 1782, he lays the cornerstone of the new mission, now called Santa Clara de Thámien after the Indian community already there, and has it blessed by Serra. A niche is carved in the cornerstone and filled with artifacts of the mission, a small crucifix, and a handful of silver coins. In that same year, Murguía is also present at Mission Dolores when Serra and Palóu lay its first stones and dedicate the second site of the mission where it now stands on Dolores Street.[15]

Working alongside the Indians, in every sense of the word, Murguía constructs a church with walls one and a half *varas* thick, about four feet, on a stone foundation. The beams and rafters are hewed from redwoods and brought down from the Santa Cruz Mountains on the shoulders of Indians. The roof is made of adobe flags well slanted for drainage, and the doors are made of cedar and redwood. The entire structure, both inside and out, is whitewashed, and the inside walls are painted with borders. The chancel and a great part of the ceiling are also painted, and the floor is paved with adobe flags. This is the biggest and most impressive mission of its time, and Serra himself calls it "the most beautiful church yet erected in California."[16]

Regardless of what Serra calls it, a few days before the dedication of this new mission, while Murguía is painting the final decorations, he falls seriously ill, but Serra, who is at Mission Dolores confirming Indians, refuses to leave his work to come minister to him. Instead, Palóu arrives to comfort the old friar, who, sick with fever, dies on the morning of May 11, 1784, five days before Serra arrives to dedicate the mission.[17] Murguía was sixty-eight years old; he'd been a priest for forty years and a missionary in Mexico, Baja California, and Alta California for thirty-five years. He'd also spent two and a half years building Mission Santa Clara. Ironically enough, Mission Santa Clara, one of the most bountiful missions, is also where more Indian deaths are recorded—6,809—than at any other mission in California.[18]

The backbreaking labor that was killing the Indians apparently also killed Murguía. He was buried under the altar of the church he'd just finished building. Both Serra and Palóu praised him as an exemplary priest and hard worker. In a letter to Mexico, Serra says of José Antonio Murguía: "I have grieved over and will continue to lament for a long time over the loss of a missionary who was so good that perhaps no one else can replace him."[19] But not good enough, it seems, for Serra to come to his comfort in his dying moments.

In a final irony, God (who else?) sends an earthquake in 1818 that totally destroys this most beautiful of all missions. Not one adobe brick of this church is now standing. And not until 1911 do workers digging a gas main for the city of Santa Clara unearth the cornerstone laid by Murguía and recover the relics he'd placed there in 1782.[20]

• • •

The purpose of every mission was to establish a productive site that would at the same time baptize and convert the Indians to "civilization," meaning Spanish religious attitudes and agricultural concepts. The missions were modeled after the *reducción* system imported from Mexico, in which the neophytes were separated from their communities and forced to live in the mission compound, under the strict supervision of priests and soldiers. The *reducción* is merely a modification of the *encomienda* system that had destroyed the indigenous people of the Caribbean and Mexico, except that with the *reducción* system, the converts were more under the control of ecclesiastical hegemony rather than a private Spanish citizen. The *reducción* was meant to be a kinder system of exploitation, but the word in Spanish means "to reduce," and it did just that to the indigenous population, in both power and numbers.[21]

There was never a sense among these missionaries of working with the Indians in their context, but only in the Spanish context. At times, the friars appear to be evil Don Quixotes battling a giant of their own creation, searching for lands on which to fight the devil. Only the devil is flesh-and-blood human beings, with their own complexities, culture, language, and traditions, who were living quite well, thank you, without Spanish civilization. The arrogance of Serra and the rest, who thought they had the Word and that therefore they would physically force it on people who had no need or want of it, is amazing to my modern sensibility. Any forced conversion to religion is oppression, regardless of how "good" the intentions might be. Even now I do not accept the premise first thrown down by Serra that the missionaries were bringing spiritual enlightenment or civilization to the natives.

Yes, it was a forced conversion. The soldiers were there to protect the priests, but also to enforce discipline and attendance at work and mass, and they dealt very harshly with those wanting to return to their communities or those who just plain ran away. Hugo Reid, a Scotsman who witnessed firsthand the treatment of the Indians, wrote a series of letters for the *Los Angeles Star* in 1852 that are quite revealing. The following is an excerpt from Letter No. 18:

> Indians of course deserted. Who would not have deserted? Still those who did had hard times of it. If they proceeded to other missions, they were picked up immediately, flogged and put in irons until an opportunity presented of returning them to undergo other flagellations. If they stowed themselves away in any of the *rancherías*, the soldiers were monthly in the habit of visiting them; and such was the punishment inflicted on those who attempted to conceal them, that it rarely was essayed. Being so proscribed, the only alternative left them was to take to the mountains, where they lived as best they could, making occasional inroads on the mission property to maintain themselves. They were styled *huídos*, or runaways, and at times were rendered desperate through pursuit, and took the lives of any suspected of being traitors.[22]

From the point of view of the priests, the Indians were paid for their labor with the benefits of civilization, which meant religion and its accompanying rituals of confession, mass, and communion. But this payment, this religion and civilization, did not cause the Indians to flourish; instead their numbers declined during the mission period from the stress of their daily lives, with half the children dying before their fifth birthday.[23]

Although in theory the land belonged to the Indians, and the Catholic Church merely held it in trust, in practice the Indians did not share in the wealth produced by the mission. So if the mission had a series of bountiful years, that did not mean the Indians received more or finer clothes or extra days off. But if there was famine because crops failed, something quite common in the missions, it was the Indians whose rations were cut and who thus sometimes starved. Yet there is not one instance of a priest starving to death.[24]

* * *

There's a saying in Spanish: "*Para muestra sirve un botón*" (For an example, a button is good enough). In this case, the daily life at Mission San Fernando is a good example of life at all the missions. The Indians of Mission San Fernando lived nearby in some seventy adobe houses. They rose at sunrise and began their day with *doctrina*, sermons or teachings; then mass; then breakfast, a cornmeal called *atole*. They worked till noon, had more *atole*, perhaps a brief siesta, and then returned to work. The men and older boys worked in the fields or shops while the women and girls were taught cooking, sewing, or spinning, or worked with the wives of the soldiers. At the end of the day there was more *doctrina*, then dinner was eaten about six, and whatever was left of the day was theirs.[25]

If one looks at the amount of cultivated lands Mission San Fernando acquired and had in production within twenty years of its founding, one can get a sense of the human hours needed to tend to this singular "garden." The total grazing lands of the mission were approximately 50 square leagues, or 350 square miles. The herds of cattle and sheep numbered in the thousands, but goats, pigs, and chickens were also raised. The Indians also planted wheat, barley, corn, peas, lentils, and garbanzos, and maintained two orchards of forty acres each surrounded by adobe walls; in these orchards Indians looked after 1,600 fruit trees: pears, apples, apricots, peaches, figs, pomegranates, oranges, quinces, and prickly pears. The mission also had a thousand olive trees, which were said to produce the finest olives in all California, and 32,000 grapevines.[26] As much as two thousand gallons of wine were produced per season, enough to export to Europe. If you take all this bounty from one mission and multiply it by twenty-one, you can get a sense of the wealth the mission system produced. The missions were like modern corporations, the precursors of agribusiness conglomerates that now exploit the land and farmworkers. Moreover, their labor cost was almost nil. The mission Indians provided the labor necessary for missions, pueblos, and presidios to survive. And it was all produced without paying the Indians so much as one peso.

Even if the missions were well intentioned, the Indians were forced and subjugated to perform this labor. It was not voluntary—who in their right mind would work like this for nothing? And yet the so-called *gente de razón*, those with critical-thinking abilities, never figured out this simple equation. It doesn't matter whether Junípero Serra is canonized or not, made a saint or sent to the devil. The Indians were enslaved, and that enslavement was spiritual, it was physical, and it was brutal. Here's something that is seldom mentioned: once an Indian entered the mission, he was never allowed to leave it again; in other words, he was a prisoner.[27] The military was always present to punish rebellious Indians or those who would run away to the hills, with floggings or days in the stockade or being shackled in stocks.[28] Men were flogged in a public square, while the women were flogged in the female dormitories by a female teacher. Considering that California Indians did not practice physical punishment, this violence must have seemed particularly brutal to them.[29] Several eyewitnesses remarked that the physical punishment meted out to the Indians seemed more appropriate to slaves than to Christians. José del Carmen Lugo, in his "Vida de un ranchero," recalls the following: "I do not know how many lashes a *padre* could order given an Indian. I believe that it was not more than twenty-five. I do not know whether or not the padres sometimes exceeded their authority in delivering punishments. I do know that they frequently castigated the Indians who had committed faults with lashes, confinement, and chains. On some occasions I saw Indians working in chains for the feet, and I also saw them in stocks."[30]

What the Indians received in return for their labor were the trinkets of civilization, some hymns to sing, and cheap clothes, all cut from the same cloth in the same style. They also received the rituals of Catholicism, including marriage and baptism. But for the thousands who were baptized and then died of overwork, disease, or other causes, there's no proof that any of them are in heaven. There isn't one painted image, for instance, showing an Indian at the side of God. Just imagine the contradiction: if Indians are in heaven, they must be working the fields while the padres drink wine and smoke cigars. And yet that was the point of the missions, to save the Indian souls, to make them candidates for heaven.

But how much did the missionaries really care about the Indian soul? There is no *campo santo* for the Indians in any of the missions, no holy ground where their bones rest. In all the missions, where exactly the Indians are buried is a mystery, and this lays bare the myth that the padres were concerned about them. Mass graves? Single plots? Each mission merely has a marker of wood or stone that says so many thousand Indians are buried here. But where exactly is here, no one knows. I imagine the missions as charnel houses of bodies and bones, with the quiet of mornings and evenings broken by the sounds of sorrowful people crying incoherent rants against punishment received for sins never committed.

Because the past is painful in California, we have fabricated a history for the missions that is pure myth. Let's just get it over with and admit that it's not only a myth, but a pretty deliberately fabricated one. None of the romance is true. The mission myth of California is the unintentional result of a novel about California Indians *after* the mission era, coupled with the more deliberate effort of magazine editors who sold California as a paradise, a land of sun, health, and romantic missions. El Camino Real never existed.[31] No royal "king's" road ever linked the missions, not ever. The missions were not one day apart, as is commonly believed.[32] The oxidized bells along the side of the freeway were the idea of a woman whose husband owned the only bell-making factory in the west. But the honor for actually placing the bells in 1906 goes to the Camino Real Association.[33] The friars wore gray robes, not brown ones (as they are usually depicted), till the 1890s, way after the mission period ended.[34] The whole "mission" myth is a Hollywood script, a public relations coup, history without substance.

The myth is started in part by Helen Hunt Jackson's novel about California Indians, *Ramona*, and then seems to take on a life of its own. This is not meant as a judgment on Helen Hunt Jackson's intentions, which were nothing but the best. John Ogden Pohlmann points out that she was a vocal advocate for Indian rights, as her other books testify: *A Century of Dishonor* (1881), and, with Abbot Kinney, *Report on the Condition and Needs of the Mission Indians* (1887). In the end, though, it's her series of articles on the missions for *Century* magazine that first solidifies the romance of the missions and sets the tone for how most other writers will approach them as romantic historical ruins (seemingly always seen by moonlight).[35] But in the sunlight, a different picture emerges.

Regardless of the stain of the missions, not all missionaries could possibly be ogres. I'm sure most of them died like Serra, owning nothing more than their gray habit and two undertunics. That they were human, yes, that their errors of judgment had disastrous consequences for native people is also true. Considering the tradition of Franciscans like Bernardino de Sahagún, the California missionaries appear surprisingly incurious about the indigenous communities they lived among.[36] They did not come to learn, to share, to commune. They came to impose their will. They had a unique opportunity to interact with native societies, in a land blessed with everything, but they approached their self-created task like brutish, bullish schoolteachers who brought discipline, work, prayer, and so-called progress (read destruction) to the native communities they encountered. The missions are a complete failure in transitioning the native people into Spanish or Mexican society—instead the indigenous communities are overwhelmed by the presence and power of the missionaries and soldiers.

The missions were never meant to be permanent fixtures, but rather temporary structures to be abolished once the Indians could sustain themselves. As usual, things never quite work out the way they're planned, and thus, not until the Mexican government insisted did the priests give up control of the missions. Even writing about the missions seems in some way to defeat their own temporary purpose. I can admire those who came here across the desert of Sonora or Baja California, hauling their meager belongings in oxcarts, and built the first pueblos. But I am not in agreement with the price that Native Americans paid so that the mission system (and later the pueblos) could flourish, so future generations of tourists could feel connected to a romantic past, intentional or unintentional.

My memories of the mission period are not in sync with what is portrayed in the myth or in the tours and dioramas that tourists see when they visit these sites. I identify with the Indians, not with the priests or the Spaniards. Why don't we romanticize the Native Americans, whose past represents the real origins of California, and who were the first settlers as it were? Instead what we romanticize is their destruction.

So, from my perspective, the "good old Mission days" never existed.

• • •

The tragedy of the missionaries, of Serra, Palóu, Murguía, and the rest, is that although from their point of view they were well intentioned, the mission system was a complete unmitigated disaster for the Native Americans. The Indians were a hunter-gatherer society, without chiefs, leaders, or specialists of any kind. Even medicine men were honored only as long as the medicine worked. There weren't even tribes per se, but communities. They distinguished only two seasons, winter and summer. But in California, really, how many seasons can you distinguish? The weather was temperate enough that for most of the year men dressed in the minimum of clothing, sometimes just a loincloth, and the women a skirt of woven grass. Although they traded for corn from the Colorado River area, they had no need for agriculture, since acorns gave them plenty of food, were much easier to gather, and did not require labor-intensive cultivation. They didn't deplete the natural resources, yet they often had a surplus food supply—of native acorns, for instance—to help them avoid famines during bad years. With a couple of hours of gathering or hunting per day, a family could survive, and survive well. The rest of the day was basically leisure time; in some ways, the indigenous inhabitants of California were the original laid-back society. So when the missionaries introduced religion and agriculture, what had been the Indians' free-flowing day suddenly became highly regimented, with work now lasting from sunup to sundown.[37] If they did not perish from disease, they perished from famine or overwork. And year by year their numbers declined. Where is the benefit in that?

Twenty-one missions were built in California, but don't kid yourself; it's not necessary to see every single one of them. About 90 percent of what you see in the missions is fake. Some of the missions are "authentic replicas," some were rebuilt totally from scratch, others aren't even the same size as the originals, and only a few of the missions have any part of the original building still standing. So in some ways what you get is not history but a cleaned-up, palatable version of history. To visit a modern-day mission is like visiting the Old West towns on the Universal Studio lot: plaster façades but no foundation to them.

Contrary to the myth that Serra's work was benevolent, Indian life at the missions was no paradise on earth. If you want to see the other side, visit Mission La Purísima Concepción near Lompoc. A five-day march from Mission San Fernando in the 1820s, it is now a three-hour drive along the Pacific Coast Highway. You approach from a small road off the main highway that skirts an Indian casino. If you stop outside the main gate of La Purísima, you are struck by its isolation. The bell tower is stark against the natural landscape, and if you squint and ignore the hum of the nearby freeway, you can almost see what the mission looked like two hundred years ago.

But to see the details of mission life you have to get up close to the machines: huge copper pots for rendering tallow, an olive crusher for making olive oil, a cross-arm rig for mass-producing tapers. It was intense labor, all done by Indians, and the finished products, along with the results of an extensive leather-hide production, were then traded by the priests to Yankee merchant captains, not to enrich the Indians, but to fill the missions' coffers. And then you should see the barracks, which were more like slave quarters, where the Indians lived cramped upon each other with hardly room to move and which were breeding grounds for dysentery, fevers, pleurisy, pneumonia, venereal diseases, scrofula, and other kinds of illnesses. Features not replicated at the missions are the stocks where Indians were shackled for days at a time or the flogging posts.

The entire history of the missions is a bloody mess. Besides the recurrent violence at San Diego, three acts of arson (burning down the mission) occur at San Luis Obispo within its first ten years, 1772–1782. In San Francisco, the neophytes rebel in 1776 and again in 1793–1794. In 1781 the Yuma on the Colorado River destroy the entire infrastructure of the mission and kill four priests and nearly all the settlers and soldiers.[38] A woman named Toyurina leads an Indian revolt at San Gabriel in 1785.[39] On the coast of California the conditions in several of the missions erupt into open insurrection in February of 1824. The Indians burn part of the church at Santa Inéz and also attack Santa Barbara. At La Purísima, the Chumash overwhelm the guards and take over the mission, holding it for nearly a month. It took a contingent of Mexican troops from Santa Barbara with a four-pound field artillery piece to put down the insurrection. After a three-hour siege, during which the Mexicans brought to bear an intense barrage of rifles and the single cannon against bow and arrows, the Chumash surrender. They had suffered sixteen killed and many wounded. The army executes seven Indians and sentences four others to ten years of hard labor at the presidio, plus exile from their lands. Eight others are imprisoned at the presidio for eight years.[40] No one has raised a monument to this revolt at La Purísima.

The failure of the Chumash apparently didn't deter other insurgents.

Mission San José feels the wrath of Estanislao, a neophyte turned rebel leader, in 1828.[41] And in 1831, Yoscolo, with several hundred followers, attacks Mission Santa Clara. He escapes to the Santa Cruz Mountains, where he holds out against the soldiers until he is wounded and then surrenders. He is then beheaded, and his severed head is mounted on a post in front of the mission church.[42]

The Indians revolted for good reason—and that reason was the cruelty and insufferable conditions under which they were forced to live. It wasn't just the priests who abused them; the soldiers were notorious for their physical abuse of the men and sexual abuse of the women. Throughout Baja and Alta California, the soldiers were considered the main source of introducing and spreading syphilis, which they called "El Gálico" or "Mal Gálico," mostly through rape.[43]

After a few short decades of contact with the Spaniards, these once robust people became sick, malnourished figures of misery. As an example, in 1765 the indigenous population of the San Fernando Valley was approximately 5,000 people; by 1890, there was barely a handful left. During the years the Indians lived in the mission under the priests, 2,837 persons were baptized and 2,028 were buried. These figures are only for the Christianized Indians; the non-Christian Indian population was depleted even faster.[44] All over California the Indian population declined dramatically after the establishment of the missions.

The secularization of the missions takes place under the Mexican government from 1821 to 1833 and brings an end to the whole mission period of California history, romantic or otherwise. What had been church land now fell under the control of the more powerful of the Californios, who had long coveted the vineyards, olive groves, and cattle ranches of the missions. Most of the assets were then either sold off or used by them or their overseers, counter to the theory that the land belonged to the neophytes.[45] This is the period of the great ranchero boom that produced men like Andrés Pico, Mariano Vallejo, and others. This shift in the nature of landholding ushers in the era of the Californios and its accompanying new myths, legends, and realities. And what of the Native Americans who'd been trapped and become dependent on the missions? They are left to fend for themselves, but since they'd lost their natural connection to nature and their survival skills, their numbers further decline.

•　•　•

Chronologically, the establishment of Mission San Fernando comes near the end of the mission period, being the seventeenth of the twenty-one missions founded in California. The mission is founded by Fray Fermín Lasuén in 1797 on ranch land that belonged to Francisco Reyes, then alcalde of

Nuestra Señora de Los Angeles. Before Lasuén and Reyes, the Shoshone lived there in a village they called Achois Comihabit. The first white men to travel through the San Fernando Valley were members of Portolá's expedition of 1769. Later, the ubiquitous Father Pedro Font, during his travels with de Anza's expedition of 1775–1776, notes in his diary that the valley is filled with oak and herds of deer.[46] He even records an earthquake that scares him half to death one night as they made camp. This mission was never an important link between the older, more established missions of San Gabriel and San Buenaventura. It was merely there.

What's missing at San Fernando, like at all the missions, reveals just as much as what is there. Although the friars taught the neophytes the rudimentaries of music, they neither built nor used formal classrooms. Perhaps to prove to themselves how "childlike" the natives were, the priests offered no classes in reading and writing. Without any attempt on the part of the priests to educate their wards, the Indians could never "progress," and therefore never develop the skills to adapt to the new society. This fundamental failure of the missionaries kept the Indians as an uneducated, subservient class, used primarily for physical labor and as a pool of unenlightened on which the priests could exercise their "spiritual" labor. It is doubtful whether two or three more decades under the Franciscans would have made it any better or easier for the mission Indians to survive the onslaught of the United States in 1846.

Perhaps because the missions were religious sites, they were dry places to live, spiritually and artistically. During their reign no miracles are recorded; no water was turned into wine, there was no multiplying of loaves and fishes, and no virgins appeared on hilltops, either. Nor were any art classes taught. The padres as a group seemed devoid of artistic inspiration, since not a single painting or even a sketch done by a padre exists.[47] In terms of religious art, the closest thing the California missions left us is a series of fourteen panels, known as the *Via Crucis*, that come from Mission San Fernando. The Via Crucis, the Stations of the Cross, which depict Jesus Christ making his way to Calvary, form an inherent part of the Roman Catholic iconography, and for centuries these scenes have been depicted in most Catholic churches. The panels of Mission San Fernando, of dubious origin, were originally attributed to an Indian neophyte for no other reason than that the artist is unknown. But recent studies by scholars cast doubt on the theory that an Indian named Juan Antonio, of Mission San Fernando, painted the *Via Crucis*; most likely the panels were painted by a priest or a soldier and later passed off as "Indian" art. It is also possible they were painted in Mexico and then shipped to Alta California. Only if they are "Indian" art would they have any historical or cultural value; otherwise, as

Western renderings, they are poor and crude. Even their original reference in the mission inventory of 1849 describes them as *"muy ordinarios"*—very ordinary. My own observations lead me to believe that several different hands were involved in the work.

Painted sometime before 1849 for Mission San Fernando, the panels disappear around 1870 and reappear in the lower room of the bell tower of the Plaza Church in Los Angeles in 1887. In 1892, they are exhibited in Sacramento and then are cleaned up, reframed, and exhibited in Chicago at the World's Columbian Exhibition. It's at this same exhibition that another California "mission" myth takes off—the Gustav Stickley style of "mission" furniture, which has nothing to do with real mission furniture, as you may suspect by now.[48]

After the Columbian Exhibition, the *Via Crucis* panels are shuffled from mission to mission, and during the 1920s and 1930s the panels are stored in a basement, then hung in a shed, at the mercy of the elements. It is understandable, then, if their condition isn't primo, and even a casual viewer will find the folds and spotting on several of the panels. Eventually, they are photographed for the Index of American Design and even exhibited at the Los Angeles County Museum of Art in 1940.[49] Thus, they are magically turned into important art. They now hang on the interior walls of the chapel of Mission San Gabriel, where I saw them one Thursday afternoon when I drove out to satisfy my curiosity about this mission-Indian "masterpiece."

Nothing in the gift shop or outside the chapel indicated any relation to the *Via Crucis* panels. Once I stepped inside the chapel, it took a few minutes for my eyes to adjust to the dim light. The chapel had nothing memorable about it, so my attention went right to the fourteen panels, which hung on the two main walls of the chapel.

The panels have a naïve style to them, which, I suppose, is understandable. The fourteen panels survive a bit dark in tone, but the colors are distinguishable. What I found most interesting were the figures, especially the soldiers with the balloon pants and Turkish-type hats and the women in medieval conical hats that give the scenes a Byzantine feel to them. The faces are interesting, grotesque almost, and crudely realized; the feet are not fully painted, and the hands awkward. Some soldiers are depicted in profile, showing just one eye, and the eye is out of proportion, making them look like a Cyclops. The overall impression is not that someone copied prints of the Stations of the Cross, as has been speculated, but that in representing the faces, the artists copied the Dutch painter Hieronymus Bosch.

If we are asked to believe an Indian painted the panels, the images of horses that appear six different times tell us nothing about the artist's relation to this beast. I find that odd, considering that horses were novelties. I would guess that someone who saw nothing unique in this animal, a priest or soldier perhaps, painted the horses. And what about panel twelve? Here we find, in the upper left, a figure of the sun and in the upper right, a figure of the moon. But the moon is a traditional side-view rendering of the man in the moon, which is a totally Western touch.

On the other hand, a native artisan might have added certain details. A half dozen of the panels have painted frames that circumscribe the action. The frame around the fifth panel is similar in design to the motif around the inside of the Mission San Fernando chapel, and a similar motif of half circles is painted around the seventh panel. We can speculate that a neophyte from the mission painted these designs, but that would require collaboration between priest or soldier and a neophyte. If we take into consideration that none of the priests showed any artistic talent or desire, a priest seems highly unlikely. So we are left thinking that perhaps a soldier or other layman worked with an Indian in the painting of these panels, but without any solid proof that this sort of social relationship existed in Mission San Fernando. Therefore, readers can decide for themselves who might have painted these *Via Crucis* panels, although the answer might not make them any wiser regarding Indians and the mission system.

Although the *Via Crucis* of San Fernando are interesting and even enjoyable works of art, they are not masterworks, especially when compared to what self-taught artists like Hermenegildo Bustos from Oaxaca were doing in the 1870s.[50] The *Via Crucis* panels of San Fernando are a mishmash of styles, techniques, and palettes. Their value is more as a curiosity because they are old rather than because they are art in the grand sense of the word.

For anyone to declare the *Via Crucis* panels masterpieces of "Indian" art would be a desperate attempt to impart a level of culture to the missions that just wasn't really there. I look at them as sad proof that the missionaries taught the Indians very little, that in truth no masterpieces of any kind were produced under the mission system.

· · ·

While I was writing this essay, I returned to Mission San Fernando to see if my memories jibed with the current reality. The present-day Mission San Fernando is a popular tourist destination in the North Valley. Buses were lined up in the parking lot, and the tourists pouring out of them filled the air with a gaggle of comments, "Oh how pretty," "We only have thirty minutes," "Where's the bathroom in this place?" I heard many languages, including English, French, Italian, and German. A quartet of Japanese tourists, in shorts, sun hats, sunglasses, and cameras, seemed unsure of whether to join the tour or not. Some of the men skipped the tour to stand outside the gift shop smoking cigarettes and staring at the sky or at nothing.

I don't need the tour of Mission San Fernando Rey de España, but if you want it, here it is. The tourists will go through the gift shop, then the *convento*, or monastery, that housed the priests, the guest accommodations, kitchen, refectory, chapel, and winery. (San Fernando has the only surviving winery of all the missions.) The *convento*'s colonnade, 243 feet long by 50 feet wide; its three-foot-thick walls; and its twenty-one arches are unique among all the missions. Also in the *convento* the tourists will step into the Junípero Serra Theater, where they might run into a gaggle of local school-children watching a film about mission life (although in mission days, children, movie cameras did not exist). Some tourists will walk through the immaculate, trimmed, well-cared-for grounds and take photographs of themselves next to the statue of Lasuén, the founder of this mission, or the one of Junípero Serra. Others will enter the chapel and look around, though the men won't remove their hats and neither will the women. At the end of the tour they might even look in the rooms that are meant to replicate the work areas of the Indians, where they'll see the spindles and looms. And they'll say to each other, "This is so authentic." Afterward, they'll head back to the gift shop and buy postcards or pamphlets; those who haven't yet, will use the restrooms. Then they'll pile back into the buses, content that they've stepped into history and seen the "good old Mission days."

I go my own way, separate from the tourists. I've come to see Monsignor Weber, who currently administers the mission. He has stepped out, so I wait in the East Garden, next to a gnarled olive tree that must be at least a hundred years old or more. As I am waiting, I think of Rogério Rocha, one of the last Indians of Mission San Fernando, who'd been born and baptized here during the first decade of the nineteenth century. He'd been trained as a blacksmith by the missionaries, and though he never learned English, he knew Spanish as well as his native tongue and could conduct church services in Latin. For some sixty years he lived in a house he'd built himself and farmed a ten-acre plot of land near San Fernando, from which, according to Spanish and Mexican law, he could not be evicted. Remember, legally, the missions held the land in trust for the Indian communities that worked them. Then in 1886, in a legal shenanigan perpetrated by George K. Porter and John Maclay, Rogério and his wife, both of whom were then in their eighties, as well as three old women who lived with them, were forcibly evicted. Deputies came one day and loaded a wagon with the old people's belongings and dumped them on the public road. With nowhere to go, they were caught in a fierce storm that lasted four days. Although Rogério survived, his wife succumbed to pneumonia. Eventually Rogério moved to a piece of land loaned to him by a Mexican, in a wild *cañon* behind the mountains, where he died in 1904 at the age of 102.[51] These stories of how Anglo California dealt with mission Indians never make it into the tourist guides. If justice existed, the street in present-day San Fernando named after Maclay would be renamed in honor of Rogério Rocha, and the junior high I attended, named for George K. Porter, would honor the Shoshone.

After lunch I find the monsignor in his office in the archival center. He is a tall, beefy man, jovial, broad of shoulders, white-haired, and dressed in black. He is a bit flippant with me when I tell him that I'm writing about the missions. Perhaps it's competitiveness between writers—he's written a slew of monographs about the missions, so to him I'm just a novice, another tourist perhaps. Or maybe it's just his personality.

Monsignor Weber is in many ways a lot like an early missionary, a man of utter faith in the church who has never wanted to be anything but a priest. And his relationship to Native Americans strikes me as not much different from that of the original missionaries. When I mention Native Americans, he responds: "Oh, there's Manuel who comes around here and says he's a Native American, but that's nonsense. He's just a fool. There are no Native Americans. I'm a Native American. I was born here." (Actually, he was born in Indiana.) I look at this ruddy-faced white man and picture the statue in the park of Junípero Serra guiding an Indian youth, and I think—it's that damn arrogance all over again. Every priest I've ever known is the same—they all think they know better than we dark-skinned folks do; they still look upon us as naïve innocents incapable of critical thought, as mere beasts of burden to be paid with a ticket to a heaven that doesn't exist.

For some reason, as if to prove my credentials to write about Mission San Fernando, I mention Mark Harrington, the key preservationist not only of the mission but of the Pico adobe a few blocks away.

"I knew Harrington just before he died," says Weber, "but he wasn't very coherent."

"Well," I respond, "when I knew him he was quite lucid."

The monsignor seems startled by my statement, and for once he seems out of words. Then I ask to see their library, and he guides me to their research/reading room, where all the books are kept locked behind glass cases, as if history is too precious for just anyone. He unlocks a bookcase and pulls out a book on the life of Mark Harrington.[52] I have it only long enough to jot down the title and author before the monsignor tells me he must return to work and snatches the book from my hands.

After he leaves, I walk through the mission grounds again, remembering what it was like as a young boy coming here on Sundays. Why is it that the sermons and the liturgies never spoke to me? And what atavistic urge, or historical memory if you will, calls me back to this place now? Wouldn't it be better to just forget the missions ever existed?

At the end of my walk, I'm drawn to the *campo santo* behind the mission chapel. I'm expecting to find all the old crosses and headstones that used to instill in me a strange nostalgia, but instead I find that the cemetery has been cleaned up and grass planted everywhere. I find just a handful of tombstones, whereas I remember many more of them. Perhaps this is a trick of memory, I'm not sure. But before leaving I discover two new headstones added to the green lawn. The dates of birth and death are modern and the names weird. Now I'm really confused. Did I create a myth of headstones back here? On my way out of the gift shop I ask one of the girls behind the counter about the new headstones in the *campo santo*. "Oh, my gosh," she says in that sing-song Valley girl way. "Those are for the monsignor's dogs that are buried there."

Outside, another bus loaded with tourists is parking. The first bus is pulling out, and it raises a cloud of dust in my face. The tourists who are leaving have not seen a thing; they only think they have. They were searching for the sun-drenched missions they had admired in postcards during their cold New England or Midwest winters, the fabled paradise that never was. None of the tourists, either coming or going, notice me standing in the shade of the *convento* arches, just as two hundred years ago the priests and soldiers didn't see me, a human being, a man, not a beast of burden. I know we have come here for different reasons. They are tourists just passing by like wind in the grass. I am pulled by the dead whose bones buried here somewhere infuse these grounds with their tragic memory.

JOSEFA OF DOWNIEVILLE

The Obscure Life and Notable Death of a

Chicana in Gold Rush California

I told the deceased that was no place to call me bad
names, come in and call me so, and as he was coming
in I stabbed him.

**—Josefa, in her own defense, Downieville,
July 5, 1851**

These words spoken by a Mexican woman on trial
for murder at the height of the California Gold Rush jumped out at me
when I first read them in a newspaper dated 1851. Who was this woman
who spoke in public so calmly yet forcefully, and for whom the only name
we have is Josefa? The tragic circumstances of her death obsessed me for
weeks, till finally, one summer day I drove out from San Francisco to visit
the Mother Lode country, La Veta Madre, as the *mexicanos* called it, the site
of this story. I crossed over the San Mateo Bridge and over the Altamont
pass, then through Tracy, headed for Stockton. But way before driving out
of San Francisco, I too, in my own way, had become obsessed with gold.
What role does it play in my memory? All the history books praise the
forty-niners, but I don't like them or their history (I don't even like the
football team named after them). I am a victim of their arrival: the forty-
niners displaced and murdered those who were already here—the Native
Americans and the Californios. My Gold Rush heritage is that Chicanos
are now foreigners in their own land. Yet at the start of the Gold Rush we
claimed the land with our names: Hornitos, Sonora, Mariposa—names that
still survive, especially in the heart of gold country.

As I drive east, I think of the events of that day in 1851, in a now insignificant town at the end of Highway 49. Of all the stories of the Gold
Rush, of incredible fortunes made and lost overnight, of violent deaths that
occurred in the goldfields with boring repetition, Josefa's is the one that
matters most to me, the one I choose to recover from the dustbins of history. It is a story of drunken vigilantes and ignoble patriots, and of men who
stood by while a woman was lynched, and those stories are never pretty. I

often ask myself what I might have done that day in Downieville. I sometimes imagine myself the hero, rushing to Josefa's rescue wielding a shotgun, and then taking her away on my horse. But I don't know for sure; I might have just closed my eyes, not wanting to see. Her violent death is an open wound in my memory, and yet I cannot right the wrong done to her. Perhaps the only thing I can do is recover her story, restore to her a sense of human dignity. And by telling the story, vindicate all good women and men, including myself, because if good people allow evil to go unchallenged, even if it's an incident a hundred and fifty years old, our perceptions and attitudes of race and gender, of right and wrong, become entrenched, sometimes forever.

A casual conversation with a friend in a Mission District café, one of those conversations fueled by coffee and cigarettes, started me on this road. Had I ever heard of the Mexican woman who was lynched during the Gold Rush? I had always thought lynching occurred only in the South, to black people. I didn't know that Mexicans were lynched in California, much less that it was a common occurrence during the Gold Rush. Our conversation drifted to other topics, and I forgot about the story. But in the coming days, at the oddest moments, I'd find myself thinking about this woman. Something about the incident infuriated me. Why was she just a mere footnote, even in Chicano history, especially when her courage is an example for all of us? Were the forty-niners really so immoral and ruthless as to have lynched a woman? Or was this just a myth, another made-up story, like the one about James Marshall's first nugget, that had now passed into the realm of "history"? But the more I followed her trail, in microfilm newspaper accounts and journals written by eyewitnesses, the more her story seemed authentic, and not just authentic, it seemed to encapsulate the story of all Chicanos in the Gold Rush. How we were pushed aside, driven out, murdered, and lynched, and how then even our names and graves were erased from the face of the earth, so as to leave not a trace that we had been here.

As I drive out to the Sierras, with the back seat of my car stacked with books, pamphlets, and photocopied newspapers from 1851, I already know that killing a Mexican during the Gold Rush years was common enough, but what the forty-niners did to Josefa is the bone in the throat of California history.

• • •

The Sierra Nevada, the matrix of the gold country, is an impressive range of burned-out volcanoes whose ice-fed streams carve the gorges and canyons of the foothills and, like a benevolent regent, nurture the San Joaquin Valley and all the main rivers in the state. It is in the Sierra Nevada that gold was created millions of years ago. The creation of gold is a metamorphic process: gold rises from deep in the earth in liquid form, usually mingled with quartz; as the gold cools it crystallizes, producing exotic filigrees embedded in the rock. The quartz, with the gold still in it, is grouted into the cracks of mountains, forming what are called veins. Some veins run for miles under the earth, others are mere pencil lines. If you know this about gold, you know where to find it. Find the quartz veins and the gold will be in it. The other place gold is found is in riverbeds. As erosion wears away the mountains, the gold, sometimes still in its quartz matrix, is washed into the gorges, where the quartz is pummeled and scraped off by the rushing rivers coming down from the mountains. Eventually, the river wears away the quartz, and what's left is the gold, a heavy, dense metal that settles at the bottom of the creek or river.[1] The metal has different forms: flake, nugget, sponge, wire—the latter being the rarest. Gold will not tarnish, fade, or wear out; it will lie in the heart of the mountain or in a creek bottom until a human hand picks it up.

Native Americans didn't care for gold. It had no value to them. None. They valued gypsum and amethyst for jewelry, serpentine for charm stones.[2] They adored abalone shell, polishing it to a bright mother of pearl, and feathers of different types of birds: condors, eagles, hawks, and hummingbirds. Once the forty-niners invaded the region, Native Americans did work in the goldfields, sometimes for wages; other times they bartered the gold for needed supplies.[3] The Californios blew hot and cold about gold. It's an old story in Chicano history that in 1842, in a canyon behind Mission San Fernando, Francisco López sat down to eat his lunch, pulled out a wild onion growing alongside the creek, and discovered clinging to the roots—¡Oro! Gold, compadre! His lucky find inspired some miners to trek north from Sonora, Mexico.[4] They worked for a while around the area where López had found gold, now named Placerita Canyon, and then lost interest in the project and moved on, south to Los Angeles or north to Monterey. Another Mexicano, Pablo Gutiérrez, found gold in the Bear River of Northern California in March 1844, but he was unable to procure a *batea* for panning, so nothing came of it.[5] The Californios who came to the goldfields in 1848 were casual miners; many were established rancheros, like Antonio Franco Coronel, who left as the troubles escalated, disgusted with the violence and the murders.

The forty-niners, on the other hand, hungered for gold with a sickness. They even described it as "gold fever." They would do anything for it. They left families, homes, everything behind; they sailed for eight months aboard leaky, smelly ships to reach California; others, captains and sailors, jumped ship at San Francisco, leaving a fleet of abandoned brigs, barks, and schooners to rot by the piers.[6] They slaughtered all the game they could find and so muddied the rivers and creeks with silt that the once plentiful salmon couldn't survive.[7] The herds of elk and deer, the food source for Native Americans, were practically wiped out in one summer. The miners cheated and killed each other in the goldfields. The newspaper accounts of the day are filled with their bloody deeds and grizzly frontier justice, or maybe it should be called injustice.[8] And in 1851, after an all-day celebration for the Fourth of July, a mob of forty-niners unleashed all their venom and hatred on a Mexican woman.

Several things disturbed me about this incident when I first read about it: the misogynist and racial implications, as well as the absence of a last name for Josefa. I, who was obsessed with names, who could spend days in sterile archives searching for even a minute reference to a Lugo, Olivas, or Murguía, suddenly found myself faced with one specific person who had no full name. In general, when writing about violence toward Amerindians or Mexicans, Western historiographers tend to use incomplete names, usually just the first name or a generic one, like "José," as if the individual didn't matter. It made me realize that it is not names and bloodlines that hold clans together, but rather their shared experience.

The eyewitness account published in *The Steamer Pacific Star* dated July 15, 1851, lists the full names of the judge, the jury, the witnesses—all of them white males—and four names for the victim, also white, a first name, a middle name, and two last names. Yet with Josefa, not even the reporter who was present records her last name, nor does it appear in any of the forty-niner journals that describe the event. Sure, no one takes notes at a lynching, but there was a pretense of a trial, with a judge and jury sworn in. All the accounts state that she testified in her own defense, and, therefore, must have been sworn in too. So what happened that her last name was never recorded, an important detail in any judicial hearing, even at a kangaroo court? Didn't anyone ask "What's your full name?"

Without a doubt, the California Gold Rush is the most written about event in the West. Yet not a single historian has questioned why Josefa has no last name. It seems that a Mexican woman in the goldfields was insignificant, not even worthy of a last name, just another "greaser." And then, over the course of many decades, historians like Hubert Howe Bancroft changed her name to fit the stereotypical Mexican image: she is now referred to as "Juanita of Downieville," which just adds insult to injury.[9] In some accounts she's even called "Juanita, the Spanish woman." So even her single name and her nationality have been distorted.

At other times, Josefa is portrayed in all sorts of romantic images, including the ridiculous, such as she "cheerfully passed away." [10] But no one has ever stood up for her. No one has ever asked why she was given such a harsh sentence, carried out so brutally, or where she learned the poise to defend herself before a kangaroo court and a frenzied mob. Where did she find the *corazón* to stand on the gallows and show more bravery than any man that day?

These questions were what set me on the road to Downieville.

• • •

In the history of Mexico and Latin America, gold has always been a double-edged sword. The Europeans, the Spaniards, and the North Americans invaded our lands, driven by their desire to acquire the precious metal. Latin Americans, Mexicans, and Californios have always, by a quirk of fate, occupied land rich in gold deposits, but we have never looked upon this metal with the obsessive avarice of Europeans. Gold might be decorative and beautiful, but in pre-Columbian America it was never the coin of the realm, and never something worth killing for.

As a young boy, I'd heard the stories of gold-crazed Spaniards: Cortés melting to ingots the intricate gifts Moctezuma had offered him, completely disregarding their beauty; his only concern was their monetary value. Or the story of the Inca, Atahualpa, who offered to fill one room with gold and one with silver if Pizarro would release him; but when the ransom was paid, Atahualpa was hung. And somewhere I have seen an old engraving of Indians pouring molten gold down a Spaniard's throat in the belief that only that remedy would cure them of their gold sickness.

So for me, gold has always been suspicious. And in spite of its allure, within my lifetime, I've seen gold lose much of its luster. As I write this, an ounce of gold on the London market is worth much less than an ounce of Humboldt green on any barrio street. So gold has an arbitrary value that is relative, depending on the importance you put on it, much like the value of a human life in the Gold Rush. But how can we compare a human life to a fistful of gold dust? I can't. I suspect few of us can. For the ancient Mexicans and Peruvians, gold was precious, but with no monetary value. For others, it's the engine that drives the wheel. And that wheel has always crushed us.

When I first started writing about Josefa, I too became obsessed with gold; it seemed that to understand what precipitated the events of that day in 1851, I had to know gold. I had to feel gold fever in my veins to understand what drove men to such frenzy over it. Is it that beautiful?

In terms of appearance, in its natural state gold is totally unimpressive. The nuggets on exhibit at the Oakland Museum as part of the California Gold Rush Sesquicentennial Project left me feeling a bit like the Native Americans. So what's the big deal here? I was looking at the very same nugget that James Marshall supposedly found in Coloma and brought to

John Sutter. The nondescript nugget was on loan from the Smithsonian and sat in a glass case. It was this nugget that had started the Gold Rush, but I was completely unfazed. First of all, I couldn't see any beauty in the metal itself. It looked to me a bit like calcified dog turd that I might hose from my sidewalk on any given morning. Secondly, I was suspicious as to how this nugget on display could possibly be the same one that Marshall found that January morning in 1848. This business of *the nugget* sounded to me a bit like wishful thinking, much like the early Christians believing in slivers of the True Cross. Regardless of what the Smithsonian Institute claims, the chances of this glass-encased nugget being the first one that Marshall found are in the realm of a billion to one, in other words, nil.[11] But 190,000 people went through the exhibit, and they all believed it was the true nugget. Gold, in the California imagination, can make people believe the implausible. It is the stuff that dreams are made of.

At the beginning of the Gold Rush, in 1848, the gold was literally lying about in the creeks and streams. A person didn't even have to pan for it. You could walk along a stream and maybe pick up several nuggets wedged between the rocks. The biggest nugget found was the size of a cantaloupe, cubic in form, and nearly pure—a twenty-three-pound gold nugget just sitting in the riverbed waiting to be picked up.[12]

At first, it was mostly locals who were in the goldfields, but by 1849 the word had spread and thousands started arriving from all over the world, from Chile and Peru, China, even Malaysia and points east. Soon, approximately one hundred thousand miners were roaming the Sierra foothills, and 7 million dollars' worth of gold was coming out every month. The totals are staggering: in 1851, the year of this story, 75 million dollars' worth of gold flowed out of California. By the end of the decade, 594 million dollars' worth of gold had enriched the treasury of the United States.[13] And the gold kept coming, year after year. During the Civil War, California gold poured into the financial center of New York at the rate of 5 to 6 million dollars' worth a month, and thereby prevented a total collapse of Lincoln's government.[14] Without that gold to feed, clothe, and maintain the Northern armies, Lincoln's *Emancipation Proclamation* might not have been worth the paper it was written on. Heinrich Schliemann, a young German adventurer, made his fortune in the California goldfields and thus financed his childhood dream—to discover the site of ancient Troy. The list is endless. With California gold, dreams were possible. Without California gold, I wouldn't be writing this, and life would be much different for all of us.

•   •   •

Nowadays, if you travel Highway 49, you will find the towns freshly painted, the main streets lined with boutiques and cafés, and tourists in khaki shorts drinking at hotel bars and paying with credit cards. But once upon a time, these same towns were ruthless, drinks were paid with gold dust, and life was worth less than an ounce of gold. Behind the present-day tourist-trap façade lies a history that is both ugly and violent.

East of Modesto, I take Highway 26 into the Sierra foothills, over Moke-lumne Hill, into the town of Mokelumne, a thumb print of history, with its narrow winding streets and abandoned ruins. Here I hook up with Highway 49. The story goes that during the Gold Rush the trail from Mokelumne to Jackson was marked with empty bottles; perhaps it's just a story, but the original name of Jackson is Botellas, Spanish for "bottles."[15]

When I reach Jackson, I stop to get a feel for the gold country towns. Jackson is typical of restored Gold Rush towns: bed and breakfast inns, antique stores—the tourist business is booming. It's the past they are selling here, not the present. And like everything else that is sold to tourists, it must be squeaky clean. The foot-high sidewalks are spotless, hundred-year-old buildings are juxtaposed with modern storefronts, and history is kept behind a glass case. Garibaldi's Camera Shop in the center of town features old photographs of Jackson in the 1880s. One photo shows Jackson in the 1930s, all lit up with Saturday night traffic. It's like looking at photos of your grandmother when she was twenty—you know it's her, but the resemblance is hard to see.

At the end of Main Street stands the National Hotel, built in 1863. The hotel bar is damp and smoky, with red globe Victorian lamps on the ceiling and the odor of spilled beer thick as a curtain. I imagine it looks much like it did in its heyday. An ornate mirror hangs behind the bar, the wooden floor is warped, and, though it is barely two in the afternoon, customers are sitting around drinking beers and shots of whisky. I'm still several hours from my destination, so I don't stay long, but I take notice of a plaque behind the bar—fifty yards east of the hotel, Botilla's (a misspelling of Botellas [Bottles]) Bordello flourished well into this century. Before leaving the National Hotel, the tattooed bartender tells me that Jackson had legalized prostitution, with several bordellos operating around Main Street until 1956, when Governor Pat Brown decided that enough was enough and outlawed the oldest game in town. This reminds me that Oscar Zeta Acosta, in his *Autobiography of a Brown Buffalo*, recounts stories of himself as a teenager, driving into Jamestown, just down the road from Jackson, to hang out with the women at Ruby's Banana Ranch.[16] So with the last sip of my mineral water I toast the memory of the old Brown Buffalo. Here in the Sierra foothills the Old West died hard—and not too long ago.

After leaving Jackson, I head north. The landscape of the gold country is beautiful: rolling hills, majestic oaks, wildflowers bursting forth in bright colors from the red earth. The present Highway 49 follows the original stagecoach route carved out of the Sierra Nevada, and it runs for a hundred miles along the foothills in a north-south trajectory. It is known as the Gold Country Highway, and the string of small towns spaced along the route form the background of many stories. One hundred and fifty years ago, the Wells Fargo stagecoaches linked the towns of the Mother Lode, bringing newcomers to the rough-and-tumble world of the goldfields and collecting gold dust for shipment to the port of San Francisco. During the Gold Rush, each of these towns was a miniature booming city. Some of them, like Nevada City, were, in their heyday, the biggest and richest cities in California.[17] But they were cities without substance, built to slake the thirst of miners, and when the rivers of gold dried up, or it became too expensive to operate the mines, the reason for their existence ceased, and these towns were abandoned almost overnight.

I'd have to look at a map to check where Highway 49 begins—somewhere near Yosemite Valley, I suppose—but I know quite well where it ends: in the little town of Downieville.

• • •

When exactly Josefa arrives in the goldfields is unknown. Most likely she is from Sonora,[18] one of 10,000 other Sonoran miners who worked and lived in the gold country. The Sonorans from northern Mexico, and other Latin Americans, had a long history of gold mining, and they brought with them the tools and techniques to extract the gold once the easy pickings were over. The Sonorans brought the wooden sluices called *bateas* for panning gold. And the Chileans introduced the *arrastra*, a heavy stone boulder that a mule drags over quartz to crush it and release the gold. They brought with them not just the culture of gold mining but the language as well; and as I'm driving down Highway 49, the Spanish names crop up like ghosts from the past—El Dorado, Placer, Campo Seco.

But the experience and success of the Sonoran miners were used against them. In 1849, the newcomers arriving from New England did not know the technique for panning or mining gold, and they felt envious of the Sonorans, who knew where to find the quartz veins.[19] The United States had just taken California from Mexico, and the forty-niners believed they were the only ones who had a right to the gold—everyone else, especially nonwhites or those who spoke Spanish, was an interloper, a trespasser, an enemy. As it was, the camps were tense, tough, dirty places. Men survived the best they could, and the weak, those who couldn't protect their claims, didn't last long in the goldfields. Moreover, the laws were heavily stacked against foreigners, men and women. For instance, nonwhites could not testify in a court of law against whites. Then, adding further tension to the situation, California passed the Foreign Miners Tax of 1850, a monthly fee of twenty dollars levied on all nonwhite miners, with the explicit purpose of running the Sonorans, the Latinos, and the Chinese out of the goldfields.[20]

The Sonorans were caught in an ironic situation. Many had been in California before the newly arrived forty-niners, and yet they were being taxed as foreigners. They were the founders of the town of Sonora, one of the richest in the gold country, and now they were being chased out. It wasn't lost on them that other foreigners, the Irish or the English, for example, were not taxed. And if the Sonorans refused to pay the taxes, the forty-niners encouraged each other to jump their claims. The Chinese turned to vegetable growing to survive, while many of the Sonorans left the goldfields disillusioned, or were run out by mobs of forty-niners. Towns they had founded, like Sonora, were abandoned; others, like Columbia, were left with but a handful of miners.[21] But other Sonorans stayed, out of pride perhaps or out of stubbornness. Some were killed; some became outlaws. Out of such conditions arose Joaquín Murieta, the legendary Robin Hood of the Gold Rush era, the hero of a tale so twisted it will take a determined scholar to unravel it.

With a typical mix of the multiple nationalities in the goldfields, Downieville, originally a camp, was founded in 1850 by a Major Downie, with his crew of ten black sailors, one Irishman, one Indian, and one Kanaka, a native Hawaiian.[22] Although the Foreign Miners Tax was repealed in March of 1851, mostly because of complaints by merchants that they were losing business, the damage had been done. By mid-1851, the once plentiful Sonorans were rare in the Sierra foothills. So for Josefa, or any Mexican woman, to have reached the gold country, she had to be resilient, brave, and determined. The last fifty miles of the road to Downieville deteriorated into a winding mule trail cut out of steep ravines along the Yuba River.[23] The journey was not only hard; it was dangerous, whether on foot or on horseback. It was not uncommon for travelers to lose their footing and plunge into the ravine, mules and all. The living conditions along the fork of the river where the camp had sprouted were primitive at best: tents, lean-tos, shanties, and ankle-deep mud everywhere. But Downieville also had two-story wooden buildings, fifteen hotels and gambling houses, butcher shops and bakeries, a theater, and plenty of saloons.

An Argentine miner named Ramón Gil Navarro came to the Gold Rush in 1849 and spent the following three years living and working in the Sierras, alternating with travels to Stockton and San Francisco. He kept a detailed diary that offers some interesting observations about the milieu in which Josefa lived. I quote Navarro because, as a Latin American, he gives a different perspective than the white-authored first-person narratives of that period, which tend to be prejudiced toward everyone of color. Navarro shows himself to be an astute observer, willing to change his own prejudices—about Indian women, for instance—if proven wrong.[24] He also looks at the various races in the goldfields through a humanist lens; his description of black slaves in the goldfields is an example.[25] The scarcity of women in the goldfields is mentioned by every writer in the field, and Navarro is no exception. He recounts in his diary the burial of a white woman, Miss Sheldon, whose horse-drawn casket is followed by well-dressed men because, as Navarro puts it: "The female sex around here sure has a lot of value."[26] Their value is not just emotional (for comfort, physical and otherwise) but also monetary, as he mentions later in his diary when he's at Sonora: "In each one of them [the hotels] there is a beautiful girl at the bar and another one at the gambling table, attempting to attract people and crowds to the hotel. Without a girl there can be no hotel, without a beautiful one there can be no business, without a woman there can be no business or anything else."[27]

Navarro also recounts the rumors that abounded of how Yankee bandits, called "The Forty," were planning to rally other miners to exterminate all Chileans, Mexicans, or Peruvians on July Fourth, 1849. He goes on to state that threats against foreigners are common on this day, causing many Mexicans to leave the towns and mines of the region.[28] Considering the Foreign Miners Tax of 1850 and the open violence toward Mexicans and Latin Americans between 1849 and 1851, also detailed by Navarro, I'd suspect that the mood of the forty-niners two years later, on July 4, 1851, had become even more patriotically belligerent.

For Josefa to have lived in Downieville during this unsettled period was an accomplishment in itself. But her courage in the face of an angry mob of forty-niners is the stuff of legend, in the same league with Joan of Arc or whatever woman warrior you want to compare her to. A hundred years from now, all the names involved in this story, including that of the writer, will be forgotten, but Josefa's name will live on. In my eyes, Josefa is an amazing woman who, through great sacrifice and courage, claims her rights as a human being on the very edge of the goldfields, in a primitive camp twenty miles from the summit of the Sierra Nevada, a place where only the toughest arrived.

• • •

After 1851, when the easy pickings were over, when the work of sluicing and panning, standing all day in frigid water, stopped being profitable, the gold business changed. More gold had to be produced to quench the thirst for wealth and profit. So hydraulic mining developed, and powerful hoses carved the mountains as if they were cakes. You can still see the sad shells of those washed-away mountains, the bleached boulders piled like dinosaur eggs along the rivers and streams near Highway 49. The debris from the hydraulic mining—mud, sand, and gravel—caused the tributaries flowing into the Sacramento River to turn into sludge channels that ruined the farmlands of the Sacramento Valley.[29] In particular, just south of Grass Valley, the Malakoff Diggings make a lunar landscape look fertile. These operations so fouled the rivers that laws were enacted in 1884 to halt hydraulic mining, but other means of getting at the gold continued to flourish. The biggest and grandest operation was the Empire Mine, outside Nevada City, right on Highway 49.[30]

About three in the afternoon I stop at the Empire Mine, an impressive network of mine tunnels that stretches for 367 miles under the earth. It's now a park run by the state of California. You pay three bucks and get a tour of the mine. During the eighty years the mine was in operation, 5.8 million ounces of gold, worth over two billion dollars, were produced. The owners had a fancy house built by Willis Polk two hundred yards from the mouth of the mine; they also owned several residences in San Francisco and often traveled to Europe. The eighteen stamps, huge hydraulic pistons that crushed the ore, worked 24/7 and could be heard fifteen miles away. The crushed ore was then slaked with cyanide to release the gold. Four thousand Cornish miners from Wales, known as "Cousin Jacks," worked the Empire Mine and its subsidiary, the North Star Mine. They were required to change clothes before entering the mines to prevent high-grading, the pilfering of a bit of gold dust, on their way out of the mines. One nugget was worth two weeks' wages, so everyone highgraded a little.

The literature at the Empire Mine State Park claims that these miners loved their work, their six days a week at the mine, their three dollars a day, and their little pasty lunches of meat and vegetable pies. Romantic perhaps, but I don't believe a word of it. Their lives were little better than those of the mules that were sedated, then lowered into the mine, where they spent the rest of their lives hauling ore carts in the darkness, without ever seeing the sun again. But even the mules refused to be abused; if they were hitched to more than seven ore carts, they would not budge. The miners, because they had families, had no choice. They descended into the bowels of the mine in train cars that carried sixty men at a time. They blasted and drilled through rock and hauled out the ore under clouds of black dust that filtered into their lungs. No one wore a mask. This is what they'd been raised to do in the coal mines of Wales, and that's why they'd been brought to work at the Empire Mine. And they worked and kept on working. Throughout the nineteenth century half of these miners were struck with fatal lung diseases. When they mixed the mercury, then the cyanide, no one wore gloves or protective clothing. In those days no one thought of safety issues. During the life of the Empire Mine, before it was closed in 1954, twenty-six men were killed and countless others died of silicosis, their lungs scarred by the quartz dust. The average life span of a miner was forty years. When looked at from a distance, the head frame of the mine, towering hundreds of feet in the air, looks like a giant gallows suitable for men of mythic proportions.[31]

What the Welsh miners have in common with Josefa is that no one recorded their names either. You can see their photographs on display at the Empire Mine, their eyes peering out of the dust that covered their rough-hewn faces, but their names do not appear. The only names mentioned are those of the owners and the superintendent. The same is true throughout the gold country: you hear about the Chinese, about the blacks, the Swedes, the Indians, the Kanakas, but you seldom find their names.

I ponder the absence of names, what happens when they are left out of history, when they are erased or ignored, or worse, distorted and stereotyped. History needs names, the names of working people, the *plebe* as it were, those who are truly the backbone of history. Without names, history is as worthless as pyrite.

By the time I reach Nevada City, the queen of the Mother Lode, the sun is setting in the west, so I hurry on without stopping. This gaudy city, the pearl of the restored towns along Highway 49, epitomizes what the wealth of the Gold Rush bought: saloons, hotels, grand Victorian houses. But there are no colleges built with Gold Rush money, no hospitals, no significant public parks; the truth is that the incredible wealth produced by the Gold Rush didn't benefit the average person. Wealth never trickles down that far. And once the gold stopped flowing, Nevada City and all the other Gold Rush towns were discarded like worn-out shoes, no longer useful to cover the feet of their owner.

Going through Nevada City, I (re)construct Josefa's story. I am driving next to the Yuba River, and the road curves and seems to double back, twisting, drawing me into the past.

There's one point about which no one argues—in the gold country, perceived crimes were dealt with swiftly and seldom with mercy. The punishment was often a public flogging or whipping, or a branding on the face, or sometimes the clipping off of an ear, any of which was then followed by expulsion from the goldfields.[32] Nearly all the crimes had to do with claim jumping, a very serious offense (unless it was a forty-niner jumping a Mexican's claim, then it was acceptable), or sluice stealing or mule stealing.

Occasionally the vigilante spirit demanded a hanging, in which case the accused were lynched and their bodies were left dangling from a tree or unceremoniously dumped in ravines. Lynching, especially of Mexicans, was quite common in Gold Rush days. At the crossing of Highway 49 and 50, in present-day Placerville—once known as Hangtown—a lifelike dummy swings from a noose outside a local saloon. This might be funny, until I discover that the first multiple lynching in California occurred right in that spot: three men, at least one or two of whom were Mexicanos or Latinos, were lynched here after being flogged to unconsciousness, based on an accusation by a total stranger that they had committed a robbery in another part of the Sierra.[33]

• • •

In the early morning darkness of July 5, 1851, while the streets of Downieville were littered with red-white-and-blue trash and the fervor of patriotic speeches still hung thick as Sierra fog, a white man was stabbed to death for abusing a Mexican woman. The day before, Downieville had celebrated the Fourth of July with a massive patriotic orgy. Hundreds of miners, would-be miners, merchants, travelers, gamblers, politicians, and even a few lawyers and other denizens of the Sierras had come together in a raucous party in honor of California joining the Union. There'd been patriotic speeches, shooting of guns, heavy drinking, several fights, even a stabbing and a flogging.[34] Except for the speeches, it had been a typical day.

Shortly after the murder, a Mexican couple fled to Craycroft's Saloon, next to the Jersey Bridge. It is possible that the man worked there as a monte dealer, which may have been why they sought this as a place to hide. But the word had already spread like venom among the miners, many of whom now gathered in front of the saloon talking excitedly, many of them urging a quick hanging. When the accused Mexicans were brought out under guard, one of them was a quiet, timid man, the other, a woman named Josefa, whom many of the miners knew. She was small, about twenty-five years old, dark and attractive, with small white teeth and thick black hair that reached her shoulders.

The general attitude of the miners (and popular historians) toward women in the goldfields, unless they were married or merchants, was that they were morally suspect. But Mexican women were even more so. Antonia Castañeda, who has written extensively on gender in frontier California, points out that popular historians stereotyped Mexican women, casting them as "fandango dancing, monte dealing prostitutes, the consorts of Mexican bandits"[35] and as "morally, sexually, and racially impure."[36] It would be logical that the forty-niners, who were less educated than popular historians, held the same biases.

Now let's see how the broad generalities of race and gender, class and sexuality were brought to bear on a Mexican woman, alone, in the middle of nowhere.

Picture yourself as Josefa. You're trying to make a living in this town, scraping by as best you can and staying out of people's way. You live your life clean; you live with a man, therefore you're not naïve sexually, but you're not a prostitute. (It is important to note here that men who personally knew Josefa all state that she was not a prostitute, that her life—in the language of the time—was without the stain of moral turpitude.)[37] Now picture your door being busted down in the middle of the night by a large intruder, a beefy man over six feet tall and weighing some 230 pounds. You yell at him, and he goes away. A few hours later there's a knock on your door. Perhaps you shouldn't answer, but you do. It's the same Americano and his friends. It's still dark outside, and the man who lives with you tells them to go away. The Americano insults you, calls you a whore. You tell him to repeat his insult inside your house. You believe he won't do it, but he does. The Americano steps inside; he is belligerent and aggressive, and shouts a demeaning slur in your face. The word whore, *puta*, is a highly charged epithet.

Now stop for a moment and think—what does the word *puta* imply at this juncture? It is both racially (because she's Mexican) and sexually (supposedly she's a whore) charged, but also infused with class prejudice (a whore works for a living by selling her body) and gender prejudice (Mexican women are whores). Furthermore, the white man says the word in Spanish (*puta*) to make the insult intimate and clearly understood, therefore metaphorically if not physically (the threat of which was obvious) violating Josefa, verbally and emotionally.

I don't believe Josefa thought in this way, nor did language exist then to describe violence of this sort, but I'm sure neither the implicit nor the explicit connotations of the word escaped her.

Josefa knew there was no man or law that would defend her if she was raped or even killed. It was just herself. Perhaps now you can explain why Josefa did what she did.

• • •

Before you judge Josefa, remember that in 1851, up and down California but especially in the gold country, a virtual war was being waged against Mexicans and Latin Americans. Josefa most certainly knew of the lynchings in Hangtown, most certainly had heard of the violence against Mexicanos, and perhaps even knew some of the Sonorans who'd been run out of the gold country with only a few hours' warning, forced to leave everything behind. She'd maybe even seen a lynching or two, or known someone who'd been lynched. And the general ambience of the camp, with thousands of single men living in a lawless state, spewing lewd comments everywhere she went, surely generated the sense of injustice and fear that kept her door locked and a knife by her bed. Everything must have been building inside her, like a trip wire just waiting to set off an explosion.

Josefa's trial unfolded like a bloody finale to the Fourth of July. When Josefa and her male friend emerged from Craycroft's Saloon, a mob of some six hundred miners, fueled on patriotism and whisky, were ready to lynch them both right then and there. But others in the mob wanted more formality, so they named a judge and a prosecutor and selected a jury, all of them white males. When a lawyer who was present—one of the few times in history a lawyer appears in a favorable light—tried to talk the miners out of their rage, he was shouted down and pummeled by the mob. After these preliminaries, the trial commenced on the same platform where the day before the speakers had praised the United States for taking California from Mexico. The judge was seated, witnesses interrogated, and declarations duly noted. At least one reporter, from the *Pacific Star*, was present, and his is one of several eyewitness accounts of what happened at the so-called trial.

After several miners claimed the deceased was of good character and was just trying to make amends for earlier breaking down the couple's door, Josefa's companion testified. His version is somewhat different; he said the Americano was abusive, and that their door was knocked down with such force as to rip it from its hinges. He also stated that the Americano threatened him with violence, but since he was small, Josefa stepped in and told the Americano to strike her instead. Then the Americano heaped abuse on Josefa, first calling her a whore in English, then in Spanish. She told him to say that in her own house and left him in the street. When the Americano followed her and was about to enter, Josefa stabbed him.

Josefa, who'd laughed at some of the white men's testimony, appears as the final witness. What happened in private and in the dark, she now declaims in public and in daylight.

Here's her version of the incident: At about 4:00 A.M. on the morning of July 5, the Americano had arrived at the cabin that she shared with her man. The Americano was drunk and had no reason for disturbing them. He'd knocked down the door and, after an angry exchange of words, had gone away—only to return a few hours later. This time the Americano insulted her, calling her bad names.

Her own words have come down to us, describing that fateful moment: "I took the knife to defend myself. I had been told that some of the boys wanted to get into my room and sleep with me. A Mexican boy told me so and it frightened me so that I used to fasten the door and take a knife with me to bed. I told deceased that was no place to call me bad names, come in and call me so, and as he was coming in I stabbed him."[38] It was that simple. Josefa hadn't gone out looking for trouble; trouble had come to her house. She felt threatened, sexually and otherwise, verbally abused, and her male companion wouldn't help her, so she defended herself as best she could.

Josefa told the truth, and it didn't go down well. After her testimony, the judge adjourned the trial till 1:30 P.M., and Josefa was taken away under guard to a log cabin behind the speaker's platform. During the break, the mob grew to well over two thousand angry miners, whose sense of justice, as it was later explained by apologists, demanded a hanging as some sort of revenge.

But more likely the miners were incensed to see a Mexican woman speak forcefully and openly, especially after having just taken the life of one of their own. In this sense, she speaks *sin pelos en la lengua*, holding nothing back, an attitude not unusual of Mexican women in pre- and post-1846 California, who, contrary to stereotypes, did act upon history, controlling their fate as much as possible within the confines of those times.[39]

After the recess, a doctor came forth who stated that Josefa was *enciente*, pregnant, in other words, approximately three months along. By all moral standards, this should have prevented her hanging. Instead, what happens next is a symbolic rape of her by the miners via three white male doctors from Marysville who, in conjunction with the previous doctor, take Josefa into a makeshift shack and reexamine her for signs of pregnancy. Since it was pretty clear to everyone that the miners wanted revenge, from my point of view, this action was meant to humiliate her. How else to interpret this? Perhaps Josefa felt that if she submitted to this degrading body exam, her life might be saved. While the so-called doctors toyed with Josefa, the forty-niners grew more enraged and were about to storm the platform when the three doctors emerged and declared that, in their opinion, Josefa wasn't pregnant. The jury retired and within minutes announced its verdict: Josefa was guilty of murder, and she should suffer death in two hours. Her male companion was acquitted but advised to leave town within twenty-four hours. It was about two in the afternoon when Josefa was led off under guard to the cabin. During the next two hours, Josefa received visitors and perhaps prayed or made her peace with God.

But why, if women were so rare, cherished, and valuable, would a mob of womanless men condemn Josefa to the gallows? Only by looking at the context of those times can we perhaps understand the reasons. Antonia Castañeda provides the framework: "The woman who is defined out of social legitimacy because of the abrogation of her primary value to patriarchal society, that of producing heirs, is therefore without value, without honor." Josefa, as a Mexican woman living with a man, was outside the scope of patriarchal society, and as Castañeda goes on to say, "A woman (women) thus *devalued* may not lay claim to the rights and protection the society affords to the woman who does have socio-political and sexual value" (emphasis mine).[40]

It goes without saying that the men who clamored for Josefa's lynching were not thinking this way (if a mob can be said to think), but this is exactly how they behaved. A woman, Josefa (read valuable), who is Mexican (of no value) can be lynched, because without value (i.e., suitability for reproducing heirs), society (read men) would not grant her the rights and protection usually accorded women, thus they would not save her from the gallows.

Josefa is lynched because she is a Mexican and a woman considered "without value" to the white male patriarchal society. If all the doctors in the world had said she was pregnant, it would not have increased her value to white society, since she wasn't pregnant with a white man's child. The miners were not even obligated to follow a civilized code of moral conduct, since Josefa was considered outside "moral" society and therefore without any rights.

Around four o'clock, Josefa was escorted to the scaffold that had been slapped together over the river, an awkward affair of timbers strapped to the bridge with heavy rope. She was tastefully dressed, and her hair flowed freely over her neck and shoulders. She appeared calm and unrepentant. By then, two thousand miners had gathered around the Jersey Bridge and along the Yuba River, waiting impatiently for the finale, as if it was some patriotic celebration.

It's hard to imagine this tiny woman walking toward the scaffold through the mob of jeering miners. What was she thinking about as she took her last walk—her home in Sonora, or the dogwoods along the river, or, if she was pregnant, that her child would also die? Perhaps she recalled the day she arrived in the gold country, her head filled with wild dreams of fortune. She might also have considered the weird fate that had brought her to this town by the river. Perhaps she cursed all the Americanos, or forgave them. But somewhere along that final walk she made peace with herself, and she strode through the mob showing no fear. Like other California women of the time (I'm thinking of María de las Angustias de la Guerra at Monterey, California, during the war of 1846), when confronted by white male violence, Josefa showed cool-headed grace under life-or-death pressure.[41]

Once on the platform, she turned to the few Mexicans who'd gathered by her side and told them that she'd killed the man and expected to pay for it. She shook hands with each of them and offered them a few words of goodbye and asked her friends to take her body so that she might be decently buried.

It was perhaps here that she decided on the act of bravery and defiance that has immortalized her. Unassisted, without fear or hesitation, she walked up the little ladder to the scaffold, where two vigilantes stood beside the noose, hoping to intimidate her. To the astonishment of the mob, she took the thick rope knotted into an awkward noose and slipped it around her neck, then arranged her hair so it would flow over her shoulders. It was more than an unmistakable gesture of courage, something every man that day would remember as long as they lived. It was Josefa's last defiant statement.

The two vigilantes pinioned her arms behind her back, which she protested. They ignored her. In their eyes, she had stopped being human the moment she stepped onto the scaffold—if indeed she'd ever been human in their eyes. They tied her dress down and slipped a hood over her head, then jumped free of the scaffold. At that point, two men axed the rope propping up the scaffold.

•   •   •

I reach Downieville at dusk and check into the Sierra Shangri-La Motel along the river's edge. The river cuts a deep ravine through the mountains that seem to rise up angrily out of the earth. There's nothing unique about the town; it consists merely of a few cheap motels and bars and the usual shops along the main drag. There's a bridge, and next to it a white brick building, which is the modern-day Craycroft's Saloon. Here, a small bronze plaque marks the occasion of Josefa's lynching with typical inaccuracy: "In memory of Juanita, the Spanish woman, lynched by mob from original bridge on this site, July 5, 1851." Thank god there are no souvenir stands offering little scaffolds with dolls in Mexican dresses hanging from them.

I've driven for nearly eight hours, but I'm not tired, so I wander around town. I know where I'm going, but I pretend it's an aimless walk. On Highway 49, the traffic is almost dead. There's a tense quiet in Downieville, as if I am disturbing something. I know Josefa was originally buried behind the theater, and that later her body was reinterred, but I don't know where. Tomorrow I will make inquiries, but I don't have much hope of finding her final resting place. The story goes that when she was reinterred, her skull was removed and used by a local secret society in an initiation ritual of some sort.[42] Though hard to believe, it's not totally implausible, especially if one considers the fate of Joaquín Murieta's own head. But I don't believe in ghosts, so I'm not sure what I expect to find here in this mean little town. By now I despise not just the forty-niners, but the Fourth of July, patriotic speeches, the American flag, and that cursed gold. I will never wear gold jewelry; I will never own so much as a grain of it.

I've read so many accounts of lynchings in which the victims were nameless Mexicans, or blacks, or Chinese, even Anglos, that perhaps I merely want to pay homage to all the nameless dead of the Gold Rush, to all those who perished here in the majestic foothills of the Sierra Nevada, yes, even to the Cornish miners who died in the bowels of this red earth so that others could become rich. Perhaps I just don't want Josefa to go into eternity so nameless, so insignificant, that not even her last name is recorded, because I despise the anonymity that is handed out to us like nooses with which to hang ourselves. Perhaps I just want to give one of these nameless dead a sense of closure. After all, every human being is worthy of at least that much. Every human life is more valuable than a mountain of gold.

In the quiet of the Sierra night, the Yuba River is rushing through the gorge. I come to the bridge, which looks dark, ominous. I know the original bridge where Josefa was lynched was washed away by the flood of 1852.[43] I also know that this Craycroft's Saloon is not the original, since the whole town was destroyed by a conflagration less than a year after Josefa's lynching, as if the gods had brought down the divine hand of retribution on this place. It doesn't matter. I stand on the bridge and look over the railing, and I can almost see her face in the water, surrounded by her long hair. I want to do the natural thing and give her a last name, my last name, make her part of my clan, so her spirit will always have a home. But she deserves the honor of her single name, because she represents all the nameless ones who lived and died here and never made it rich, all the nameless faces in the photographs. In some way, perhaps, she is the Saint of the Mother Lode, martyr and inspiration to all Mexicas, symbol of our courage. No matter how hard they have tried to erase our names from history, our stories have endured.

There's no place on the bridge for a cross of flowers with her name on it, but the river is eternal. I toss a sprig of wildflowers that I've picked along the road into the frothy currents. It floats for a moment before it disappears beneath the roiling water. I am finished. I have told her story. I have returned her name to the dark mountains, buried it in La Veta Madre, like ancient gold returned to its matrix, undisturbed. I say her name one last time—Josefa. And I walk away from the bridge.

TRIPTYCH

Memories of the San Fernando Valley

I

When I first return to the San Fernando Valley, I am that strange breed of native son who has no inkling of his landscape, no insight into his history. I lack the basic knowledge most six-year-olds would have of this culture, as if I've been dropped from another planet, and my tongue has never spoken a single word of English.

Eventually, years later, I will learn this history. One day in 1915, my grandfather Agustín Lugo brought my grandmother Ramona and my Uncle Carlos, then three years old, to the border town of Juárez, Mexico. They had come by train from Chihuahua, Chihuahua, fleeing the Mexican Revolution that had been raging for five years and still had five to go. At the border, Agustín paid three cents apiece for each of his family members to enter the United States, nine cents total for crossing over. They spent that first night in a dingy hotel in El Paso with only his *sarape* for a blanket. The next morning they headed for New Mexico, where Agustín contracted work for the Santa Fe Railroad, eventually reaching the status of foreman. A few months later he sent for my great-grandmother Epigmenia Najera Olivas, born in 1871, also in Chihuahua, to join them.

The history of Mexicas working on the railroads is a long one and well documented. Usually, contractors would hire the individual workers and then assign them to a particular task, either to lay track or to repair it. As part of the maintenance crew, Agustín repaired tracks up and down New Mexico and into Texas. The railroad workers lived in converted boxcars with "Santa Fe Railroad" stenciled on their sides that were rolled onto unused sidetracks outside of town. These boxcar housing projects form the basis of many southwest barrios, such as Wilmington in Los Angeles, El

Hoyo in Arizona, and Belén in New Mexico, where my family lived. My mother, Soledad, and all my aunts and uncles, except for the oldest and the youngest, were born in boxcars.

In 1925, Agustín Lugo made the move to the San Fernando Valley, hauling seven kids and whatever furniture he could pile onto a Model T Ford pickup. They came to California in part because the Olivas side of my family was already long established in the Los Angeles area, near the first plaza, La Placita, where Los Angeles was founded, and today the oldest barrio in the city. The Olivas were also established in the Valley, having arrived at the turn of the century.

Agustín Lugo settled in what was then called Roscoe, but the Mexicas called it Horcasitas, named after Felipe Horcasitas, who owned the land bounded by Stagg Street, Lankershim, Arleta, and Buckney. Later, when I was born there in 1949, the neighborhood was known as North Hollywood, and the barrio was called Orcas, a name it carries to this day.

My grandfather by this time had seven kids: Carlos, Juan, Soledad, Ignacio, Antonio, Carmen, José, and one more on the way, Agustín. He rented a dilapidated house from Horcasitas and moved his family in. At that time a dozen families lived in the barrio, all Mexican except for one Anglo family. There were no paved streets, no electricity, and no running water. Kerosene lamps were used for light, and outhouses were used for the basic necessities. The houses were mere wooden frames plunked down on the dirt without any foundations. When my aunts and uncles played hide-and-seek as children, anyone hiding behind the house was instantly spotted through the widely spaced slats of the walls.

My grandfather made his living with the Model T Ford one-ton pickup on which he had loaded the family when they came to the Valley. He would drive out to a chicken farm in L.A. that had a million egg-laying chickens, and he'd ask for some of the chicken manure that must have been piled several feet high. The chicken farmers were only too happy for him to haul the shit away. So my grandfather would haul the chicken manure to the Valley and sell it to the Japanese farmers to use as fertilizer for six dollars a truckload. Then, during the harvest season, he'd go to these same Japanese farmers and ask if he could haul off all the leftover produce in the fields, the carrots, lettuce, turnips, and whatnot that for whatever reason had been discarded. He'd fill his truck with these leftovers and sell them to the dairy farms in the Valley, for six dollars a load, to use as feed for their milk cows. So, in a way, he was surviving off the fat of the land, off the leftovers and scraps that no one else wanted.

This must have been a good business, because pretty soon he purchased a piece of property from Felipe Horcasitas on Troost Street. This house wasn't a house at all, but a former dance hall without any interior rooms or partitions of any kind. It goes without saying that there was no running water or electricity either. But this was the first house the Lugos would own in the Valley. Over the years, two bedrooms were built to accommodate the family, and a bathroom was added, along with indoor plumbing and even a chimney that my Uncle Antonio built. Even so, with nine kids to raise, life was tough. Eleven people were living in what was basically a four-room house.

This house is still standing on Troost Street, and it is still in our family. The last child of Agustín and Ramona, my Uncle Agustín, was born in this house, as were my older brother, Raymond, and I. The house is so small one person can fill it up. The biggest room, the living room, measures about ten feet by fifteen feet. Of the two bedrooms, the largest is eight by ten, and the other one is seven by nine. The fourth room, the kitchen, is at the back of the house and measures six by ten. The toilet and shower are next to the kitchen in a little cubicle no bigger than a closet. The total living area of this house is about three hundred and fifty square feet, which is not much bigger than your typical contemporary studio apartment. But, remember, this was a house for eleven people.

Besides the tough times and the housing crunch, there was one other problem—my grandfather was a serious alcoholic. Ever since I can remember I've heard stories about him, how when they were still living in New Mexico, he'd gotten drunk and fallen asleep while watching a pot of beans, and the boxcar had caught fire and burned to the ground. Maybe this was the reason they left New Mexico. Later on, one afternoon when he'd been drinking, his truck stopped right on the tracks that ran through Lankershim and Sherman Way. I don't know the details, but he was still on the tracks when a train barreled through, and the impact totaled his pickup. Perhaps because he was in shock or because he was so high he didn't care, he walked away from the accident without telling anyone. When the train engineers jumped out to survey the wreck, they found the pickup turned into an accordion, but no driver. When my grandfather didn't appear at home, he was presumed dead. It wasn't till days later, after he'd come down from his *paranda* spent at a friend's house, that his family discovered that he'd walked away from the wreck unscathed. I heard other stories about him—drunken binges, abuse of my grandmother, fights with my father—but I did not know him then.

When I knew him, his wife, my grandmother Ramona, was already dead, and he was a teetotaler. He lived in San Diego, in the barrio of Logan Heights, with his second wife, who was in a wheelchair and took aspirins like a kid eats candy. I remember he liked to work in his little garden, growing tomatoes and bell peppers, and on Sundays he ushered at Our Lady of Guadalupe Church. My brother and I were living in Tijuana then, with our paternal grandmother, waiting for her papers to come so we could join my father in San Fernando. My grandfather would drive across the border in his 1952 Chevrolet to pick up my brother and me so we could spend the weekend with him. By then my mother had already died in a car accident, and he was the first of the Lugos that I remember. He was soft-spoken and kind, a typical *abuelo* who doted on his grandchildren. When I turned five, he gave me the first birthday party I remember, a cake with candles, and he took a photograph—which I still have—of me with that cake. He only spoke Spanish to me, so I don't know how fluent he was in English.

Abuelo never spoke of it, but I knew he had this troubled past with alcoholism. His children, my aunts and uncles, were estranged from him; perhaps they blamed him for Ramona's death because of the hard life she'd led with him. Perhaps they resented his behavior while they were growing up and resented how he straightened up too late for them. But I never saw him touch a drop of alcohol or smoke a cigarette. It was as if he had no vice but his past.

It was because of Agustín Lugo that my clan reestablished itself in California and sank roots in the San Fernando Valley, thus halting our disappearance and bringing us back to this story. To this day I can recall the sense of security and peacefulness that his house imparted, even the scent of myrrh that permeated the rooms. As far as I can tell, he was a full-blooded Indian, very dark, and he looked like Geronimo's twin brother. All his children were dark, as were his grandchildren, myself included. You'd have to go back to my great-grandmother Epigmenia, mother of Agustín's first wife, Ramona, to find light skin.

· · ·

Over a million and a half people now crowd into the San Fernando Valley, from movie stars to working-class people. Some neighborhoods have million-dollar homes while some barrios don't have running water. In my own lifetime, I've seen the Mexican population, once marginalized around San Fernando, explode with a terrible vengeance that has swallowed the suburbs of Van Nuys, Panorama City, and North Hollywood.

Although citrus orchards dominated the landscape for the first half of the twentieth century, very little is recorded about the citrus industry in the San Fernando Valley. Even a fairly recent volume, *The San Fernando Valley: Past and Present*, includes details of prehistoric and indigenous life, but it does not devote one word to the citrus industry. Chicano historians focus their labor studies mostly on grape workers or cannery workers and ignore the citrus workers. Since many Mexicanos and Chicanos worked in this important industry, it seems to me that this era can be a rich source for investigations. From interviews with my clan, I can postulate that the origin of the word "Chicano" comes from first-generation Mexican Americans who used this word in reference to Mexicanos (without the pejorative sense), much like Mexicanos referred to us as "Pochos" (but with the pejorative sense). And we never crossed the border illegally, surreptitiously, or as part of some great adventure through the mountains, fighting bandits, and so on. On the contrary, my clan crossed quite casually, as if there was no border, as if we had never left.

•   •   •

My Aunt Carmen, the youngest daughter of my grandfather, lives on the outskirts of Sylmar. Although it's a middle-class neighborhood, with fenced and well-tended yards, there're no sidewalks, and the wind blows dust in your eyes. Thirty years ago she and her husband owned perhaps the most successful real estate office in the San Fernando Valley. Even now, though she's retired and out of the real estate business, she owns apartments and other property. She's also quite talented with a paintbrush, and the paintings that adorn her living room—desert scenes, lake scenes, flowers, gold fish—are quite exceptional, though only if she's asked will she admit to being the artist. If the Latina Woman of the Year award had existed during her prime, she might have been selected three or four times.

When I'm on the trail of this book I come to visit her, hoping to fill in the gaps of what the Valley was like in the thirties and forties. My aunt is about 5′2″, proportional in weight, and is wearing a beige jumpsuit and white adidas® that look as if they just came out of the box. In her driveway sits a white Jeep 4x4 (white has always been her preference for cars) and in the garage, a partially restored 1932 Ford coupe, the kind teenagers love to turn into hot rods.

She hasn't always been this comfortable. And although she doesn't want to speak of it, I will speak of it, and hope she will forgive me if I betray her past, which is also my past. When she was a little girl, there were times when she had no shoes to wear. Or if she had shoes, she'd cut out cardboard to slip inside so the holes wouldn't show. When she was in high school, she worked cleaning the house of a rich white woman for $1.25 a day. But she makes me stop the recording when she tells me these parts of her life because, as she says, "I don't want to talk about that; I just want to talk about the pretty."

The perception of historians, sociologists, judges, and other social commentators is that we are victims of this society, condemned to poverty, miseducation, and all the worst that society can inflict on us. Just don't say that to my aunt. I think in our heart of hearts, we do not see ourselves as victims, because victims cannot act, cannot control their destiny. Yet my family has always acted, has launched projects and business ventures. And at the risk of offending many, let me say that the women in my family, although hurt by this society, are not so much victims as they are survivors, like all my clan. Aunt Carmen has been a survivor since the day she was born in a boxcar.

I've come to listen to her story about the San Fernando Valley, but before we can talk, we must have lunch. She has prepared some sandwiches, and she serves them with a handful of chiles serranos from her backyard. Then we sit in the living room, brightly lit by the afternoon sun, and I turn on the tape recorder. She speaks slowly, choosing her words carefully, sometimes pausing till the right word comes to her. She speaks at such a pace that I don't really need a tape recorder; I can transcribe her story by hand as she tells it. To start the interview she has brought out her birth certificate and is reading it to me:

"My name is María Carmen Florinda Lugo, and I was born September 26, 1923, State of New Mexico, County of Valencia, school district of Belén, town of Trujillo. When I was born, my mother, Ramona Olivas, was thirty-two, and she was born in Chihuahua, Mexico. My father, Agustín Lugo, was thirty-one years old and was also born in Chihuahua, Mexico. My father was a foreman for the Santa Fe Railroad.

"This is what my grandma told me: I was born in a railroad car, 'cause that's where we lived right there in New Mexico. This is interesting—my certificate of baptism at Our Lady of Belén Church in Belén, New Mexico, is dated the twenty-ninth of September, 1923, so I was only three days old when I was baptized. My *padrinos* were José María Maestas and Lugarda Sánchez de Maestas.

"I just remember my grandmother on my mother's side; her name was Epigmenia Najera Olivas. I never met or even knew the names of my father's parents. My mother had three brothers, Jesús Olivas, Vicente Olivas, and Juan Olivas, and my mother's name is Ramona Olivas. My father, Agustín Lugo, had two sisters, Francisca Lugo and . . . I know he had another sister, but I never met her. I only met Francisca.

"I was told that Epigmenia was born in Chihuahua, Mexico, and that my mother was the oldest of her children. I was the eighth child, and my mother was thirty-two when I was born. If my mother was the first child of Epigmenia, and she was thirty-two at the time, you can figure out when my grandma was born, you see?

"Epigmenia lived with us part of the time. When one of her sons came into the Valley, then she moved in with her son. But she lived, when I was a very young child, she lived in our home with us.

"Epigmenia was very strict, and I'd stand very straight when she scolded us, because she had blue, blue eyes, blue like the sky, and I felt when she scolded me she could see right through me with those bright blue, blue eyes. And she was very fair complexioned, very fair. When I was a child, she had premature gray or she had blonde hair. I don't remember dark hair on my grandma. She always had platinum hair, and I just assumed it was gray hair. But she had a fair complexion, so maybe she had light hair. My mother: black hair, black eyes. Coming from the old country, it must've been a mixture of blood from the early settlers.

"Only my oldest brother, Carlos, who is now eighty-six, was born in Mexico. The rest of us were born in the U.S. So that would be Tony, Ignacio, Soledad, Juan, José, then there was Manuel and myself—all born in New Mexico. I believe that I was about eighteen months old when we came here, right to the Valley, to North Hollywood. I know that my grandmother had some nieces who lived in Los Angeles: Jesusita, Rosario, Guadalupe, Nicolasa were their names. And these would be Olivas. And I believe that at that time, even then Los Angeles was Los Angeles, and I think there was encouragement from my grandmother's nieces, living right in the center of what today is Los Angeles, La Placita and all that. They'd lived there in Los Angeles a long time, almost forever, and I know they're all gone now, and they all died there. I don't believe it has anything to do with our family history, but two of the original families in Los Angeles, one was a Lugo and one was an Olivas, it just so happens they had our family name.

"But I also think it was an adventure—coming here I mean. Because we didn't live in Arizona or Colorado or anything like that. I can remember the little wood-framed house we first lived in. The house was already old when we came there. It had wood floors, no cement floors, rickety floorboards, and rickety stairs to get in. Just a small house for such a large family. I suppose we were poor, but as children you don't realize you are poor. I remember going through cold winter nights. I realized when I was in high school, most particularly in high school, I realized we *were* very poor. But I think that the love my mother had for each of her children made for a happy home. I remember meals, particularly dinner—there was a family togetherness. I knew there was radio then and radio stations, but that doesn't mean that we had a radio. Of course, television was unheard of. I think I remember hearing a telephone in school, but those things were not thought of. The neighborhood had no streets and no gas. There was no running water—to tell the truth, I don't remember where we got the water.

"This first house was located just about a block from Lankershim Boulevard. And we never moved away from that area, never. Before even going to school, before kindergarten, and then right through high school, we still lived in the same block, just a different house, but we never moved away from there.

"Okay, so my mother had eleven children and when we came from New Mexico to North Hollywood, I think, like I said, I was about eighteen months old, and then after that, Augie was born and then two little girls were born. Both of the girls died. A woman doctor from Burbank came and delivered the babies right there at home. I don't remember the births, I'm sure they figured a way of getting all the children out of the house.

"When I was about seven or eight years old, a man would come around in a little Model A truck, and I remember he would bring vegetables and meat, fish, poultry. Then a little later on there was a little country store; but we didn't go to the store every day, everything was homegrown. We didn't know what bread was, I didn't see bread till the time I went to school and saw the kids eating sandwiches. We had home-cooked meals every day, very healthy food; my mother knew how to stretch what we had. Later on, when I was twelve or thirteen, we used to walk two, three miles to get to Roscoe, and there was a department store there where we could purchase towels. But we all each used to make our own clothing.

"My father started out with one truck, and he used to buy fertilizer from the Runnymede Poultry Farms, and he sold it to the Japanese farmers because then you didn't use chemicals, no nothing like that. And then, I guess business was pretty good, because soon we had a second truck. He did well because his trucks served two purposes: the selling of the fertilizer, and then the farmers, the Japanese farmers, would let him come in after the crops. If it was carrots they worked on that day, he could load the trucks with what remained. Then he would take the carrots, the lettuce, or the beets to the dairy and sell it as feed for the cows. That's when life started to get a prettier picture. We had a little bit of an income then. Prior to that, I don't know what his occupation was. I know he left a good job, because he was a foreman of the Santa Fe Railroad. But, of course, at eighteen months, I don't remember the trip to North Hollywood.

"The Valley was beautiful then. There were no paved streets, obviously no telephones poles, no electricity. I remember the kerosene lamps. No smog. It seemed to me that the sky was bluer, and it seems to me that the stars at night sparkled like diamonds. You don't see any of that anymore. Not only was there a lot of vegetable farming, but California, most particularly the San Fernando Valley, was known for its lemon and orange orchards. Lemons and oranges as far as the eye could see.

"But life was beautiful. Everyone got along, there were no gangs, no fear of going out at night. Walking the lonely streets where there were no street lamps, and most particularly, I guess we were a healthy group because everywhere you went you walked.

"And there were lots of Japanese farms. It seemed to me that vegetables were shipped by freight train, because there weren't just two or three acres of farms. I mean there were miles of planting, so how did they keep the vegetables fresh to reach Florida or Chicago? That part I don't know. But I know that they were put on freight trains because there weren't enough people in the Valley to need this much produce. Because this was miles of vegetables—tomatoes, cucumbers, lettuce, radishes, turnips, beets—you name it and it was grown here in the San Fernando Valley.

"At that time in the Valley there was Roscoe, now Sun Valley; there was Burbank; and North Hollywood was then called Lankershim. There was a Mr. Lankershim, and that's where the name comes from. And, of course, Los Angeles and Pasadena. We never heard about Hollywood, where was I? I should've known about Hollywood, but I didn't. But most definitely Pasadena, Los Angeles, those were big towns. I guess it wasn't till my teen years that I heard of Long Beach, San Pedro. We were very limited as to the distance we could travel, so a kid doesn't pay too much attention unless you were going to go there.

"The one grammar school that I can remember was in Roscoe, now Sun Valley. I went to Roscoe Elementary School, a two-story brick building that I think was built in 1919. It still stands there, the same building. It was walking to school—the two miles to and from—rain or shine, there was no school bus, you walked it. That's another thing. We looked forward to going to school because there was the togetherness of walking to school and the togetherness of walking home from school. So we always appreciated school. Like I said, the teen language then was so different, the words that come out of our kids nowadays . . . I don't know, we didn't have much, we were poor but rich in good health, year-round happiness, and it didn't take too much to make a child happy.

"We had no elaborate birthday parties or teen dances, I mean, like dancing was for adults. A couple of musicians would get together—maybe someone who knew how to play the accordion, another the violin, guitars—and I remember the dance hall came way later. I remember the first birthday celebrations: they would water the yard or the patio real well the day before, sweeping it with brooms and taking out the little rocks 'cause there was going to be dancing and so it wouldn't raise any dust. There were no folding chairs, like sometimes you see in western movies; there were benches, but the benches weren't built, they were just boards. I remember they put some bricks and two-by-fours to hold the boards across where the ladies sat. These celebrations would usually be at someone's house.

"You know, I don't remember any Sixteenth of September. I remember the Fourth of July, because we were taught that at school. But there were no firecrackers or no picnics that we'd get together and go to—we just knew the history. The Fourth of July celebrations came many years later. Being born and raised here in the U.S., there was no Cinco de Mayo, Dieciséis de Septiembre; we didn't know they were celebrated elsewhere. *Quinceañera*— what was a *quinceañera*? We didn't know. Because my grandmother and my mother, my family, they did not bring the *costumbres de México* with them. They really did not.

"Yes, we grew up speaking Spanish and only Spanish before we went to school. See, as a child, we spoke to our parents in Spanish, but at play, whether at school or at home or in the neighborhood, we did not speak Spanish, our only language was English. But when we went to school . . . we were not allowed to speak Spanish. They hit us. Of course, I was a very good girl. But I remember some children being hit on the hands with a ruler if they spoke anything but English. Now, in my home, we were always taught, my mother always told us—you must always obey your teacher, because she is your second mother. I know in my home, my parents would never have tolerated rudeness from us against our teachers. Absolutely not. We were to respect our teachers as if they were our second parents.

"There was no junior high when I attended school; grammar school was from the first to eighth grade and high school from the ninth to the twelfth. I went to North Hollywood High School, and I enjoyed high school very much. We were never playing hooky from school, I think because we got on the bus, and then they drove us straight to North Hollywood. And there's nowhere to play hooky. Where were you going to go?

"This is real cute. Every Saturday night, one of the better trucks that my dad had was scrubbed with soap and water and washed and everything. Then in that truck, all those that wanted to go to Sunday mass were welcome. There were only three churches, Santa Rosa, San Fernando, and Guardian Angel in Pacoima. And that's where I first learned of, not *kermeses*, those came later, but of *jamaicas*.

"And there was food and dancing in the parking lot of the church. And we used to look forward to that. And then there was a dance hall in Pacoima, and then, oh dear, here they come. That's when I first heard the word 'zoot suit' and 'zoot-suiter,' and there were fights among them. It was more the dress, though, the style of their dress than the meanness in them. And some of the girls, young ladies at the dance, it was quite the thing if they danced with the fellow with the balloon pants. I don't really know how they slipped their foot in their pants, 'cause the cuff was so tight. I never saw any zoot pants close enough to find out, either. My brothers did not dress like that. And the second dance hall that I can remember was in Glendale. And of course to get to those you had to either have a friend, or a brother, or maybe your own parents would drive you the distance. And then, about that time, there was the El Portal in North Hollywood that now they're trying to make a historical monument on Lankershim Boulevard.

"And, oh my, we listened to the best bands in the world. By that time there's the Palladium, and we'd hear Harry James and Tommy Dorsey. I remember we went to the Palladium, and I said to my sister, 'Oh, my gosh, there's this guy, and all the girls are crazy over him. He's all right, and I guess he's gonna make it.' And it was Frank Sinatra. But now, when it came to Harry James, I thought he was really attractive.

"And then, just before the war, my closest friends, my dearest friends were Japanese. How many families were in Horcasitas then, seven maybe? So our friends were Japanese, and it was very sad when they just uprooted them and took them away. Of course, I wasn't a child anymore, but they were very good citizens and they had no allegiance to Japan; I don't think they did. They were good Japanese Americans. There was Ted Yoshiwara, the Yamanoris, the Sakaguchis; in fact, my very doctor now is a Sakaguchi. Intelligent people, the six Sakaguchi children are doctors and dentists. Lilly Sakaguchi was the only woman research scientist sent to Japan to study the effects of the atomic bomb.

"Then all of a sudden they were all gone. It was like a thief in the night. Till we read it in the papers and stuff. We thought they had taken them off to war some place. We didn't know they were being interned here in Manzanar or other places. Actually, I asked myself, what happened? I didn't know immediately, of course; it was frightening, December seventh, Pearl Harbor Day. We knew it was the Japanese, but we didn't associate our neighbors with the enemy—we'd been childhood friends and grown-ups and all of a sudden they were gone. We didn't know immediately what happened to them. Their farms? They all dried up. Because when the bracero program started, it wasn't for farming, it was for the great loss of citrus here in California.

"Of course, they did come back, but not immediately. By this time I was married, and I was away from North Hollywood—I was in San Bernardino. In fact, of my Japanese friends, I just recently got to see my friends the Sakaguchis. I didn't look them up, and they didn't look me up; it's just that they got so well known in the field of medicine and research. And one of them is now my doctor; they should all be retired, but they're all still practicing medicine.

"My brother Nash, my brother Juan, and my brother Augie all served in World War II. My brother Nash was in the army, but he was never sent overseas because he was injured here during military training. And then my brother Juan went in the navy. And he used to do a lot of hitchhiking from San Diego to North Hollywood, and when it was time to return to base, there was a kind of anxiety till that first letter came. Because there was no phone, we had no phone at home so we could not have knowledge of it. But anyway, one time my brother Juan was robbed and beaten pretty badly and was left in a lemon or orange grove near San Diego, where the navy base was. And he was hospitalized for quite some time. And so, then again, that one was not sent to war. To this day, I don't know if there was a court hearing or what. But my brother Augie was sent, and that was hard on my parents to send three of their children to war. That really, really was painful for my mother. In fact, she died of a cerebral hemorrhage, and her baby didn't even get to come to her funeral. My brother Joe was called, but he was sent home 'cause he had flat feet, and we always used to tease him about it. My other brothers were married, and at that time they weren't taking married men.

"I graduated from high school in 1942, and there were only two other Latinos in my class. One difference that I see regarding schooling, I didn't know one to drop out. According to the paper, we have so many dropouts, and yet we didn't have the opportunities we have now—student loans, transportation, so many things are available now that we didn't have then. When I graduated, we had parties and proms, but my boyfriend was in the service, in the navy, so I didn't feel much like dancing. So I chose not to go.

"So ours was one of those wartime marriages. We went to Tijuana and got married on one of his leaves; he didn't want to go to war and leave his sweetheart. And then we had to get married here again, because they requested the marriage certificate in order to send the monthly service pay. Then the navy lost our certificate of marriage, and that was in '43. So then his next leave in '44 was a week, so we got married here because the navy didn't want to accept the Mexican wedding because a lot of sailors were crossing to Mexico to get married, and we were one of them. Well, Steve, my husband, was in the navy. I was so happy 'cause I had the one child. I was back in North Hollywood. I was married in 1944. And the war was over in '45. My first child was born in '45, and my daughter Anne was born in '50.

"During the war, I was with Security Pacific Bank, but anyway, I always stuck to banking. I started working for Bank of America at the Burbank branch while I was still in high school. There were no computers then, and all the bookkeeping was done by hand; later on, I was the head bookkeeper at the San Fernando branch.

"The first coat I ever bought with my salary was a beautiful gabardine coat. I was so proud of that coat. And one day your mom asked—'Can I borrow your coat?' I said, 'But Sally, I haven't worn it any place yet.' She said, 'I'll take good care of it.' I said okay. Then I wondered why she covered it when she hung it up the next day. She'd put a man's shirt on it. She'd burned a hole in my brand new coat. I didn't even know she smoked. How could she? Like Dolly Parton's 'Coat of Many Colors.' That was my first, I'd never had a new coat in my life. How could she do that?

"In Burbank, at the B of A, I was the only Latina. Even afterward, after I graduated from high school. Then they transferred me to the San Fernando branch, and I was still the only Latina working there. And there were more Spanish-speaking people in the San Fernando Valley than in Burbank, where there were no Latinos.

"And here's a cute little story that happened there at the San Fernando branch. This lady, this Mexican woman, came in and wanted to open a savings account. And so they called me to the front desk, because I was the only Spanish-speaking employee, and I said, 'Sit down and I'll take the information.' And she said, 'But I didn't bring my money with me. I'll be right back.' And she left. I didn't know what to make of it. And after a while—here's this little old lady pulling a red wagon, a squeaky red wagon. And she had sacks full of coins. And she told me she sold handmade corn tortillas, and she used the little salt containers to keep her money. And she said, 'You people count it, and I'll come back tomorrow and find out how much it is.' And she pulled that little red wagon full of money through the barrio and the center of town, and do you see how life was? Nobody bothered her. I wish I could remember the exact amount, but it was several hundred dollars, all in silver dollars and silver quarters.

"Let me tell you something—when I went to work for Bank of America, I realized that there was a mortgage on our home, and I thought—let me lighten the burden for my mom and take over payments on the house. A gentleman by the last name of Horcasitas was the owner of that land . . . I mean that's not the registered name of that little town, it just stayed Horcasitas. So he used to come around for the payment. Then later on, he moved to Las Vegas, Nevada, so I used to send the payment over there. The payment was seven dollars a month. And I thought I'd like to do that for my parents. So one day I said to Mr. Frazer, the bank manager where I worked, 'Can I talk to you a few minutes after work?' He said, 'It doesn't have to be after work, you can come in the office and talk to me anytime you want.' So

I told him I was paying the mortgage on our home, and that the monthly payment was seven dollars a month. I was a young girl, I didn't know how to go about increasing the payment; naïve, I thought I needed an application. 'Oh absolutely,' he said. And of course, he just thought—what a wonderful thing this girl was doing. So big deal, I made it to where it was $21 a month, but don't forget, I was just making about $159 a month wages. So $21 a month was cutting a chunk out of my paycheck. My folks never asked me for money, but I just felt like it was the obligation that I had . . . kids nowadays don't think that way. So I gave money to them, and now and then I would pick up the utility bill. But I was so proud when I paid off the family house. This is the house on Troost Street—we moved from that first little wood shack to Troost Street, and that was it. Those were the only two places we ever lived. I can remember my sister and I planning the first bathroom that house had. Being able to bathe in the bathroom and not go to the outhouse, we were very proud of that—my sister and I did that. Then I remember that we remodeled, and it was all because of that little young lady who worked at the bank. You're looking at her.

"I'm a Mexican American. I hate the word 'Chicano.' Don't call me a Chicano. And don't call me a Hispanic. What's the definition of a Hispanic? I am a Mexican American. I'm of Mexican descent; my parents were. Let me put it this way: my two children had already graduated from high school, my son had already gone to the service and back when I first heard the word 'bilingual.'

"I've left the San Fernando Valley—I've lived in Calistoga, in Napa. And I've been to Europe three times, and when you're over there, you realize the U.S. is in its infancy. In fact, I can remember the beautiful brick buildings that were in Los Angeles when we'd go to see aunts, relatives of my grandmother. And I used to see these beautiful brick buildings; gosh, the first general hospital in Los Angeles was a brick building, and here we knock those buildings down. Knock them down. Make new structures and those beautiful buildings are gone forever . . . I don't know if you know the City Hall in Los Angeles? Those marble stairs, that beautiful art they have there. They're not appreciated. They're fighting to keep City Hall even today.

"And I'm backtracking now, I'm getting a little bit off the subject. I remember when I was working full-time at Bank of America; I was already there my last year of high school, so I wasn't going out looking for a job, I already had a job. And I told myself: only the best of shoes. I don't care if I don't have a car. I don't care if I don't have twenty skirts or thirty blouses. But I'm going to have good shoes, and I'm going to have coats. And I remember having to walk quite a distance to get the bus on Lankershim Boulevard to take me into North Hollywood—to get on the streetcar to go to Hollywood to buy shoes. I didn't have shoes when I was a little kid. And that's always, even to this day . . . a little bit of sadness.

"Anyway, to this day I refuse to wear shoes that are uncomfortable. I'm seventy-seven, and I still like good shoes."

II

My father, Enrique García Murguía, is a different story. He was born in the dusty Mexican town of Autlán de la Grana, Jalisco, in a small house, #24, on Calle Benito Juárez, in the year 1918. When my father left his hometown in 1936, his eternal wanderings were just beginning. In his pueblo, he was the fastest sprinter, leaving all the other barefooted boys in the dust. The governor of Jalisco, General García Barragán, offered my father the chance to run in the prelims for the Pan-American Games, so he boarded the morning bus for Guadalajara, never to return to Autlán. In Guadalajara, he ran like a scared jackrabbit in the 220 and the 440, and though my father ran barefooted, he was good enough to earn a spot on the team. But when the coach insisted Enrique use cleats, he couldn't get used to them, and that was the end of his track career. After that, he went on to Mexico City to care for his mother and work on the orange streetcars of the Azcapotzalco line.

My father held chauffeur's badge 4530 in the Sindicato Nacional de Transporte. This was the era of Lázaro Cárdenas, and Mexico seethed with political intrigue. During a strike of the streetcar drivers, police found a corpse in front of his tram and busted him on a framed-up murder charge. He spent a month locked up with thieves and cocaine sniffers, political prisoners and gangsters, bedbugs and lice. In jail, he befriended Jacques Mornard (Ramón Mercader), who, following Stalin's orders, had buried an ax in Trotsky's head, but all they talked about was soccer. Once the strike was over, the gates of Lecumberri Prison opened for Enrique, and he went back to work. No charges were ever filed against him.

In that glorious decade of the 1940s, my father carried himself with style in nightclubs and cabarets, his favorite haunts. He favored Domit shoes with French toes, double-breasted pinstripe suits, red silk ties, and a snap-brim fedora turned down at a rakish angle. He'd been a tailor in Autlán, and he cut his wool suits from whole cloth, the pinstripes perfectly matched around the collar, the sleeve stripes aligned with the shoulder ones. A *catrín*, slick as a *lotería* card, he danced the sexy *danzón* at all the fancy ballrooms: El Salón México, El Colonial, Los Angeles, and on Sundays he went to the bullfights at the Plaza de Toros, where he once sat next to Agustín Lara and the legendary film goddess María Félix.

Who would ever have dreamed that one day Enrique would wind up in the San Fernando Valley? In La Capirucha (Mexico City), Agustín Lara had 99 percent of the Sunday evening radio audience tuned in to his show on XEW, and Libertad Lamarque burned up Latin America with her songs— in those faraway days of 1940.

In the spring of 1941, while the streets of Mexico City teemed with people whistling Lara's latest hit, "Farolito," and the front pages of the *Gaceta de Policía* were splashed with photos of beautiful women like María Félix or Toña La Negra, the newsreels showed the *Luftwaffe* bombing London into rubble and Hitler's panzers slashing across Europe. In Mexico City, on Reforma and Insurgentes Avenues, the rich flew two flags on the antennas of their Packards: a Mexican flag and a swastika. But after Pearl Harbor and Operation Barbarossa, Mexicans became intoxicated with the romantic notion of a "Good War." So Mexico joined the Allies and sent the 201st Air Squadron to the Philippines to fight the Japanese—which was a laughing matter. In that same war, Chicano-*pochos* would chalk up Medals of Honor by the fistful for good ol' American pie and mothers back in barrios, while the zoot-suit riots were just around the corner of Fifth and Broadway.

●　　●　　●

In 1944 my father left his job as a streetcar conductor, and set out to vagabond through Mexico. He eventually reached the border, a thirsty traveler just arrived from Mexico City. As he strolled the south side of Nogales, Sonora, a warm rain fell on the powdery dust that dirtied his Domit shoes. The narrow streets of the small border town were lined with curio shops painted pink, orange, and white; hotels with iron-grilled balconies; cantinas; and Mexican restaurants offering *menudo* and Carta Blanca beer. Produce trucks and jitneys rattled through the dust, and oxcarts and burro trains hauled wood. Across the street was a row of brick office buildings, hotels, and stores: Nogales, Arizona—the fabled United States. No flags flew that rainy day to clearly define the border. From the Mexican side, he could see the north side of International Avenue and the red-and-white front of Foster's Drugs, with its hand-lettered sign in the window—ROOT BEER FLOAT. My father knew the English word for *cerveza*, but he was curious about this root beer. So, confident as Bogart, he strolled past the sleepy gringo guards in the *garita* and crossed the street (and the border) with suitcase in hand. He always laughs when he tells this story, says his destiny was sealed by a root beer float.

On his way out of Foster's a young black girl called him over. She was barefooted and wore a flour-sack dress. The girl lived up on Cemetery Hill, the black quarter of town, and could not be served inside Foster's. So my father went back in and bought her a sundae. Then he found he could get a one-day visa to travel on the U.S. side of the border to Tijuana. He filled out the form in the drugstore. Then he gave the black girl her sundae and, without thinking twice, he boarded a Citizen Auto Stages bus to seek his brother Arturo in the flourishing bars and gambling dens of Tijuana.

He didn't stay long in Tijuana and soon hitched a ride to L.A., still using his one-day visa. That first day in Los Angeles, Enrique rented a room, and the next day he went searching for work. Eventually he landed in Pico Court, a bracero camp of white-washed adobe barracks and a modern packinghouse from which they shipped the pride of California—"sunkissed" oranges—to destinations all over the world.

Sunkist Growers Association owned and ran Pico Court. The camp housed maybe two hundred braceros in those adobe barracks. The men lived there without women or family, leading lonely, desolate lives that revolved around working the citrus fields. All the administrators were Anglos. Ninety-eight percent of the workers were Mexicans. An occasional gringo or Pakistani would try picking oranges but would inevitably give up after a day or two. Only the hard-working Mexicans hung in there, day after day, season after season.

The men worked six days a week picking fruit, through summer days of hundred-degree weather, bandannas wrapped around their heads, exhausted and dirty from crawling among trees and climbing on three-footed ladders for lemons, two-footed ones for oranges. Sometimes they'd be picking right in the ranch owner's backyard, and as they strained with the heavy citrus sacks, not twenty yards away, in ranch-style mansions, barbecues would be going on, the big-bellied men in shorts and the women in bathing suits, dipping their toes into the heart-shaped swimming pool or licking ice cream cones.

At night, the men gathered around guitars in the barracks rooms and, with voices filled with nostalgia, sang *boleros* about unrequited love and wasted lives. They spent their weekends killing time in camp or going into town to see Mexican movies at the old San Fernando Theater. These were single men, their belongings packed in cardboard boxes, here only to labor, always looking over their shoulders, unwelcomed in this land because they were dark and Mexican.

•   •   •

My parents met at a *kermés* in North Hollywood, at the church of Nuestra Señora de Zapopan. My father worked picking oranges and had ridden in from Fillmore with a friend, admiring the Valley dense with citrus groves along the way. The night was filled with the fragrant aroma of orange blossoms and the chirring of busy cicadas. When he arrived at the modest church, the entrance cost eighty-five cents and beers were a dime. The Mexican community was out in strength, the *kermés* in full swing, entire families raising money for the war effort. The dance organizer, the dynamo of the event who went from table to table supervising and encouraging, was a cinnamon-skinned, big-eyed beauty named Soledad Lugo.

My mother could not have been more different from my father. A tireless fund-raiser for the war effort, she organized the monthly war bonds *kermés* of the Chicano community and sent weekly packages to her two brothers in the service. Soledad lived an independent life; she drove a car and paid on her own house. She emceed the program that night, introducing each act and raffling war bonds during intermission. The ten-piece Navarro Brothers Orchestra, decked out in flashy zoot-suits with balloon pants and ducktails, was the featured attraction. Juan Navarro, a flamboyant trumpet player whose style resembled that of Cab Calloway, full of eye rolling and hand waving, led the band. At the start of their second set, my father requested a popular *danzón* that year, "Juárez," that he dedicated to the emcee, señorita Soledad Lugo. She refused to dance that first *danzón* my father dedicated to her, but he was neither deterred nor offended, understanding her reluctance to dance with this slick stranger from the biggest city in the world.

A pretty, sought-after woman known throughout the Valley, Soledad Lugo led an active social life filled with dances and war bond rallies. She worked at the Veteran's Hospital and drove a royal blue 1939 Plymouth coupe. But Soledad's independent streak did not prepare her family or the barrio of Horcasitas for the summer evening in 1944 when she casually stepped out of her house wearing a pantsuit. Pants made her legs look long—that's what she liked about them—and she was the first, besides Lauren Bacall, to wear them on Ventura Boulevard. *Tsss*, the old women in the barrio shook their heads: What was the world coming to if a woman wore pants? But my father could admire her classy elegance and the sharp cut of her suit. The night they met at the *kermés*, my father dedicated a second *danzón*, "Nereidas," to her and when she accepted his invitation to dance, they already knew their histories would cross, two streams of the same culture that would eventually form one river, creating something new. That something new is what I am.

None of Soledad's friends or family liked my father, didn't like that he was a *catrín*, a well-dressed man from Mexico City. They told her he'd never stay, that he'd leave and go back, and probably had a wife in Mexico (he didn't). But he proved them all wrong.

A few weeks after that fateful *danzón*, they drove the Plymouth coupe to Ensenada, and the darkness caught them on the road, so they spent the night in a motel, within earshot of the crashing ocean. Since technically my father had ruined her virtue by keeping her out all night, they had a justice of the peace marry them in San Diego before they returned to L.A. They came back to live on Troost Street in North Hollywood, in the barrio of Horcasitas, where I was born years later.

In 1957, my father took me to see the last game the Hollywood Stars, of the old Pacific Coast League, ever played in Gilmore Stadium. And on the way back, driving over the Mulholland Pass as we came over the mountains from L.A., my father pointed to the Valley lit up by thousands of house lights, like one big Christmas ornament. "When I arrived in '44 there was nothing but orange trees; at sunset their scent filled the Valley and seemed to stay with you the whole night. That was the year I met your mother." This was the first time he'd ever spoken to me about her. He said it in a moment of weakness for him, of nostalgia, yet even my eight-year-old mind could tell how much he missed her.

What little I know about Soledad Lugo is hearsay: She was gregarious; everyone in North Hollywood loved her. She died in a car accident in Mexico while my father was driving. Her funeral procession stretched for blocks. I don't think my father ever recovered from the shock of losing her or from the guilt. Twenty years after her death, at the funeral of my Uncle Juan, the priest brought up her name and mentioned how much she was still missed in the barrio. But I know her mostly from photographs—her big, smoky eyes like some dark tropical flowers—or from people who said she was beautiful enough to have been a movie star. The photos I have of her prove they are not lying. She did leave me with something, a certain sensation, something without words that I have carried my whole life, like a helix or a vortex carved from air that every now and then reminds me I'm her son.

• • •

I didn't always get along with my father. In my younger years, when I lived at home, we fought often and hard. But age has mellowed both of us. And now each time I return home I ask him to tell me about his life. I don't know that I'll ever truly understand what made him so hard when I was young, so in some ways he'll always be a mystery to me. But I carry his stories in my heart, the ones of old Mexico and of the Cristero Wars, of when he met my mother, of the Valley when he first came here. Some of these stories I've taped over the years; others are recorded in my memory. He is eighty-three years old now and still remembers with exacting clarity events and names from sixty and seventy years ago. We are sitting in his backyard, under a pair of towering palmetto palms. It is a balmy summer night, the crickets are almost as loud as the freeway. As he speaks, the rumble of traffic on freeways in the background breaks the stillness of the San Fernando Valley, and I lean forward so that I catch every word. He speaks in Spanish, rapidly, the words tumbling out as he recalls the stories. The interview that I made for this book is translated from the original Spanish, but it is true to his vocabulary and cadence.

I turn on the tape recorder, sit back, and listen to him tell this story, his memories of the Valley in the 1940s and 1950s. He clears his throat before beginning.

"I arrived in Tijuana, in transit from Nogales to San Ysidro, on July 3, 1944. Tijuana then was just a small, dusty town where servicemen would go spend weekends getting drunk in the cantinas. My brother Arturo worked in one of those cantinas, and of course, he set up poker games after hours. One time he won $7,000 in one night, only to lose it all again a few days later. He'd told me he could get me a job in Tijuana, but a week after I arrived, I still had no *chambe*. A relative of ours came to visit friends in Los Angeles and then had swung by Tijuana to see us. We met him at the bar where Arturo worked and then went out to the bullfights. Afterward Florencio asked me if I wanted to see Los Angeles, and I said sure. But I already had information as to where the camp for *contratados* was located. It was on Fillmore Street and San Fernando Road. Alexander's Court it was called. I had a passport with an entry visa to come in and out that they'd given me in Nogales so I could cross over in transit to San Ysidro. In those days, the road on the Mexican side was *brecha*, so it was better to travel through the U.S. side. It was a provisional visa for twenty-four hours.

"We crossed over in Florencio's car. There wasn't a checkpoint or anything on the border, just a little *gabachito* there. I'd already gotten my Social Security number in San Diego, because my compadre José Morán wanted me to come over and work, and so I had applied for it and they'd sent it to Arturo's address in Tijuana.

"I told myself—I'll just look around and return the next day. I had about twenty-some dollars in my pocket. Florencio was a bit drunk and side-swiped another car over by San Juan Capistrano, and we went into a ditch by the side of an orange grove. Then, what a problem we had getting the car out.

"Once in Los Angeles, I decided to stay, and I rented a room on Alameda Street between Sixth and Seventh. I paid $1.25 for the room. After breakfast I asked the waitress where I could get the bus to San Fernando. So I went where she told me—there was a sort of circle at the bus station with doors indicating the destinations, El Monte, Alhambra, etc., and one that said San Fernando. I came on the bus and arrived at the contractor's at noon.

"I came in and asked for work and told them I had come from Merced and that I had worked on the tracks. And they asked me some questions, like how much does the hammer weigh and a bunch of other stuff I didn't know, so they realized right away I hadn't worked on the track. So I told them the truth, the whole story about how my brother had invited me to Tijuana, and how I couldn't get work, and now all I wanted was a chance to earn some money so I could go back to Mexico City.

"They invited me to eat there at the *contratados*, and as we were eating *albóndiga* soup, the *cocinera* recognized me, although I didn't recognize her. 'Aren't you so-and-so who used to live on such-and-such a street in Mexico?' she asked me. And I replied, 'Yes. I lived on Francisco Díaz Covarrubias #97.' And she says, 'Well, I lived right in front of you. I even got on your train several times.' It turns out she was married to a guy named Chencho Jaramillo, who was a foreman at the camp. Right away she says, 'I'll tell them that you're a relative of mine so that they'll give you work.'

"Antonio Quevedo, who was in charge, then asked me about Mexico City. He said I could stay if I was from there. And I said, 'Sure, I know the whole city.' And he started asking me about all the places, like El Agua Azul, El Tranvía, and all these *caberetuchos*, real dives. Of course, I knew them all, since the trolley I drove made stops at all those places.

"Then he told me to pay attention to how the workers arrived at the end of the day. And they started showing up all covered with dirt and sweaty and with just their eyes and teeth showing. 'I don't care,' I said. 'I want to work so I can go back to Mexico.'

"So Quevedo asked me if I had any money, and then he took me to J.C. Penney's to buy my work clothes. I had arrived at the camp wearing a dark blue double-breasted suit, with white shirt and red tie, and red hanky in the pocket, and Domit shoes that were very popular back then. At Penney's I had enough for a work shirt and pants but not for shoes. 'So with what shoes are you going to work in?' he asked me. And I said 'With these,' and I pointed to my fancy Domits.

"They got me a room with a guy from Aguascalientes that they called 'El Pirrín.' And boy did his feet smell—that's why he bunked alone. It was one of those double bunk beds, and I slept on the top. I didn't stand it more than a few days before I moved to another room.

"The first day they told me I would be working with Chalo Aragón, who had truck number 7. And I said, 'That's a lucky number.' So I went to pick oranges. The first day I picked seventeen boxes at ten cents a box. My expenses for room and board came to $1.75 a day so I didn't even break even. That's how I started out. One day I picked seventeen, the next eighteen, but not more than twenty boxes a day. And I was all scratched up, hands, arms, everything.

"One day Chalo says, 'Tomorrow you're going with Johnny Flores to Ventura. When you see him in his truck, jump in the cab with him. There's more fruit over there, and you might do better.' I guess the truck driver didn't like driving all over the grove to pick up my one or two boxes.

"So I went to Santa Susana, over by Simi Valley, with Johnny Flores, who'd been here three years and drove the trucks that picked up all the orange crates from the fields. And it got better for me there. The first day I picked thirty boxes. I arrived there the 28th of August, and by the time the harvest finished, about mid-November, I was picking sixty to sixty-five boxes a day.

"During the time I was in Santa Susana, Chalo came by the camp one Sunday. He was wearing a gray-and-green checked suit, with a pink shirt and a yellow tie that looked like *cagada de niño*. *¡Qué bárbaro!* 'Oye, mariachis,' 'cause that's what he used to call us Mexicans, 'who wants to go to a dance?' Seems there was a *kermés* back in the Valley. But nobody wanted to go. Finally, I said, 'If you wait till I shower and change, I'll go with you.' So I showered and put on my dark blue double-breasted suit and red tie. And when Chalo sees me, he says, 'You're not a mariachi.' And I said, 'Why not?'

"'Well, look how you're dressed. Where'd you learn to knot a tie like that?'

"I tried telling him how you knot a tie, but he couldn't get it, and finally I said, 'Here, let me do it.' Later Chalo told me he used that tie for years with the same knot, he'd just slip it over his head without unknotting it.

"So just the two of us went to the *kermés*.

"The emcee at the *kermés* that night was señorita Soledad Lugo, and she had these huge dark eyes. It was, as they say, love at first sight. I asked Chalo, 'Who's that girl?'

"And he said, 'Forget it. *Esa pulga no brinca en tu petate.* She's real serious.'

"'I bet I'll dance with her. You'll see.'

"'Naw. She won't dance with you.'

"It turned out that one of the musicians was a guy I knew named Rodolfo Asunción. He played a real nice clarinet, and he'd joined up with a local group called Los Hermanos Navarro. So I talked with Rodolfo, because Soledad, being the emcee, was near the band. They charged a dollar to play requests, and I told Rodolfo, 'Play the *danzón* "Juárez."' He said they had other songs to play first, and I said that was fine. Then I turned to Soledad and said, 'When they play "Juárez," you're going to dance with me, right?' But she just ignored me.

"So they played other songs, and I just hung around waiting for the song I requested. When they played 'Juárez,' I came up to her and asked her to dance. 'Come dance with me, you said you would.'

"She looked at me really angry. 'No, I said no such thing.'

"'Yes you did.'

"'No I didn't.'

"But I insisted so much that she went out and danced a little bit, then went and sat down. They played some more songs, and I insisted she dance with me, but she wouldn't. Finally, she said, 'Why don't you wait till the dance is over, and I'll go eat with you. And then only because you came with Chalo, and I know him real well.'

"So we were eating when her brother Carlos showed up. And she introduced me, 'This is one of the Chicanitos who came from Mexico.'

"And Carlos said, 'You come from Mexico?'

"'Yes.' I said. 'Why?'

"'It doesn't look like it. The Mexicanos I know aren't dressed like you.'

"'That doesn't matter. I come from a town in Jalisco, and I used to be a tailor.'

"So we kept talking till Chalo said he was leaving. But Carlos said, 'Stay a while longer and I'll take you back.' We spent most of the night talking about Mexico, and when it was time to head back, I told Soledad, 'Next Sunday, why don't we go to Los Angeles?'

"She said, 'I'm too busy. But if you like, when my brother takes you, see the way and you can come back next week.'

"The next day in camp Chalo asked me: 'How did it go with Sally?'

"'What Sally?' I said.

"'You know, Soledad. Sally is what everyone calls her. She was the maid of honor when I got married. I know where she lives. I'm going to take you next Sunday, and you knock on her door. She has a car, you know.'

"So he took me the next Sunday, and I knocked on the door, *tun-tun*.

"She came out and said, 'What are you doing here?'

"'You said to come look you up.'

"So we went to the Cine California in L.A., and we played bingo and I won. And when I stepped up to claim my prize, they asked me my name and where I was from. When I said Autlán, a bunch of people came out and said they were from Autlán too. One guy even said my father had lent him money to come up north. When we got back to North Hollywood, Soledad told her family everything that had happened and how it was true that I was from Jalisco 'cause everybody knew me.

"I returned to the Valley about the beginning of November, which was after the orange season was over. I stayed at Pico Court, and on Sundays I'd go into San Fernando to see a movie. The theaters here were nothing like the fancy ones I was used to in Mexico City, like the Teatro Chapultepec that had a fountain in the lobby. In those days, the theaters here were segregated, and the Mexicanos had to sit in the back. And the first time I went I told myself, 'Why am I going to sit in the back if this is just a shitty little theater.' So I told the Raza sitting back there, 'Come on, sit wherever you want.' And all the men sitting in back got up and moved up front. And after that they didn't bother us anymore; we could sit where we wanted.

"Sometimes I'd hook up with Chalo, and we'd go to a *kermés*, or we'd play cards or shoot dice in camp. So he asked me to join his *cuadrilla* when the lemon season started. We were paid twenty-four cents a box for lemons, but with lemons, you don't pick that much because you have to use a ring to measure the fruit before you pick it.

"Actually, there's two reasons why I stayed in this country. The first, of course, was meeting Soledad. Because I never meant to stay here. Up to that time my intention was to earn enough money so I could buy a taxi license in Mexico City and go into business for myself.

"The other reason had to do with work. In Santa Susana, there was this guy who could pick 100 boxes a day. His name was Villegas, and his face was pockmarked. Chalo used to call Villegas '*de la cruz*,' because he didn't know how to write his name and so he'd put an X on the boxes he'd picked. They'd rotate the pickers up to Santa Susana where there was more fruit so they could make a little extra money. When I went up there, I saw that Villegas was the best. Everyone else picked 70–75 boxes a day, but he always picked more. So I thought to myself, What's he have that I don't?

"After a few months, once I got the hang of it, I was right up there with him. I was working with Chalo's *cuadrilla* at the time, and we went to pick a ranch in Granada Hills. One day, Villegas picked 80 boxes, and when Chalo asked me how many I picked, I said 80. And he looked at the two of us, and the competition was on. It was so intense sometimes that if I didn't break to eat or drink, Villegas wouldn't either. One time, there by De Soto and Nordoff, I picked 98 boxes every day for a week and couldn't break a hundred. And he couldn't either. Till finally one day in Santa Susana I picked 125 and he picked 123. Nobody had ever picked that much.

"In those days, you'd climb up any hill in the Valley and you'd see green, nothing but green. Maybe a little ranch house someplace and that was it. San Fernando only reached to Laurel Canyon Boulevard, and beyond was orchards. All the area around Holy Cross Hospital was orchards. North Hollywood was vacant lots and lots of peach and apricot farms, because the soil is sandy there. Glen Oaks was empty land and rocks. Pacoima was a few shacks and unpaved streets. Canoga Park had two streets, and they were both dirt.

"I didn't come as a bracero. I stayed a year and saved up some money and I left. I took a letter from the packinghouse saying that I had worked there. And Antonio, Soledad's brother, gave me one saying I had worked with him as a bricklayer and that I had a job whenever I wanted. So I went to Tijuana and deposited $900 in the bank. Then I sent for my papers from Autlán, my birth certificate and all that, and I had my brother Luis get me a letter of recommendation from the Sindicato de Transporte. By mid-October I had all my papers.

"So Soledad went to visit me there in Tijuana. She was on vacation from her job at a hospital on Balboa and Van Owen for the wounded men coming from overseas. She was a secretary for a doctor there, or for a general, something like that. In Tijuana we went to a nightclub called Negro y Blanco, and Arturo told the waiter to load up Sally's drink. And he gave me the sign, like, let's get her bombed.

"Soon the musicians were dedicating songs to her and that sort of thing. Then Arturo leans over to me and says, 'Now that she's a little *quemadita*, why don't you take her to see Mexico? Ask her if she wants to know Ensenada.' So we went to Ensenada, just the two of us, and on the way back she was a little too high to drive. We had no choice but to stay at a motel. But she says to me, 'I'm going to stay not because I'm drunk. But I won't return to my house unless I'm married.'

"Then I said, 'Fine. We'll do it.'

"The next day she called her work, told them she couldn't come in, she was sick or something. 'In that case,' I said, 'why don't we stay a few days.' I called Arturo at the cantina, and he said, '*Ahí te mando unos centavos.*'

"When we crossed over at the end of the week, we got married in San Diego. Soledad arranged everything. We had blood tests, everything. By December I was broke, so I came over on the Greyhound for Christmas and worked at the packinghouse for seventy-five cents an hour. That's when I got a letter from Arturo that all my papers were ready. I waited for Saturday so I could get my check and have some money. But when I arrived at the consul's, my appointment had already expired. Just then a lady stepped out who used to dance at José Morán's bar, and she asked me what was happening. She knew how to cut the red tape, so when the consul showed up, my papers were ready to go, and I got in line. The doctor, a relative of the young lady, passed me right away. By four o'clock my *mica* to immigrate— which is the same one I've had my whole life—was ready, and it was sent to Troost Street.

"I worked for a while at the packinghouse stacking empty crates, but I could make more picking. The boxes then were paid at ten cents for orange, eight for grapefruit, and twenty-four for lemon.

"I still went back and forth to Tijuana. One time, coming back, I was driving Soledad's car, a '39 Plymouth, on Highway 15. And just past Escondido the Border Patrol pulled me over. I had this other man from Pico Court with me. His name was Félix Padilla. Right away they separated us. They asked for my license and everything, but when they saw my papers were in order, they let me go. But they took Félix away. Later, at Pico Court, I received a letter from him. He was in Mexicali, and he sent a picture of himself. The Border Patrol had beaten him to a pulp, and in the photo he had a black eye and looked like a real mess.

"In 1948, the field man, Vicente Bustamante, who was a Spaniard, asked me to be foreman. Most foremen then were fifty to sixty-five years old, and I was what? thirty-five? thirty-six? I carried twenty-five men normally, but sometimes over thirty. The thing I always tried to do was figure out, to estimate, how many boxes we would pick. That was good for the *trokeros* because then they knew how many empty boxes they had to bring and not make so many trips. And I got so good that I could tell the rancheros how many boxes of oranges they had on their trees. After a while, many of the rancheros wanted only me to come. They'd ask for the one with the '*bigotito*,' the little mustache.

"Now and then I would even bet the rancheros a carton of cigarettes or ten dollars on how many boxes would be picked. There was a time when I'd tell Sunkist, the grower's association, look, there's so much at each ranch. And the big guys would come, and my estimates would be right. Even the biggest rancheros, Kay and Mulholland, wanted me to pick their ranches. Perry Mulholland, the son of William Mulholland, had a ranch of navel oranges over by Nordoff and DeSoto, and one year I told him, 'You have 17,000 boxes.'

"'No, Henry,' he said. 'That's too many. Can't be more than 14, 15 maybe, but not 17.'

"So every morning he'd come by and see how we were doing. And I'd tell him how many trees and how many boxes we'd picked. It turned out we picked 17,005 boxes that year. By the next year, some rancheros insisted that only I could pick their ranches. I picked all the ranches in the Valley—the Mulholland, the Porter, the Mackay, El Sombrero—all of them.

"A few years later I told Mulholland to scar the trunks of the trees when they started flowering, because then the tree would feel injured and would put out more energy and produce more fruit. The next time I came to pick I told him, 'You have 23,000 boxes.' He couldn't believe it so we bet twenty dollars, since he didn't smoke. He'd come by every morning about ten o'clock. He was president of the grower's association too. When we passed 17,000 boxes, he just shook his head. The trees had not only more fruit but bigger fruit too. Well, we didn't reach 23,000 boxes, but we didn't miss it by much. But it turned out that they caught this guy who was driving a pickup at night into the ranch and stealing oranges that he'd later sell at a fruit stand. It was because of him that we didn't reach the amount of boxes I'd estimated.

"One time at Mulholland's ranch, I climbed a tree to pick three or four oranges that had been missed. He happened to come by and asked me what was I doing. And I told him, 'Well, figure it this way. If you miss one orange per tree and you have so many thousands of trees, and then figure how many oranges per box, you can see how many boxes you're losing.'

"And he said in Spanish, 'cause he spoke a little Spanish, having studied in Guadalajara, '*Oye*, Henry—what did you work at in Mexico?'

"'*Sastre.*'

"'Tailor?' And he just scratched his head, wondering.

"The last time we picked at the Porter Ranch, it was late in the year, and the men were picking about ten trees a day. But then the temperature dropped to eighteen degrees, and we had to stop. When the men went back, the few lemons still on the trees were all black in the center, all burned. After that the men couldn't pick one box from ten trees. They lost over a million dollars' worth of fruit that year, and all because the ranch foreman insisted that I pick the ranch. But I was picking others, and when I was finally free, the frost hit and it was too late. That was in 1961.

"And eventually what happened was that they passed laws so that the rancheros couldn't use the kerosene furnaces in the fields to fight the frost. They had to use the big propeller-driven defrosters that didn't work at all; they just made it colder. And once the growers started losing money on the harvest, they started selling out one by one. And one ranchero would sell for $7,000 an acre and a few years later another would sell for $14,000 an acre. And then the next one would sell for $40,000 an acre, and like that.

"But everything you see here in the Valley was an orchard at one time. San Fernando High School was an orange grove. Chatsworth and Sepulveda the same thing. Over where the Bear Pit B-B-Q is was a strawberry field. And on the other side where the motor inn stands was an onion field. All along Devonshire was navel oranges; the same thing where Ralph's Supermarket is—I picked there too. You can still see a few little trees left over from that time. But that's what happened: World War II ended, and they started to knock down trees.

"Then the earthquake of 1970 finished off the rest. There used to be a big hotel in San Fernando, on Brand Boulevard, a big hotel with high arches, and after the earthquake they knocked it down. That hotel had walls of adobe, maybe three or four feet thick. And they tried to knock it down with a cable and tractor, but the cable would only slice through the walls, but nothing would happen. They had a hell of a time knocking that old building down."

• • •

We've been sitting for two hours in my father's backyard, talking above the humming noise of the freeway. As the night wears on, he grows quiet, lost in his own memories of 1940, and the scent of orange blossoms seems to dust the hours and the years long past and fill my head with all those stories of how much the Valley has changed. And sadly I realize what is gone and lost from his life: the hopes he had with my mother, the Valley fragrant with citrus dew, the baked white adobe houses of the bracero camps, the men in the poolrooms plucking boleros and remembering tropical nights back home in palm-thatched cafés getting stoned on tequila and cinnamon-flavored señoritas—all this is but a fading memory and will soon not even be that.

Enrique García Murguía is one of the last surviving *veteranos* of those citrus-field days, those men who stayed to live out their lives on Kalisher Street or haunt Martínez's Café, that old rundown bar and whorehouse that used to be the center of activity forty years ago. Men like my father, with hands that could crush walnuts, spent their entire lives talking of going back to Mexico, but they never did. My father lived his life dreaming of another time, and of the woman he loved, my mother. He never returned to Mexico, perhaps because he couldn't stand leaving her here, alone.

This is my father, a cynical and righteous Mexican who understood the world from his Mexico City nights and his orange-field days that he took me to share with him when Soledad, "La Sally," died and there were only his two sons and his crooked hand left to care for.

III

My memories of the San Fernando Valley are not the same as those of my aunt and my father. I grew up in Pico Court, the bracero camp where we lived, and in those sun-baked days there wasn't much for a kid to do. Nothing but dust, that's what I remember, no grass, no flowers, only a couple of date palms that looked out of place. I thought I'd go crazy living under those cloudless, boring skies, the monotony broken only by the whirring of motorplanes crossing the blue expanse that seemed to stretch forever. The first time I entered those adobe barracks of Pico Court I was six years old, and the smell of sweat and camphor and strong tobacco overcame me so that I wanted to vomit, or run away. If despair has an odor, it must be the smell of those labor camps.

The only other kid in Pico Court was Tony Rosas. He collected baseball cards, and later, behind the pool hall, taught me about Lucky Strikes. Tony's father, besides being a *trokero*, owned two pool tables set up in a corrugated iron bungalow in one corner of camp. On Sundays, the barber dusted off a chair in the pool hall, and the men would sit through haircuts that left them all *trasquilados*, as if a lawnmower had cropped their hair. Tony and I would rack up the pool balls and collect the money for the tables, and we'd pay attention to how the men chalked their cue sticks. Later we'd imitate them, an unlit cigarette behind our ear as we leaned over the table shooting eight ball.

I learned early to take care of myself, learned to make my own lunches: sandwiches of cheddar cheese and mayonnaise that stuck to the roof of my mouth or the common peanut butter and grape jelly, food I never cared for. When the refrigerator was empty, I just went without. The first time I cooked bacon I burned it to a crisp, sending greasy clouds funneling out the kitchen window. The men in the camp rushed to our house thinking there was a fire, but the fire, as I would later learn, was all inside me.

• • •

Sometimes, for the adventure, I would spend Saturdays in the citrus orchards with my father. I would rise before daybreak and go out with him to the big tarp-covered trucks still misted with morning dew. Out of the darkness of the bracero camp, men would appear from the mess hall with their *café con leche* and brown-paper-bag lunches.

Soon after sunrise we'd arrive at a citrus ranch, somewhere in the foot-hills of the Valley. The citrus groves were laid out in neat, seemingly endless rows of trees. The men would jump off the truck and stretch, then hit the orchard, my father directing them. In the fields, they worked fast till noon, then had lunch over a campfire shaded by giant eucalyptus trees that served as windbreakers. A half hour later they were back picking fruit till sunset, then into the boxlike camp trucks, big canvas-topped Fords with clumsy steering wheels. My old man often helped load the produce trucks as they came through the orchard, 250 crates to the truckload—the sweat of a hundred hands heading for the packinghouses of Fillmore and Saticoy, and from there all over the world.

I'd spend the day wandering in those vast fields, watching flights of

crows in the sky or a jackrabbit that would suddenly scamper out from
under a tree; the air would be scented with the pungent smell of rich earth
just turned or the sweet fragrance of orange blossoms. But I also remember
the men caked with dust and sweat, their work shirts stained front and back
with sweat. My father carried a jar of salt tablets in the truck in case a
worker collapsed of dehydration or sunstroke. To this day, the mere sight
of a salt tablet will bring back those days in the citrus fields, as vivid as if
I'd just left them yesterday.

•   •   •

The men of Pico Court were a microcosm of Mexico, each of them stamped
with their peculiar regional habits. Rosario, from Sinaloa, never went without his Brooklyn Dodgers baseball cap, and he could fill a hundred boxes a
day with oranges and still have energy to organize a pickup baseball game
in the dirt lot of the camp. El Pato was a cigarette-smoking dude, cool and
suave, who wore his hair slicked and scented with Tres Flores pomade. And
there was Guadalupe, who once scuffled with three *pachucos* in a Pacoima
bar; he was holding his own—till he slipped. Some time later, Guadalupe
spotted one of the *pachucos* stopped at a red light. Lupe rushed the sedan
flashing a *filero*, the blade glistening, and before the surprised *pachuco* could
raise his window, Lupe stabbed him three or four times in the chest. Lupe
fled after that and returned to his pueblo in Jalisco. One day in the *placita* a
vaguely familiar *greñudo* calls him over, "Hey, ése . . . don't I know you from
Pacas?" The *vato* approached Lupe with a song and dance, hustling him for
some *jando*, 'cause he was broke and 'sides, ain't they homeboys? Lupe
instantly recognized the *vato* as part of the gang who'd jumped him that
time in Pacoima, and he pulled out a .38 from his coat and made the *cabrón*
get down on his knees and beg forgiveness.

•   •   •

It was these same tough men who organized the camp's social activities.
They celebrated all the traditional Mexican fiestas, special *pozole* dinners
for Cinco de Mayo and big patriotic celebrations for Sixteenth of September, complete with baseball games, raffles, foot races, and *palo encebado*, or
greased pole. You have to actually see the *palo encebado* to appreciate the fun.
First, the men would get a telephone pole and grease it heavily with lard
and oil and anything else that was slippery. Then they'd attach a prize to
one end; it could be an envelope filled with money or a transistor radio.
After this, the pole would be set up straight, solidly in the earth like a regu-
lar telephone pole, with the prize at the top. Then a bunch of men, sometimes twenty or more, would attempt to shimmy up the pole, but since the

pole was heavily greased, they wouldn't go more than a foot or two before they'd slide down. But no matter, that was the fun of it. They'd keep at it, sometimes for an hour or more until some greasy, lucky guy finally made it to the top and claimed the prize. Once I saw my father in a foot race during a Sixteenth of September fiesta. A distance of a hundred yards was marked out on the asphalt of the bracero camp. Ten men were running for a $20 prize. My father took off his shoes and ran barefooted and beat them all by a good five yards.

But other fiestas were more solemn. On December 12, Nicolás, the gray-haired camp cook, organized the fiesta in honor of La Virgen de Guadalupe. A candle-lit procession would weave through the bracero camp, followed by midnight mass at the mess hall. I'd sit enchanted by the ritual and the glowing candles, my memories whisking me to Mexico City and how we used to celebrate the Virgen's day with firecrackers and skyrockets. It was these little rituals, these celebrations of being Mexican, hearing the men speaking Spanish, that kept me in touch with myself during this time of alienation. These were my links to a world left behind. Every region of Mexico was represented in Pico Court, the very *corazón* of Mexico surviving in the desert of California.

• • •

Every September before school started, my father bought me two shirts, two pairs of pants, and one pair of shoes. These were meant to last till the following September. I washed my own clothes in tubs of soapy water, squeezed them through a wringer, and used wooden clothespins to string them on a line. This world held not the slightest bit of affection. My day-dreams centered on running away from Pico Court to some foreign place where life was dangerous and exotic. Though I dreamed of adventure, I hungered for affection; I don't ever recall a kiss on the forehead, not even a pat you would give a dog. The men in the camp scoffed at kindness as a weakness. These were hard men without the time or inclination for dialogue, or books, things they considered a waste of time. The worst sin, if you weren't drunk, was to admit feeling lonely, abandoned, exiled. So I grew up as angry as a scorpion stinging itself.

And school was a disaster. San Jose Elementary School and later George K. Porter Junior High were an endless tedium of teachers without a spark of imagination, without a love of learning—cranks who hated their dark students who spoke with thick accents and wore the same clothes to school day after day. The Chicano kids were put in the slow classes; we were reading Dick and Jane and Spot in the fifth grade. And I was bored; I knew intuitively that I had to ignore and break the rules if I were to survive. I saw school as punishment, with detention handed out for the slightest infraction. That's how Chicanos socialized—we all met in detention.

I survived those years with the help of big, bad Tony Rosas, his waterfall conk fixed in place with Tres Flores pomade, a pack of Lucky Strikes twisted into the sleeve of his T-shirt. Tony was a head taller than I, so I looked up to him in more ways than one. He skipped school as much as possible, and soon I was doing it too. We became masters at forging letters from our parents. In the seventh grade, Tony and I managed to stay out a whole month. My father left early for work, so he was never around in the morning. I'd go meet Tony, and we'd wave to his mother as if we were off to school. Instead, we'd go to the hills behind the San Fernando Mission and roam the vacant fields, throwing rocks at blackbirds and picking fruit from yards that said No Trespassing. When Tony's mother went to visit relatives in Mexico, we spent a whole week at his house watching *Our Gang* on TV and smoking his father's Lucky Strikes. We'd do anything to stay out of school. Even then, I knew I had to rebel, that I would not follow my father's steps. No way.

One day, I came home from being truant, and my father was waiting. I knew something was wrong; he never arrived home till six in the evening, and now it was only four. The house was dark, the curtains drawn, and he was sitting in the living room that was also my bedroom. He held a letter from school that he waved in my face. I knew he couldn't read English, but somehow he had figured out that I'd been absent for a month. Now he had to appear in school, at a meeting with the principal, a situation that embarrassed him.

He asked me where I'd been all these weeks I hadn't gone to school. I told him the truth, that I couldn't stand school, that they didn't like Mexicans, and that I didn't want to go back. His voice trembled with anger at what I had done. I would go in the next morning and apologize to the teacher, or else, he said. Not knowing what "or else" meant, I pictured my humiliation in class, and so I replied, "No, I'm not going back to that dirty school."

He whipped the belt out so fast the leather hissed through his belt loops. Then he came at me. I tried to jump out of the way, but he caught me across the legs with the first swing. I stumbled to the ground, and he stood over me waving the belt. "So you won't go back to school?" he shouted in a mad rage. The word "No" had barely formed in my mouth when the belt came down again and again, on my legs, on my back, on my shoulders. I rolled on the floor, my arms over my head, trying to avoid the belt, but he kept swinging, ten, fifteen, twenty times, the belt stinging like dog bites. He stopped when his arm grew tired, or maybe he realized he might kill me.

But I never said "Yes" to him. The next day when he marched me into the principal's office, I couldn't sit down, my legs and butt were one ugly purple bruise. But he was the one who apologized to the principal in broken English, not me.

He hadn't broken me, and he knew it. If he couldn't tame me at age twelve, it was too late to tame me at all. For years we fought almost daily, arguments and threats and curses, till the time when I was fourteen. By then, my older brother was out of the house, already headed for Viet Nam. I'd been out joyriding with Tony and some of the other *vatos;* we had finished a quart of Bacardi, and I swaggered in past midnight. My father was waiting in the living room again, all red-eyed from lack of sleep, and he asked me where I'd been. I just shrugged him off. That set him off. We exchanged words, and he raised his hand to smack me, but I blocked his blow with my forearm. Crazy with anger, he came at me, but I pushed him back and raised a table lamp ready to smash it in his face. He never expected that. I stood my ground, ready to fight it out with him. I was his size, but younger and faster. He was almost fifty years old, and life had never been fair to him. I didn't want to hurt him any more than life had, but I wasn't going to let him beat me. He didn't know what to do—he went to pull out his belt, but I told him he'd have to kill me before I'd let him whip me like when I was younger. He stood there for a moment thinking about it, then he turned and retreated silently to his room and never told me what to do again. That was my Independence Day, my Sixteenth of September and Fourth of July all rolled into one.

But I can't blame him for what he was; he knew no other way. His only days off were Sundays, and the only thing I remember him having energy to do on those days was sleep. I had to move quietly around the house, could not make any noise, and I'd peer into his darkened bedroom where he slept during those Sunday afternoons to see if he hadn't died. He'd be stretched out on the bed, snoring, a crack of light coming in through the curtained windows, and I'd tell myself I didn't want to be like him; I didn't want his life of endless work, with one day of rest to recover the strength to work another six. I didn't know how I would make my life different, but I knew I had to escape the bracero camp, get away from his world, away from his dead-end life.

My father had this little ritual he'd put me through whenever we were together for periods of time, like when the rains came and work slowed down at the packinghouse, and he'd be at home brooding. The ritual went something like this: he'd ask out of the blue, "What you gonna be when you grow up, *mi'jo?*" And I'd answer whatever came into my mind, "A doctor." Or maybe I'd say it just to piss him off, to make it seem that I'd be better than he was. He'd laugh. "You'll never be a doctor—you ever seen a Mexican doctor in this country?" I knew he was goading me, knowing that life for a Mexican kid in this country was going to be tough, and if I was going to make it, I'd have to be tougher than most.

One time he told me, "I never wanted you to grow up here, because in this country there's not much chance of a Mexican kid moving up." I understood then why he was making me tougher than I had to be. And I swore I'd make something of myself and show him what kind of son he'd raised.

• • •

The one thing Tony Rosas was really good at was being bad. He knew all the thrills that restless young *vatos* crave, and he did them all with a flair I envied. He'd sneak bottles of Hamm's beer from the cooler his father kept in the pool hall and come knock on my door. We'd drink them behind the eucalyptus trees that surrounded Pico Court, often going through a six-pack each. We'd talk trash about girls, or of places no one had heard of. He'd say something like, "I want to be the first Chicano in Dar es Salaam." And he'd start describing a city, and he'd invent details like the pawnshops or marketplaces, and in my head I'd go far away to exotic cities with brave men and dangerous women. He was a year older and a complete failure at school and proud of it. I copied his don't-give-a-damn attitude and his style of smoking, letting the *frajo* hang from my lip.

From Tony I learned to hand-roll joints of Mexican *yesca*, weed that we scored from the older *vatos* for a couple of dollars. We practically lived in after-school detention, and the *yesca* made it seem bearable. At home there was nothing but dust and my taciturn father, so every evening I'd seek refuge behind the eucalyptus trees and smoke my *yesca* till I felt I could touch the stars. I knew that as long as I could get my hands on those matchstick-thin joints, I could make it through the drudgery of Pico Court till I could get away. I even slicked my hair with Tres Flores and hung out with Tony on the street corners of the barrio, my stance an affirmation against this society, declaring for the world to see that I, too, was an outlaw, a *vato* machine, *loco y pachuco. Y ¿qué? Punto y total.*

When I was thirteen, Tony showed me the outlaw thrill of joyriding. Using a wire coat hanger, we'd break into cars—Tony favored 1950 Chevrolets because you didn't need to hot-wire them, you could turn the ignition with your thumb and they'd fire right up. Tony drove with a cigarette behind his ear. He'd pop the clutch and burn rubber for a quarter mile down Sepulveda Boulevard, and he'd take corners so sharp the car would tilt on two wheels. We'd siphon gas from parked cars and go riding around the Valley, sometimes even to East L.A., where we'd pick up *cholitas* on Whittier Boulevard and take them to Elysian Park, getting plenty out of them with our stash of beer and *yesca*. We'd sit in the park, our arms around a girl we'd just met, and Tony and I would talk about running away to Polynesia, Afghanistan, Madagascar—names as exotic as our dreams. What would I have done without Tony Rosas? My life would have been truly lost, a waste; if nothing else, he taught me to dream, to imagine a world unknown, a life away from the camps. After these parties, we'd head back to the Valley, then abandon the car on Rinaldi Avenue, over by the cemeteries, and walk home exhilarated, high as the stars.

At fifteen, Tony appeared in Pico Court wearing this stunning crimson jacket with a silver crown in back, topped in Old English script with the words "Los Reyes." So I started hanging out with Tony and Los Reyes at garage parties where I filled my head with purple *yesca* smoke and slow-danced with tattooed *pachuconas*, their eyes made up like Egyptian queens, blue tears on their faces. At these parties, I learned to French kiss, to squeeze and feel a woman for the first time, to slip my fingers into that furry triangle of desire. Tony and his *carnales* in Los Reyes—El Puppet, Spider, Johnny Rojo, El Oso—were bad, bad dudes who wouldn't hesistate to kill any sucker who offended their honor. These were the *vatos* who would later do twenty years in Folsom and San Quentin, who would die in gang ambushes, or who would fly off the road into telephone poles while loaded on reds, downers, or barbiturates and would be buried accompanied by a cortege of lowriders and a dirge of oldies: my generation.

Then, just before my initiation into Los Reyes, for which I had to tattoo a blue cross on my left wrist, Tony was busted for joyriding. For some reason, I wasn't with him that night, but another *vato* we called Perico was. The police pulled them over on San Fernando Road. Perico panicked, made a run for it, and in the chase was shot and killed by the police. The city held no inquiry; it was assumed that all Chicano youths were criminals, as guilty as original sin. Tony took the rap. He didn't have much choice. He'd just turned sixteen, and they sentenced him to five years in the California Youth Authority. By the time he was released, I was involved in other things and never hooked up with him again. Years later I heard he overdosed on heroin: he was twenty-two, and they found him with one hand on the wheel of a slick lowrider, the needle still in his arm—a fate he didn't deserve.

After Tony was busted, I drifted away from Los Reyes. I discovered I didn't like being part of a gang, didn't like being just another faceless Chicano kid. And I knew that whatever statement I'd make with my life, it would have to be on my own, *yo solo, solito*.

I can't exactly say when the dual-headed serpent of language first bit me, but sometime around my fifteenth birthday I started to pay attention to words. I was sitting in English class, ostracized as usual to the back row, and the teacher said something like ". . . the destiny of so-and-so." I didn't exactly catch what she was saying, and I didn't care. But after class I went to the library and looked the word up, and I knew that's what I'd have to find—my destiny. And it wasn't going to be in their books; I wasn't in those pages, it wasn't my story. The next week I returned to the library and found other words, like "desire" and "tropics," beautiful words that helped define my world and who I was. Eventually, I discovered the words to express this story I am now writing. But it has been a struggle to get here. In the end, I was the only one of my barrio to survive. I know each sentence I write is a rebellion, a miracle of survival.

· · ·

My father and I tolerated each other during my teenage years, but after our last fight, he was even more distant, more aloof. And when he spoke, it was never about the things that mattered. I wanted to know about my mother, but he could never find the words to tell me. On Sundays, when he wasn't sleeping, he played his old Mexican music, *danzones* and boleros, that ever after I will associate with him. That's practically the only memory of him I cherish. Perhaps I didn't realize that he was trying to relive the best times he'd ever known, the times before my mother died.

Only once do I recall him drinking. I was still living with him, and I must've been sixteen or so. It happened one Sunday night. I had my feet up on the sofa and was watching *Peter Gunn* out of sheer boredom. He came in from his *compadre*'s house, where he'd had a few tequilas. He sat down in front of me and started talking. I turned off the TV. I was amazed; he'd never done this before, and I wanted to listen. At first, he was happy, but then somehow he turned toward sad subjects. He told me how much he loved my mother, told me how her death had changed his luck forever, that he'd never been happy since, had carried on only for our sake, for me and my brother. I could see the conversation was driving him beyond the limits. He was just being honest, being human, but this embarrassed me. I didn't want to see my father, this rock in my life, so hurt and mortal. Then he told me not to be like him, not to work as a mere laborer, to study, to do something with my life. "Here, look at these hands," and he showed me his calloused palms, ripped from years of work, especially the crooked finger on his left hand, swollen and as red as raw meat. He was fifty-two years old, and the juice of life had been squeezed out of him. And I wanted to hug him, because I knew he had worked his life away. Instead I made up my mind to leave.

· · ·

After the citrus groves were ripped out to make way for the suburban flood of the 1960s, Pico Court closed down, and my father moved us to a house on Memory Park, a few blocks away. He's lived the rest of his life there, a proud and lonely man, struggling on his own. Even in his eighties, when his shoulders are rounded, he still keeps his mustache neatly trimmed out of vanity.

Once I had saved enough money, I stuffed my clothes into a cardboard suitcase. I was playing out my destiny; whatever fate had in store for me, I was ready for it. The Santana winds were blowing to scorch the skin that day, and the thick curls of my greased waterfall conk scented the air with Tres Flores pomade. There I was, a young *pachuquillo* with the Valley dust thick on my shoes, and when I pulled out of the driveway, I turned my face to the sun and I never looked back.

Years later, one smoggy sunset, I went back to Pico Court. The gates of the old bracero camp were chained up, so I crawled in through a hole in the fence where Tony Rosas and I used to hang out. I walked through the abandoned adobe barracks, searching for something of my youth, of my past. I looked for the palm tree where I'd once carved my initials, but now only a charred stump remained to mark the spot. The field in front of the mess hall where Tony and I had played baseball with Rosario was overgrown with weeds, and the roof of the mess hall had caved in, leaving the rafters showing like bones. My past was already a crumbling ruin, and in a few more weeks the tractors would obliterate this part of my life forever. I pushed the door to our old house, and it swung open, rotted on its hinges. It was empty but for trash and broken bottles and cobwebs. I stepped inside the white-washed adobe rooms one last time, the rooms where I had fought with my father, where I had laid out the plans to escape from his world, and as I did, the odor of sweat and camphor that had filled those days in Pico Court, where I had lived out my years of desperation, returned to me one last time.

In spite of everything, I love my father and regret that I have never told him. Such simple words. But somehow I think he knows.

GATHERING THUNDER

On October 21, 1955, I crossed the border from Tijuana to San Ysidro, completing a full-circle journey that had taken me from North Hollywood to Mexico City and back. California is my *tierra natal*, but my first memories of life are of Mexico City: El Mercado La Merced, Chapultepec Park, the songs of El Cri-Cri on the radio, and *fotonovelas* of El Santo, the legendary masked wrestler. I was five years old when I left "La Capital" and came to the border town with my older brother, Raymond, and my grandmother. We rented a yellow house on Calle Segunda, next to the Librería Mérida, and waited for her immigration papers to come through.

The house on Calle Segunda had a front porch and a dirt yard where we used to play marbles. Behind our house stood the burned-out shell of an apartment building where fifteen people had died. These ruins towered over the barrio, and they fomented recurring nightmares of arms and legs falling through the flames, nightmares that I still recall quite vividly.

Tijuana is a city where things happen, perhaps because it is a transient city. People walk fast, and disappear just as fast. During my short stay in Tijuana, a momentous event seemed to unfold every day: One day I entered first grade, another day I smoked my first cigarette, another day I kissed my first girl. I recited poetry for the first time, standing on a balcony overlooking the entire student body of La Escuela 16 de Septiembre. It was October 12, Día de La Raza, and I delivered in memorized rhyme "Las Tres Carabelas," the tale of *La Pinta, La Niña y La Santa María*.

Our schoolyard games were shooting marbles or spinning tops on the hard dirt. Sometimes we bought dry ice from street vendors outside the front gate and blew the gas through rolled-up papers, pretending we were smoking. Other times we smoked real cigarettes. Sometimes we got into rock-throwing fights with gangs from other schools.

Although the school was coed, each grade was separated into two classrooms, first-grade boys and first-grade girls, and so on. I was barely five years old when my grandmother enrolled me in first grade so I could attend at the same time as my older brother. There was a disparity in ages among my classmates—I was the youngest; the oldest boy in our first-grade class was fourteen. Sometimes a kid went to school for only a few weeks, and then we'd never see him again. Once, the two oldest boys in the first grade, Pelón, who was fourteen, and Chato, who was twelve, got into a fight in the back of the classroom. The fight ended with Pelón driving a sharpened pencil into the right temple of the other boy. Before anyone could stop him, he ran out the classroom, climbed over the fence, and took off. He never came back. Neither did Chato.

Flash floods that winter forced classes to be canceled in the middle of the day. My brother and I were the last to leave school, and by then the streets were already flooded several inches deep. As we got closer and closer to our house, the water levels kept rising. By the time we reached our block, there was no way to cross the street. We were rescued by a man in thigh-high rubber boots who picked us up like we were bags of groceries, one under each of his arms, and took us across the intersection so we could get home. We were the lucky ones. That same flood wiped out several cardboard shantytowns in the hills above Tijuana, leaving dozens dead and hundreds homeless.

On Saturday mornings, Raymond and I would go to the Cine Maya around the corner and exchange our milk-bottle caps of La Vaquita for a ticket to the matinee. These childhood Saturday mornings began my love affair with movies. A special treat was the day we went to the opening of the Cine Roble, at that time the most luxurious theater in Tijuana; my grandmother, Raymond, and I got to sit in the new plush seats, and when Pedro Infante sang, all the women in the theater sighed. Then the first televisions came out, and the whole neighborhood gathered at a neighbor's to watch a beauty contest on a six-inch screen.

The streets of downtown Tijuana were ablaze with splashy, dazzling neon signs, exploding like firecracker castles on the Sixteenth of September: signs that expanded in rings or that flashed off and on like electric fireflies in pastel colors, or the sign of a winged horse flying above a gas station. One in particular was in a class of its own: the neon flamingo that advertised a liquor store in magenta colors. The flamingo hung over a dark street that I had to cross on my way home from school, and its electric wings, flapping as if taking flight, illuminated the dreary tenements and buildings. Every time I passed by, I'd stop and gaze at the long-necked bird scattering neon light, and the ominous street would seem to glitter with a soft pink glow of beauty and wonderment.

In my memory, in spite of tearful farewells from friends and neighbors, the day we left Tijuana is sunny and bright. My father had borrowed a car to drive us back, and my grandmother had been packed for days. My brother, the champion marble shooter of our neighborhood, invited all our friends over, and in our front yard, tossed all his marbles in the air. It was a mad scramble, a free-for-all fight for his prized shooters. With our luggage stacked atop the car, we drove out of Calle Segunda like a band of gypsies. As we passed the ziggurat-shaped marquee of the Cine Maya and, next to it, the neon flamingo, I said to myself, "I'll be back soon," but it would be thirteen years before I returned to Mexico.

•   •   •

At the crowded international border (a figment of one's imagination, since there is no border, only a white stripe painted on asphalt), we waited our turn, then suddenly, without any fanfare or strobe lights, we were back in the U.S.A. We crossed the border like thousands of other immigrants from Mexico moving to the north: legal and illegal, counted and uncounted. There was no statue with a fake torch for us, none of that "Give me your tired, your poor, your huddled masses. . . ." California was no melting pot, but a boiling cauldron where we'd get scorched, collectively and individually.

We arrived that long ago October day at Pico Court, a bracero camp in the San Fernando Valley, when the Valley was still pretty much one large citrus orchard. The camp was within walking distance to the town of San Fernando, located just outside the border of the city and county of Los Angeles.

My first day at school was as bitter as cod liver oil swallowed with the nose pinched. Although I was native born, the six-year-old kid who crossed the border didn't know *papas de inglés*—didn't know diddly, in other words. In Spanish, I could read and write in longhand, also add and subtract and do multiplication tables, but in English I knew nothing. To my utter shame, I was enrolled in the first grade, where students were adding one plus two and learning to print the alphabet in block letters. But worse, the teacher (a horse-faced Mrs. Hofsteader) changed my name. I couldn't even pronounce what she said, much less relate to it. I could accept starting over in the first grade. I could accept the loneliness and alienation I felt because of my failure to communicate. I could take all that, but I couldn't take losing my name. I ran home and refused to go back to school. My father, who spoke no English, insisted I return to class. I went back the next day, but with no pretense of enjoying myself in that environment. Eventually, I learned my first words of English through an advertisement jingle. One day I stood at a hamburger stand half a block from Pico Court, proud but unsure if the man would understand me. I still remember those first words I uttered in English—"Pepsi, please." When the man set the soda on the counter, my joy was boundless. I had finally communicated in this bastard tongue.

Then I fell in love with a pair of blue suede shoes I saw in a store window in San Fernando. My father thought them too flashy for school, but he bought them for me anyway. Later I heard of Elvis and the rest and learned about rock 'n' roll, rhythm and blues, and oldies.

But the best example of what a Chicano could aspire to in this country, Ricardo Valenzuela, known as Richie Valens—who sang in Spanish or English—would die tragically while still in his teens at the close of the 1950s. Years later, I would attend the same high school, San Fernando High, where his presence and spirit could still be felt in the halls and classrooms. The handful of songs he wrote and sang were still played on the radio, but his own live voice was stilled forever that February morning when, along with Buddy Holly and the Big Bopper, his plane went down in a snowy cornfield, and a generation lost its music.

•   •   •

San Fernando is built on land once owned by a Mexican rancher named Celis, who sold it to John Maclay, who in the 1870s had his friend Leland Stanford build a railroad through it. On weekends, we sometimes walked to San Fernando from Pico Court, and I'd pass by the Pico Adobe, a once majestic, now crumbling, two-story adobe house where Andrés Pico presided over the last days of Mexican California. Another half mile down the road, on Brand Boulevard, stood Mission San Fernando Rey de España, founded by the Franciscans in 1797. Now when I look back at where I grew up, it seems that I was fated to confront California history.

Back in the 1950s, the San Fernando Valley was one big citrus orchard, and buried amidst the big ranches that occupied the land—the Mulholland, the Porter, the Lankershim—were three small towns full of Mexican braceros and Chicano *pochos*—San Fernando, Sun Valley, and Canoga Park.

Kalisher Street in San Fernando was the center of the Valley for us. The street was lined with skimpy trees that offered little shade, but it was *el barrio, la mera cosa*. On weekends, *vatos* would come from East Los Angeles, Encino, even San Pedro; the bars and hangouts would be filled with *pachucos* and braceros, the barrio sidewalks crowded with squats in khaki pants and zoot-suiters. *¡Qué vatos más locos!*—with tattoos and ducktails, French-toed shoes and one-button rolls, masters of the tongue known as caló, the argot of the Chucos.

Ramírez Pool & Bar stood on the corner of Kewen and Kalisher, a block up from Martínez Café, an ancient bar and whorehouse. Across the street from Ramírez Pool & Bar, music and tequila spilled out of Carmen's Cantina, where, one Saturday, Jaime, a friend of my father's, was snuffed over nothing. There had been a fight, and Jaime had beaten a man pretty hard, and the loser, nursing his damaged machismo, returned with a *cuete* and shot Jaime once in the chest. Poor Jaime fell, his eyes rolling toward the sky, as if asking God, "Why?" He was dead before his skull hit the sidewalk with that awful sound.

•   •   •

I was always looking for Mexican and Spanish surnames to identify with in the popular culture of the 1950s. Through my childhood friend Tony Rosas, I was introduced to baseball cards and new heroes like Ted Williams and Willie Mays. But above all the others I admired Bobby Avila, the clean-hitting second baseman of the Cleveland Indians. He wasn't a home-run hitter, but he won the American League batting crown in 1954 with a .341 batting average. It was good to know one could play second base *en las ligas grandes and* win the batting title *and* be Mexican. Years later, after I had lost all my baseball cards, I paid $6 for a 1954 card of Bobby Avila in a batting stance and his Cleveland Indians uniform. I just had to have it as a memento of my childhood. But I had other favorites. Roy Campanella, the scrappy catcher of the Brooklyn Dodgers, was one of the great players of that era, and I associated with him. I figured someone named Campanella must have a little Latin blood in him.

One summer night in September 1957, my father and Rosario took me to my first professional baseball game: the Hollywood Stars versus the San Francisco Seals in Gilmore Stadium near the present-day Farmer's Market. I remember the wooden stands, the clear September night, the talk of the Dodgers and Campanella coming to the coast the following year. This was the last game the Hollywood Stars ever played, the last game of the Pacific Coast League, and the feeling in the stands was that this was the end of an era.

That same year, 1957, would also be the beginning of the end for the big citrus ranches. Within a handful of years, my father would be unemployed and eventually enter the construction trade. The huge ranches were sold, one by one, to developers armed with chain saws and bulldozers, who turned the Valley into little communities named Granada Hills and Northridge that sprang up overnight like hallucinogenic mushrooms.

Late one winter's night, a solemn Rosario came over to visit my father. He brought the news that Roy Campanella had been badly injured in a car accident on an icy eastern road. Campanella would survive the accident but be confined to a wheelchair the rest of his life. He would never play catcher for the Dodgers in Los Angeles.

Many things ended with the fifties; Dwight Eisenhower was finished, so were tailfins, toreador pants, the Hollywood Stars; the braceros would fade away, and Pico Court would disappear, plowed over for Simi Highway 118.

• • •

Soon after the citrus orchards gave way to the suburbs, we moved to Memory Park Lane, where I first learned of California history from the renowned archaeologist Dr. Mark Harrington, who lived across the street from us. At the time I knew Dr. Harrington, he was already in his seventies, a huge, ponderous man whose size hid a gentle nature. He lived in a beautiful adobe house that is still standing, with an enclosed patio and fountain, shaded by pepper trees and surrounded by an impressive wall of opuntia cactus. He moved slowly around his house, dragging his right foot with its shoe that had a sole four times as thick as the other to compensate for a physical defect caused by polio.

For several years I spent at least one Saturday afternoon a month with him. I would rake his yard, split his firewood, clean up the fallen cactus leaves. Afterward, the two of us would sit in his kitchen or living room, and over a snack he'd made, he'd tell me stories of his early work in Cuba or in the deserts of the Southwest, where he'd uncovered important clues of early man. His house was like a museum filled with Native American and California artifacts, and over his fireplace hung a family heirloom, a musket from the Revolutionary War of 1776.

He didn't treat me like a *patrón* would; instead we were more like friends. I like to think he envied my youth as much as I respected his age. And since he couldn't get around much, he depended on me for help, just as much as I relied on his checks for spending money. But beyond our pragmatic friendship, he introduced me to the world of Native Americans and Californios, worlds apart from the working-class barrio that was my turf. Dr. Harrington knew Native American songs, in particular Chumash songs, and he'd sometimes sing them to me, one hand shaking a rattle while he chanted *Teh-yeh-yeh-yeh, Teh-yeh-yeh*. It must have been an odd scene: a thirteen-year-old Califas kid listening to an aged white man singing Native American songs. But the rhythms of the songs have endured in my head all these years—as have the creation stories of Chiniginich, the Chumash god who went to heaven while dancing.

In his living room, Dr. Harrington also placed early California in my hands—Chumash baskets, Pomo flints, Californio saddles. He explained to me the construction of adobe houses, how the bricks were built of straw and mud, the rafters fixed with wet rawhide strips, even taught me how to mix limestone with water to use as whitewash over adobe bricks. These first-hand history lessons are my earliest memories of California's past, and I absorbed them like air.

It was here, too, where I first realized that schoolbook history didn't always coincide with my history. At that time, the accepted premise was that man had been in the Western Hemisphere not more than three thousand years. I remember being taught this all through my public school years. But with Mark Harrington, I learned different. One autumn Saturday, after I had split some oak logs with a sledgehammer and wedge and had brought the wood in, he invited me to have some refreshments. I kindled a fire in the fireplace, and as we sipped mulled cider, he started on one of his stories. For most of his professional life, he'd accepted that man was a recent arrival on our continent. He'd even dismissed obvious proof at several digs, including one in Cuba, where he'd found clear evidence that man had lived in conjunction with animals that were now extinct—that man, in fact, had lived in the Western Hemisphere at least ten thousand years ago.

Finally, in 1931, he could no longer deny the evidence. At an archaeological dig at Gypsum Cave, Nevada, some fifteen miles from Las Vegas, he found irrefutable proof. Digging through layers of soil, animal dung, and human artifacts such as atlatls and darts, pre-bow-and-arrow weapons, he reached the oldest layers of the cave. There he found remnants of a fireplace, and mixed with human weapons, the atlatls and darts, was hair and dung of the ground sloth, an animal of the Pleistocene Era. It was unmistakable proof, he told me, that man had been here since at least since 8,500 B.C. Then, in the 1940s, he excavated an obsidian site used by various Native American cultures at Borax Lake in Northern California. The artifacts his team from the Southwest Museum found, arrowheads and metates, dated the site from 10,000–15,000 B.C., possibly older, maybe 25,000 B.C. This placed the presence of humans in California farther back than any previous archaeologist had dared contemplate.

He finished his story by the heat of the crackling fire, then he reached for something on the mantelpiece. "Look," he said, "here's something for you." He placed in my hand a small chipped piece of black stone, shiny as glass, with a groove in the center. It was barely two inches long, weighed as much as three or four feathers, and I saw no significance in it. "It's a Folsom point from Borax Lake, the oldest of its kind. Your ancestors used it to hunt bison fifteen thousand years ago."

That night in my bedroom I studied the point carefully, turning it over in my palm, tracing the sharp edges. This chipped piece of obsidian, worked by hands not much different from mine, transported me back to when people like me roamed the lush valleys now turned to deserts, and our clans gathered around campfires, and memory was all we had to link us to the past. After what seemed like hours pondering the arrowhead, I placed it under my pillow and went to sleep.

That night my dreams were filled with mammoths, camels, and sloths moving through the savannas of prehistoric California, and I was there with them with my obsidian points. I awoke to the sad realization that this had all been a dream, but within the sadness was the joy of knowing my roots were much deeper than I had ever imagined.

•   •   •

Besides being a pioneer in the study of early man in the Western Hemisphere, Mark Harrington was also a direct link to Mexican California. A grand two-story adobe house stood three vacant lots from my own house. This adobe had been part of General Andrés Pico's ranch during the 1800s, and Harrington had actually owned it for a while during the 1930s, had authentically restored it, and had lived in it for several years before donating it to the state. Around 1947, Harrington had his own adobe house built true in every way to the early California architecture, and he lived in this adobe house when I knew him.

The Pico adobe was a place with which I was very familiar. It was usually open to the public during Easter Week and other holidays; but I also visited the place with Dr. Harrington, and he'd point out what room had been *el comedor*, *la sala*; how he'd brought in mining carpenters to do the work of rebuilding the rafters. I soon became curious about Andrés Pico, the general who defeated the United States Army at the Battle of San Pasqual on December 6, 1846, the only victory for our side in that war. Pico was a native Californio, the brother of Pío Pico, the last Mexican governor of California. His mother was a *mulata* and his father a mestizo. Photographs of him reveal a ranchero turned soldier by necessity, no different from any civilian forced to take up arms, like John Adams or other New Englanders in the 1770s. He defended what was his without really defending the political power of distant Mexico; what he was defending was California, his native land. After the U.S. intervention, Pico adapted well to the new politics, serving in the state legislature and even as a general of the California militia. In his most famous photo, he is dressed in an outrageous vaquero outfit that must have been strictly for holidays and feast days; no one could possibly drive cattle in such elegant, almost royal, clothes. The jacket has fancy braids all across the chest, and the pants are bell-bottoms, with a strip of satin to widen the cuffs—a dandy's outfit no doubt. But his face is without arrogance, his nose is as round as an apple, and he is very dark; he seems sympathetic, jovial, someone who liked to laugh and was totally without pretensions. Andrés Pico was also an expert horseman and general. At San Pasqual, though his forces were outnumbered 2–1, he led them to victory, inflicting seventeen dead and eighteen wounded on the Yankee troops without suffering a single loss of his own. In the midst of the battle, Pico fought head to head with a U.S. cavalry officer, dismounting the Yankee with a thrust of his lance.[1] Pico's countenance is one of quiet confidence; he does not impose his presence, but he will not let anything be imposed on him. It is the attitude I see in my father, the universal dignity of man.

After the missions were secularized in 1832, Pico bought an interest in the ex–Mission San Fernando ranch and lived in the *convento* building for many years. The adobe that bears his name stands about a quarter mile from Mission San Fernando. Although he never lived in the adobe, he did remodel it in 1874 as a wedding gift for his son Rómulo. Eventually, in the early 1890s, the adobe was abandoned by Rómulo and Catarina Pico, the last of their clan to live there. Over the years, the adobe's roof caved in and vandals stole much of the brick and woodwork.

In the 1930s, Harrington was looking for a place to restore and live in, and when he saw the ruins of the adobe, he fell in love with it. He brought the old *casona* back to its former grandeur, working on it with his wife and son, pitching a tent on the grounds till he could move in. He uncovered beneath the rubble the original mission tiles used on the floor, and he even had adobe bricks built on the grounds to strengthen the walls and replace those that had fallen. Harrington lived in the Pico adobe while he guided the restoration of Mission San Fernando, a project that he worked on through most of the 1930s. At one time, Mission San Fernando had been in almost total ruins, with the roof missing and as bare inside as a saint's tomb. Some efforts were made to save the ruins from falling to dust, and Harrington was key in the restoration work of that project. Among the many things he did on the project, he acquired one of the old bells and had it rehung.

It's possible that Harrington might have known Rómulo or Catarina Pico, direct descendants of the old general, but if he told me, I can't remember. Regardless, each time I visited the Pico adobe with Dr. Harrington, it was pretty obvious to me that history was not something for books alone—dates and names were kept in history books, and that was fine, but something seemed to be lacking. I already knew more California history than my teachers, and yet at school I always seemed to be excluded from the points of reference. There was hardly a mention of Mexicans or Native Americans in California, as if history was created without us. It wasn't one particular day, but most likely a series of days and seasons of being surrounded by the memory of early California, that led me to realize that I belonged to the history of this land.

• • •

After the Californios had fallen into decline and had lost their land, power, and prestige, one member of my clan, José del Carmen Lugo, recounted his story for Thomas Savage, a scribe hired by Hubert Howe Bancroft.[2] José del Carmen Lugo was born on March 19, 1813, in the pueblo of Los Angeles. He was a third-generation Californio, grandson of Francisco Lugo, the old soldier who'd come from *la otra banda*, in other words, Mexico. His great-aunt, María Antonia, was claimed in marriage at the time of her birth by Ignacio Vallejo, whom she in fact married when she was fifteen. She was the mother of Mariano Guadalupe Vallejo, who later plays a key role in Northern California.

His narrative, published as *Vida de un ranchero*, reveals intimate details of California life and customs, but more important, it details a legacy of resistance. He recounts numerous historical events, including rebellions by Californios against Mexico, Indian uprisings, and a vivid account of the flood of 1825 that caused great damage to Los Angeles and his father's ranch, San Antonio. He also mentions the rebellion of 1835, when the insurgents of Monterey declared California independent of Mexico (although it didn't last), and the strained relations between Californios and Mexicans whom he did not look upon necessarily as allies. During the U.S. invasion of 1846, although Lugo is merely a ranchero who disdains politics, he is basically drafted to defend California. And he does so with courage, defeating Yankee insurgents at Chino, the westernmost position of the war. During this engagement, which he leads, he dodges a volley of bullets while riding horseback to procure a torch used to set fire to the ranch where the enemy is entrenched. He captures some forty to fifty Yankees and turns them over to authorities in Los Angeles.

His testimony reveals several causes for the defeat of the Californios. A Mexican named Segura absconds with the funds raised to fight the United States, pulling the rug out from under the Californios. Also, the Californios are fighting on two fronts: one against the United States and one internally against Indian uprisings that occur at the same time. Lugo, in fact, is fighting Indians in December 1846, while Andrés Pico faces the invaders at San Pasqual, a few miles away.

After the war, Lugo serves as the mayor of Los Angeles in 1849. But, like most Californios, he has a hard time under the new government. His rancho is attacked and looted in 1851, but he tracks down and kills all the gringo bandits at El Cajón. He has a sharp memory for detail, and his accounts include everything from the type of buttons worn to all sorts of manners practiced and even songs popular with men and women. His narrative is political and personal, yet it creates a communal memoir; he even details the custom of a man placing his hat on a woman's head to show affectionate approval of her dancing skills. But soon after 1853, according to Lugo's own words, "I had the misfortune to loan my signature as bondsman for other persons in whom I had confidence, and these, for one reason and another, left me as they say vulgarly, 'on the horns of the bull,' and I had to sacrifice my property and even the house in which I lived to meet these obligations."[3]

He recounts all this in a very humble way, often stating that because he mostly stayed on the ranch, he was "poorly informed on events in this country."[4] The scribe, Thomas Savage, states that Lugo was destitute when Savage took down the narrative in 1877. But Savage totally fails to grasp the irony of Lugo's statement of being "poorly informed," and in spite of having written down Lugo's rich and detailed memoir, Savage writes in the introduction, "I was quite disappointed—soon discovered his ignorance on history and most other things. . ."[5] The ignorant one here, without a doubt, is Mr. Savage.

•   •   •

The last time I went to Pico's adobe with Dr. Harrington I was about fifteen. By then I knew who Pico was, and I was also very familiar with Mission San Fernando. I had a sense that the adobe and the mission were about me, but I hadn't yet determined what my relationship to them was. I was up on the second floor, looking out the window toward the mission, while Harrington, on the first floor, was describing the restoration of the adobe to a group of visitors. I could see the arches of the *convento*, much as Pico must've seen them when he threw lavish hunting parties for his friends from Los Angeles. Pico also would have seen the vineyards and olive groves that at one time were said to be the finest in all California, whereas all I saw were the houses across the open lot on Columbus Avenue.

I could hear Harrington's voice coming up to the second story, and in my imagination it seemed to intermingle with the voice of old general Andrés Pico. I stood still and quiet, listening to the rafters creak, transported by the scent of oleanders that ringed the adobe, and I felt that just as Pico was a part of the adobe and of the mission and of California, so obviously Harrington was a part of it too. So where did I fit in? Here I was in the old adobe, in the house of Pico and Harrington, standing where they had stood.

We had this shared experience, this similar vision of the landscape. They were my history, and I was a part of their history, and now our lives had crossed and intermingled. We had touched the same artifacts of obsidian and leather; had stood, in fact, on the same ground; had breathed the same air in the same spot; and, most importantly, the three of us had loved this land. And this love for California, for this little piece of earth where I was born and where the rancheros Pico and Lugo were born, united us (and also Harrington) and made our struggle one continuous unbroken line of love and resistance.

• • •

The 1960s began for me on the chill January morning of John F. Kennedy's inauguration. Though Kennedy seemed liberal, in retrospect, he wasn't such a great thing for us folks from the tropical latitudes. For Latinos, Kennedy means the Bay of Pigs; the Cuban Missile Crisis; blueprints for fallout shelters; the Alliance for Progress, with its technocrats in torture; plus escalation of the conflict in Viet Nam, the war in which so many young men of my generation cashed in their chips—a heavy price to pay for the dubious distinction of living in Camelot. Another dubious distinction was being the first of your race to endure slurs and epithets at college or at the lunch counter of your neighborhood five-and-ten.

And California in the sixties was racist and segregated, though few people nowadays want to remember that or admit it. San Fernando was divided into the Mexican side and the Anglo side, and the boundary was San Fernando Road. If you were Mexican, you didn't cross over to the Anglo side of town, where the streets were clean and the lawns manicured. I never even knew this part of town existed till I was halfway through high school. But I especially felt racism in junior high, mostly because I didn't attend a barrio school.

I was one of a handful of nonwhite students at George K. Porter Junior High in Granada Hills. I don't recall any black students, perhaps one or two Asians, but that was it. My brother did fine; he got along with everyone, and he was well liked, a good student, and a good athlete. I, on the other hand, who was shy and self-conscious, felt totally isolated. As I was without a doubt the most dark-skinned person in the school, I stood out like a fly in a bowl of milk. I had issues, a couple of fights on the playground, and I was called names like "spick" and "beaner," but I also had a few Anglo friends, or so I thought. Till it struck me in the face that some of those I considered friends were nothing but racist dogs.

It was a cold morning in 1963, I was in the eighth grade, and I had walked to school, my breath puffing frost. At the side gate where I usually entered stood three guys I knew. They were lanky gringos, taller than I was, and we had played football together in after-school sports. As I came up to the gate—and I'll never forget this—one of them, his name was Craig, stepped in front of me, blocking my way. "You can't come in," he said. "We don't allow niggers here." Stunned by the slur, I didn't know what to say. Then all three of them burst out in howls of laughter. I shoved my way through, blinded by anger, their hazing like a whip stinging my back. For days after, I felt dehumanized, and it seemed that every white person in that school was looking at me with scorn, telling me with their eyes that I didn't belong in their lily white classrooms. That was fine with me. Years later, when I was in college, I would encounter that same racist look in the eyes of white administrators who'd never seen a dark person on their campus. And on two occasions in my life, a cop has aimed a gun at me point-blank, and in the officer's eyes was that same pinpoint of racism I encountered that morning. If you see that look once, that blatant stare stripped of any pretense, you never forget it, and you're able to spot it when people hide their racism behind a smile that don't mean shit.

If the early sixties were the time of a mythical Camelot, its false dreams were shattered that November day when Kennedy's motorcade passed under the shadow of the Texas School Book Depository. And later, television provided a front-row seat to Jack Ruby firing point-blank at Lee Harvey Oswald's gut. You could hear in your living room the Dallas detective holding Oswald's arm cursing, "Jack, you S.O.B!"

· · ·

Marking time in high school (a ghetto school with a mixture of Chicanos, blacks, whites, and Asians), I was more into driving two-door sports coupes and chasing mini-skirted girls than digging classroom scenes. Although my friends were *vatos locos* from the barrio, we liked to read: Henry Miller and Sartre; *Les Misérables* and *The Story of O*; Aldous Huxley's *The Doors of Perception* and *Heaven and Hell*. We hung out at Brand Park but also at the Los Angeles County Museum of Art, and we'd seen the work of Van Gogh, Toulouse-Lautrec, Picasso, and Dalí up close and with our own eyes. One Saturday on Sunset Boulevard, I witnessed the Hollywood riots and saw police clubbing white teenagers and buses burning long into the night as rock 'n' roll fueled the energy like gasoline. I got turned on to the craziest Chicano hipster of them all, Frank Zappa and the Mothers of Invention, the creators of acid-rock music. On Thanksgiving of 1966 I dropped my first Owsley, the original street LSD, and spent my trip peering through a telescope at Mars and Jupiter; on other acid trips I wrote poems and dug Dylan's "Subterranean Homesick Blues" or John Coltrane's "A Love

Supreme." Like many teenagers, I owned a car, a '58 Chevy Impala, with hand-polished chrome and a touch of primer on the fender, *ése*. I cruised Whittier Boulevard when that legendary strip was in its prime, my car radio blasting "oldies but goodies," Martha and the Vandellas, Ronnie and the Ronnettes, and Lil' Julian Herrera. I caught the shows at El Monte Legion Stadium, the Avalon Ballroom, Machinists Hall, and Carpenters Hall, where I saw Rosie and the Originals, Cannibal and the Headhunters, and one memorable night Lil' Willie G and Thee Midnighters. We were finger-snapping, bopping, bumping, and rolling. An Egyptian-eyed *ruka* had her head on my shoulder as we spun around the floor at the Palladium while Lil' Willie G. sang "Are You Sorry?"

After our late-night romps, which sometimes ended with *chingazos*, we'd meet at Hat's Jungle Burgers on San Fernando Road, where we'd continue the party. We drank Ripple wine and twisted *yesca* in zig-zags that we blasted in our low-slung *carruchas*. In those days, we measured a lid of grass at a hundred joints to the lid, and it would set us back ten or fifteen dollars. We had garage parties and sometimes things got out of control, and more than once a *vato* OD'ed, or a *ruka*, loaded on downers, pulled a train on a pool table or on a sofa while the other *vatos* checked it out. I preferred the privacy of the tuck 'n' roll backseat of my '58 Chevy Impala, the most classic of all lowrider cars. In my memory, the sweet kisses of the young *rukas* I made out with spin like old 45s, out of sequence and intertwined: Stella, Rhonda, Linda—where are you now? Pills, thrills, and several spills, fender benders, bennies, and reds, *mi querida Vida Loca*.

But nothing stays the same forever, nothing did, not the barrio, not the city or the *raza*. Never again would the barrio style be that classic, that solid and heavy, so original and daring. Our scene gave way before the onslaught of malls and suburban culture. The *vatos* went from spit-shined shoes and khakis to the slick, continental style of slacks and knitted sweaters. The classic *chuco*, bred during the more violent era of the forties, and survivor of the deadly fifties and early sixties, faded out. But lives were marked forever by what went down in the barrios, by a tattoo between thumb and trigger finger, or on the inside of the wrist. Those oldies but goodies will forever remain the catalyst of memories that many years later will dance out of a radio on a Sunday afternoon, in a city a thousand miles from where all this happened, and then you will relive again the streets, the dances, the songs, *vato loco* to the end, *ése*.

•   •   •

My father went as far as the sixth grade in Autlán, Jalisco, but he's not slow. He never told us how to go about getting an education, perhaps because he

didn't have one himself, but he always insisted that his sons get an education. Back in those days, an education meant a high school diploma. I didn't
know one person in the whole barrio who'd been to college. I don't believe
I ever heard the word "college" used in our house. The only thing I was
sure of was that I didn't want to be a car mechanic—so I always avoided
auto shop, where all the Chicanos were enrolled. The only reason I went
to college after high school is because my old high school art teacher,
Mrs. Grace García, bless her heart, was determined to save me from both
the draft and the drugs that destroyed my generation.

The summer I graduated, in 1967, was the "Summer of Love," when
young people gathered in Monterey to hear acid-rock with flowers in their
hair. Just to bring things into perspective, it was also one of the most
intense summers of the Viet Nam War. I was hanging out with David Lee,
the main acidhead of our group. He was on a bad flashback after taking two
hundred psychedelic trips, and his genius seemed burned out on paisley
visions. I was planning to pack my '58 Chevy with everything I owned and
head as far south as I could. I was waiting for the summer to end, for the
party to be over. A week before my August birthday, Grace García showed
up at my apartment on Heliotrope off Melrose and talked me into going
across the street and signing up for junior college.

Thus, September 1967 found me at Los Angeles City College, with
autumn in the air. The old, ivy-covered, red brick buildings pretended an
eastern prep-school ambiance, but it was just a ghetto college, like high
school had been a ghetto school. I hung on in college because outside the
classrooms I found something more interesting and educational.

The first Chicano student organizations were being formed on campuses: Mexican American Student Association (MASA) and United Mexican
American Students (UMAS), and although they still carried the Mexican
American tag, they were the campus wings of the barrio, the intellectual
instigators and proponents of change. I witnessed the East L.A. blowouts at
Garfield High in the spring of 1968, and I was amazed that Chicanos two
years younger than I had the balls to take on the Board of Education.

We talked of La Raza, of self-realization, self-determination, identity,
and of searching for points of reference in our history: Cuauhtémoc, Cinco
de Mayo, the Mexican Revolution of 1910. And everywhere you went you
saw that ubiquitous poster of Zapata with the famous quote, "It's better
to die on your feet, than . . . ," and you had to admire the dude's eyes, *ése*,
that intense, sincere look, and that mustache, *¡qué brocha!* I also relearned
history from new perspectives, such as the Treaty of Guadalupe-Hidalgo
and Ricardo Flores Magón. Here's what I had been searching for all these
years. The movement was more than a feeling or an inspiration. This was

action, the gut-splitting, soul-curling *grito* of our liberation, "*¡Que viva La Raza!*" we shouted. "*¡Viva Villa, cabrones!*"

But apart from the theater of protest, there was something concrete the movement gave you: a celebration of yourself, your culture, your roots, your family, your parents, and your language. The most important thing I got out of going to college was not a degree, because I didn't get one; it was being a part of the Chicano student movement, rediscovering my roots, and getting back in touch with the Spanish language. Invariably, when someone of my generation—Chicanos or Mexican Americans or Hispanics, whatever they call themselves—speaks against bilingual education, it's a given that they were not involved in the student movement. While we were on the barricades, cracking open the piñata of higher education, they stood on the sidelines, waiting to collect the candy, the scholarships, or, later on, the grants and fellowships. In college, I took back the name stolen from me in the first grade, took it back with pride, *con orgullo*, like an heirloom coat once hidden, now worn like a magnificent quetzal-feathered cape. And ever since, I have spoken Spanish or caló in private and public places, rolling my *r*'s, popping my *p*'s without shame, understanding that being bilingual is fundamental for me.

•   •   •

On holidays like Cinco de Mayo, our student group MASA at Los Angeles City College organized forums at the student union. This is where I first heard Guadalupe Saavedra recite poetry and Reies López Tijerina talk of the courthouse raid in New Mexico, and saw Luis Valdez and the Teatro Campesino perform "Los Vendidos," probably the best *acto* Teatro Campesino created. I also dug Luis Gasca blowing trumpet with Mongo Santamaría and met an *L.A. Times* reporter named Rubén Salazar.

These years were the heyday of Chicano Power, a movement misunderstood by our parents, who feared our militancy, and often by our peers, who feared the same thing. But the movement wasn't really all that radical. Our demands were mostly in the realm of reform. We wanted the right to speak our language; we wanted Spanish and our history taught in the schools. Some of us demanded more: we wanted control of the political power so we could determine our own destiny; we wanted release from the exploitative economic system of this country; and we wanted a free Aztlán, the ancient mythical homeland of the Aztec Mexicas, which we claimed as the Southwest of the present United States. We were rich in rhetoric but poor in practice. Thirty years later, few believe in the pipe dream of a free Aztlán; some of our young people haven't even heard of Aztlán.

The best dreams and aspirations of my generation were wasted on the fields of Southeast Asia or beaten down by the hysterical clubs and guns of "law and order." While the war in Viet Nam kept escalating, the Tet offensive brought it all home, leading many of us to take to the streets, angry that we were the ones dying. No way, LBJ. One, two, three, four, what are we fightin' for?

My brother, Raymond, like so many other Chicanos, was shipped to Viet Nam. Television again replayed history in living color, interrupted only by commercials: the burning villages and napalm strikes of that dirty little war; Robert F. Kennedy as he moved through the backstage corridors of the Ambassador Hotel shaking hands before the ambush. Raymond would return from Viet Nam with all the trimmings—Silver Star, Purple Heart— and all the contradictions of having to reintegrate into this fragmented society torn apart by that war.

On the campuses and in the barrios, the four horsemen—Law, Order, War, and Death—approached. Brown Berets fought back in the barrios, and Black Panthers prowled the ghetto. Real bullets were fired at us, not phony Hollywood blanks like those used by the B actor who governed the state, but real death-in-the-barrio bullets, in an attempt to keep the lid on urban concentration camps named East L.A. and Watts. And we marched and marched and shouted to a foot-stomping beat, "Free the East L.A. 13," "Free Los Siete de La Raza," "Free Huey," "Free North America." Student strikes like those in Paris and Mexico City would ignite also at San Francisco State, where students of color for the first time demanded the novel concept of Ethnic Studies, which is nothing more than an investigation of the world, history, literature, and the rest from a nonwhite perspective. In those days, to question that all truth and knowledge emanates from Europe was a radical concept. For some, even today, this idea is still radical and unacceptable.

After San Francisco State, U.C. Berkeley students of color went on strike based on the same demands. These strikes dragged on for months, and we devoured all the news we could get about them. At Los Angeles City College, the UMAS formulated a series of demands for the administration to add classes relevant to Chicano students. I was a member of the steering committee of UMAS, and we worked in conjunction with the Black Student Union (BSU), and sometimes formed tactical alliances with Students for a Democratic Society (SDS). The modern reader must understand that in 1969, although Chicanos were dying at a higher rate in Viet Nam than any other group, we couldn't get our foot in the door of government jobs or even of colleges. It was as if we had never paid taxes or supported this government and its institutions, so in a way, all we wanted was our money's worth. Likewise, that's all we want now—give us our money's (taxes') worth, or else don't tax us at all.

During this same time in Los Angeles, one Chicano a month died while in police custody. If the press mentioned it at all, they called it a suicide or an accidental death. Yeah, sure, accidentally on purpose. And if by luck or accident, someone like me made it to college, it was the same old story: subtle and not-so-subtle racism, hostility, slurs, and a curriculum that emphasized only one perspective and only one view of history. You take a guess whose perspective and whose history.

In March 1969, as UMAS and BSU negotiated with a hostile and intransigent L.A. City College administration for more community access to the campus, a series of events propelled us to a violent confrontation. Several of us in UMAS had met with members of the Third World Liberation Front that had been on strike for five months at San Francisco State over similar demands. We heard the stories of the Tac Squad clubbing students and tear-gassing community people who came to show support. My own friend at U.C. Berkeley, Ysidro Macías, took a billy club to the head that almost killed him. And we saw that, sooner or later, it would most likely come down to a strike on our campus too. Then, unexpectedly, violence erupted in the predominately black high schools of Compton and South Central L.A. The police attacked some black students who were holding a demonstration, and protests quickly spread to other high schools. The BSU on our campus, a very militant group of dashiki-clad brothers and sisters, wanted to go on strike in solidarity with the high school students. They came to us and asked for our support. After several nights of meetings, during which we went back and forth, pro and con, looking at the issue from many angles, UMAS took a vote. It was not unanimous, but the majority of us felt that if we were going to strike, now was the moment. SDS joined us, and the strike was set for Thursday morning, March 13, 1969.

I don't think I slept much that Wednesday night, between making picket signs and worrying about what would happen and wondering if we were doing the right thing. But that morning when I showed up at eight o'clock, I was ready for whatever came down. The first thing I realized was that nobody was honoring our strike. I was posted, with a ream of leaflets to hand out, by the side entrance, next to the cafeteria, and students and teachers were just walking through our picket lines, ignoring our calls to stay out of classes. Then I saw Patricia, an SDS member, being shoved aside by a reactionary poli-sci professor. Suddenly, she hauled back and punched him in the nose. Damn, I thought, I guess that's what it's going to take. I dragged one of the cafeteria benches toward the entrance and flipped it over. "Come on," I yelled to the other strikers. "Help me build a barri-cade." In a flash, several other students were hauling tables, newsracks, and anything else we could find and piling them in front of this entrance.

Within half an hour, another barricade blocked the front entrance to City College—folding chairs, overturned patio tables, their blue-and-white umbrellas pointing like Don Quixote's lances against the windmills—and behind the barricade we stood, angry, defiant, daring the system and at the same time imploring it to listen to us. What happened next was totally unplanned on our part. A group of right-wing students, organized as Rea-gan supporters under the banner of Victory in Viet Nam Association (VIVA), attacked us. A melee broke out between the strikers and the strike-breakers, a freewheeling fistfight that raged up and over the barricades, until the LAPD stepped in. Confronted by the helmeted and billy-club-armed protectors of the state, we had no choice but to retreat. But in our retreat, we wrecked havoc on the campus: we set trashcans on fire and stormed through the hallways breaking windows, pounding on doors, dis-rupting classrooms, and shouting, "On Strike! Shut It Down!" Our senti-ments that day were the result of extreme frustration, the futility that no one was listening, and the feeling that we would always be denied the resources of this society. So we reacted violently—our motto became "If the institution will not serve us, then it won't serve anyone." You, my friend, may not agree with what we did that day, but what did you do when the sweet life of our people was snuffed out?

. . .

In April 1969, Corky González put the call out for the First Denver Youth Conference, so the Chicano movement headed for the snows of Colorado. Corky, formerly a boxer and a member of the Democratic Party, had split from traditional politics to form his own organization, the Crusade for Jus-tice. Along with Reies López Tijerina of New Mexico and César Chávez, Corky was one of the key figures in our movement. He was also the author of the epic poem of Chicanos, "I Am Joaquín," which he recited during the conference. On the last day of the conference, we marched to the state capi-tol for a rally at the Colorado State Building. As I stood on the steps of the State Building hearing Corky speak, surrounded by many at the rally wear-ing brown berets and khaki jackets, I spotted someone waving a Mexican flag. In a moment of inspiration, I told him, "Come on, follow me." We ran over to where the Colorado State flag was hanging and took control of the flagpole. Then, with a group of *carnales* providing security, I lowered the Colorado flag, hooked up the Mexican one, and raised it. Shouts of "Viva La Raza!" thundered from five hundred ecstatic Chicanos, as if this was the flag raising at Iwo Jima. Even if it was just agitprop, at least for that moment we had reclaimed our land. It was a dramatic closure to the First Denver Youth Conference, and photos of the flag raising were flashed all over the country.

But on a more important level, the conference produced "El Plan Espiritual de Aztlán," a manifesto for our liberation. I'll quote a key passage from the preamble:

> We, the Chicano inhabitants and civilizers of the northern land of Aztlán, from whence came our forefathers, reclaiming the land of their birth and consecrating the determination of our people of the sun, declare that the call of our blood is our power, our responsibility and our inevitable destiny.
>
> We are free and sovereign to determine those tasks which are justly called for by our house, our land, the sweat of our brows and by our hearts. Aztlán belongs to those who plant the seeds, water the fields, and gather the crops, and not to the foreign Europeans. We do not recognize capricious borders on the Bronze Continent.

The "Plan" concludes with this statement:

> With our hearts in our hands and our hands in the soil, We Declare the Independence of our Mestizo Nation. We are a Bronze People with a Bronze Culture. Before the world, before all of North America, before all our brothers in the Bronze Continent, We are a Nation, We are a Union of free pueblos, We are Aztlán.[6]

But for me, two years at City College seemed like two years too much. Perhaps it was impatience with the traditional approach to change, perhaps it was that first day in elementary school so long ago, or that racist incident in junior high—whatever it was, I felt that school wasn't for me. In reality, my friends turned me on to a wider range of authors—Federico García Lorca and César Vallejo and Bob Kaufman—writers I found much more interesting than those I was reading in my college courses. But more importantly, I realized that although I believed in revolution, the Chicano student movement did not. After a while, the movement became merely about who was going to run the Equal Opportunity Program or some other program, and no longer was there talk of liberating anything. Professor Carlos Muñoz Jr., recently of U.C. Berkeley and an activist from those days, put it quite succinctly in his book *Youth, Identity, Power: The Chicano Movement*: "But priorities shifted as these activists moved from involvement in the politics of confrontation to implementation of programs, and their emphasis often shifted to institutional politics."[7] He also describes the decline of the

Movimiento Estudiantil Chicano de Aztlán (MEChA), the key Chicano student organization: "Still another factor in MEChA's decline was the fact that many of the activists had neglected their studies because of their political involvement. Many of these students were placed on academic probation and were thus forced to shift their personal priorities from MEChA to academic survival. Attendance at MEChA meetings suffered a noticeable decline."[8] So *that's* what happened to the revolution. My, my.

It was at about this time that I pulled away from the student movement. I decided to head south, so I hopped on a Tres Estrellas de Oro bus headed for Mexico, stopping in the little town of Autlán, Jalisco, to pay homage to ancient family roots. Then on to Guadalajara, and my return to Mexico City. The blood in Tlatelolco from the Olympic massacre was still fresh. Mexico seemed to be going through an identity crisis, with everyone trying to scrub the Mexican away, trying so hard to be North American, but the dark roots showed beneath the peroxide hair. Easy for me in Tepeyac, where the shrine of the Virgin of Guadalupe is located, or the barrio of Tepito, where no one suspected I was from the other side, but there was no crossing the class lines in the Zona Rosa, where I was refused entrance to ritzy nightclubs because I obviously wasn't upper class, and besides, I was as dark as earth.

When I returned to the States, I entered through Tijuana, just as I had that day back in 1955. The shock hit me all over again as my papers were scrutinized, antagonistic questions were thrown at me, and I saw, once again, the racist slurs in their eyes. Was this the land where I was born? By then, college was out for me. I had wanted to major in languages, writers, and writing, but I realized it would lead to a dead end in the reading room of some dusty library. So I hit the road again, Highway 101 to Big Sur, San Francisco, and Berkeley, where I was teargassed at Sproul Plaza on the U.C. Berkeley campus while protesting Nixon's escalation of the war into Cambodia. I stayed in Berkeley in part because I felt L.A. was getting too hot for me. Then, with the staff of *El Pocho-Ché*, one of the first Chicano political-literary-arts magazines, I went back to Denver for Youth Conference II. We crossed the snow-covered Rockies in a VW van, taking turns at the wheel and driving nonstop: Ysidro Macías, Roberto Vargas, and "Teen Angel," an eighteen-year-old politically correct Califas Chicanita. At the conference, Cha-Cha Jiménez and the Young Lords, with their purple berets at cocky angles, blew everybody away. Spanish-speaking Ricans, *¡Coño!* For many of us, this was our first exposure to Latinos from eastern barrios. On the last night of the conference, Alurista, Lalo Delgado, Roberto Vargas, myself, and others read poetry, but I was already getting turned off by the rigid and constricting nationalism pervading the movement. It seemed stupid to me not to consider the Chicano struggle part of the struggles of Latin America, if not of those all over the Third World.

Now the big push in Aztlán centered on a massive antiwar rally, the Chicano Moratorium, set for August 1970 in East L.A. Our battle cries became, "*Chale* no, we won't go. No more Raza dying in Viet Nam." In San Diego, New Mexico, Texas, and Colorado, Chicanos organized against the madness of the war. In Oakland, I worked for an antiwar organizing committee, and through some stroke of luck, we were able to pull together radical, shotgun-toting militants of the Chicano Liberation Front, Berkeley students, and local working-class barrio *gente*. Three months of work culminated in July 1970 with a rally at San Antonio Park, in the Fruitvale District of Oakland. Families came out, fathers with their kids, even radical organizations, as well as the winos of the park. We also organized caravans for the East L.A. Moratorium.

Around this same time, Roberto Pérez Díaz, a Berkeley Chicano with a bushy beard like that of Camilo Cienfuegos, told me about the Cuban *zafra*, the sugarcane harvest, with the Venceremos Brigade. The brigade was leaving in mid-August, so if I went, I would miss the moratorium in East L.A., but the chance to learn directly from a Latin American experience won out. The brigade included a handful of Chicanos and African Americans, some Asian Americans, and a Native American or two. We headed cross-country by bus, and I saw the breadth of this continent, crossed the Mississippi River at St. Louis, checked out the dingy streets of Chicago and the steel mills of Pittsburgh, went through New York's barrio, and on through Vermont and Maine. More *brigadistas* joined us in Chicago and New York, including a large contingent of Puerto Ricans. In St. John, Canada, we boarded the Cuban freighter *Conrado Benítez*, named after a schoolteacher who'd been assassinated by CIA-trained *gusanos*. For security reasons, the *Conrado Benítez* pulled out of Canada in the middle of the night.

Three days later, while I sat on deck a few miles off the Florida Keys, the transistor radio brought us the news: the Chicano Moratorium had erupted in a police riot, and Rubén Salazar, my friend and an *L.A. Times* reporter, was killed by police in the Silver Dollar Café on Whittier Boulevard. I cannot describe the shock I felt on hearing this. The freighter seemed to stop in mid-sea, and the wind dropped, the air hung still, motionless, suffocating. The Florida Keys dragged by, with their tranquil white hotels in the bright tropical sunlight oblivious to the tragedy, until the last of the mainland slipped from view, and only the stunned silence remained—the knowledge that my city was burning, and it seemed I was headed for exile.

Those scorching days of August 1970 were the turning point for the student movement I had belonged to. Never again after August 29 would it be so strong, so fearless, or have so much balls! The struggle continued, as it must, through La Raza Unida Party, the Farmworkers Union, and all the rest. But the Chicano movement would never pull off anything as big as the moratorium again. Some of the *compañeros* from those days disappeared underground that summer, to reappear years later with tales of hiding out and being on the run. Others would be assassinated in police setups or killed in barrio tragedies. Some just simply disappeared, the way students disappear in the streets of El Salvador. I would pass through L.A. on other occasions, but I would never live there again. What had been my involvement with the Chicano movement was over. The movement reached its apogee during those three days in August when East L.A. fought from behind barricades, and fires burned on Whittier Boulevard. Unlike the mythical phoenix, it has never risen from the ashes.

Now, over thirty years later, those scenes from my student days come back to me like scratchy black-and-white archival footage of World War II. As I write this in La Mission, San Pancho, Califas, Aztlán, the sun outside my window is burning through a sulfurous yellow haze, and in my heart of hearts, the embers still burn. The rural San Fernando Valley has long been overrun by an exploding population and covered by sooty smog drifting from Los Angeles; and Mexico City, which the Valley will one day resemble, is deadly with pollution. These cities barely resemble what they were three decades ago. But then again, neither do I. And my friends, what shadows do they cast today? Mario Bañuelos, dead in a gang fight on San Fernando Road; Mike Bustamante, killed in Viet Nam. Should I count the dead first, or the dead among the living? And I can't help but wonder: What are the tangible fruits of our infatuation with rhetoric, our student strikes, our Chicano studies? Are we better off as Raza, as a *familia?* And what exactly does it mean to be Chicano these days? (And do I spell it Xicano?) Does it mean you take a principled political stance? Or is it just a tag to grease whatever hoop you're jumping through? What mistakes did we make in our youthful arrogance? Where did we detour to founder in dead ends? Where did we mark well the trail? I admit that we were so shortsighted that when the revolution didn't happen that summer of 1970, most of us turned our backs on meaningful social change and opted for slipping into the system.

Yes, this is the sad part. But there is more, much more to the story: many memories of my generation not yet recorded, struggles and battles fought, and a lot of *gente,* good *gente,* to be remembered and honored. Who's the keeper of these memories? We all are in a way. Those who lived through the years of the *movimiento* remember and remember well. For now, though, our memories reside mostly in our heads, indelible mementos of time and landscape. We also keep the unquenched fire of our youthful dream archived in cardboard boxes, our movement documented in faded posters and leaflets now crumbling to dust in garages and basements throughout Aztlán. For our parents and our children—for all our relations—we will remember.

TROPI(LO)CALIDAD

Macondo in La Mission

During the 1970s, the Mission District in San Francisco teemed with painters, muralists, poets, and musicians, even the occasional politico or community organizer who acted beyond the rhetoric and actually accomplished something. We called it La Misión, or La Mission, and we spoke *español*, caló, Spanglish, or just plain unadorned English. We had no problem being understood because La Mission was a microcosm of Latin America, and the whole barrio seemed in perfect sync. A cutting-edge music scene, fueled by musicians like Carlos Santana; the Escovedo Brothers (Pete and Coke); and groups like Malo, with Jorge Santana, brother of Carlos, and Luis Gasca and their song "Suavecito," kept us moving day and night. Although "renaissance" is too grand a word to describe the scene, the Mission District was a cultural force that pulsed with the unique sensibilities of a community too hip to last.

I came to the Mission District from Los Angeles because of political reasons: the FBI was after me. My crime? I'd visited Cuba the summer before. A few weeks after I returned to L.A., a team of FBI agents had raided the house on Vermont Street in South Central where I was staying. When I answered the knock on the door, they'd swarmed in, guns drawn, badges on their lapels, making their declaration of "FBI." They also carried with them a photo album of various political outlaws they were after, people like Mark Rudman and Bernadette Dorn. I knew *who* they were; I just didn't know *where* they were. Even if I had known their whereabouts, I'd learned one thing a long time ago—in the barrio you never snitch, no matter what. I didn't run with the Weathermen, but I knew which way the wind blew.

After showing me several mug shots, one of the agents asked me if I knew Alejandro Murguía. With a straight face, I coolly denied ever hearing the name, but inside my heart was racing. That evening I borrowed thirty dollars from my housemates, packed the few clothes I owned, and hitched a ride to the airport. I took one of those ten-dollar midnight flights that Pacific Southwest Airlines used to offer. You'd show up at LAX about 11:00 P.M. and form a line with a bunch of other people who wanted out of L.A., and if you were lucky, you'd get a ticket to fly. I carried no ID; I was truly anonymous, nameless you could say, a fugitive hiding behind the alias I gave at the airport ticket counter—Pancho Villa.

I arrived in San Francisco in February of 1971, already weary and battered by the life I'd been living. I was six months past my twenty-first birthday and looking for a refuge, someplace to recharge my batteries. It was also for me that heady time of youth when everything seemed plausible and possible, and La Mission, the little barrio I had chosen, seemed like the perfect place to experience life.

· · ·

It was almost two in the morning when I picked up my bag at the San Francisco airport, and I didn't want to drop in on my friends at that hour, so after the bus ride to downtown, I walked from North Beach to La Mission, waiting for the sunrise. I was used to living out of a duffel bag, sleeping on floors, staying up all night, having nothing to eat, but as long as I was involved in something creative, life was grand. I also suffered from the political angst common to restless youth everywhere, fostered by the Viet Nam War, racial conflicts, and the search for my own true identity. I had dropped out of college in L.A.; had traveled several times by bus to Mexico and back; had lived in Berkeley, then Oakland. During the summer of 1970, I'd worked on the Isle of Youth in Cuba with the Venceremos Brigade and had walked the streets of Havana. On my return, the FBI was waiting at the dock at St. John, Canada, and as we came down the ramp, they photographed every single one of the seven hundred *brigadistas* that had gone to Cuba. Besides it being political harassment, I felt it was a waste of taxpayers' film. I stayed in New York after that, giving the FBI the slip, living for three months in the Lower East Side, getting a feel for the city and the Puerto Ricans who lived there. I was searching for a place to call my own, and when I didn't find it back east, I returned to L.A. during the winter of 1971. A few weeks later the FBI came knocking on my door.

Those first months in La Mission I crashed with Ysidro and Veronica Macías at their pad on Bartlett Street near Twenty-third. They lived on the third floor of a Victorian in a flat with about eight rooms. Ysidro had been a key student leader during the Third World Liberation Front student strike at U.C. Berkeley and also the editor of *El Pocho-Ché*, a mimeographed magazine that published radical Chicano and Latino writers and artists. He'd also written an essay, "The Evolution of the Mind,"[1] in which he discussed the stages of evolving consciousness. According to Ysidro, the intellectual development of the radical went from being a nationalist, a narrow concept, to a broader Third World concept, to an even broader internationalist viewpoint, and finally to an inclusive approach that would embrace all of humanity. His ideas were basic, but I felt they were right on. We'd been to Cuba together, and he'd offered his pad if I was ever in the City. I unpacked my duffel bag in a room with a view of Horace Mann Junior High, not knowing how long I'd stay in La Mission.

That night I attended my first reception at Galería de la Raza, at that time located on Fourteenth Street between Valencia and Guerrero, in a storefront that is now a furniture repair shop. The energy was electric that night, the place packed. A young Mission band called The Ghetto was playing in one corner—what else but "The Ghetto"? I reconnected with old friends that I'd known through *El Pocho-Ché*: Roberto Vargas, who was a community organizer for the Neighborhood Arts Program, and Rene Yáñez, who was the curator of the Galería. The energy was so high, I'm not sure anyone needed wine, but the wine did flow, as did the conversation; one minute I was talking with Rupert García, the next minute with Ralph Maradiaga or Irene Pérez. I was sure there wasn't a place in the world I'd rather be, not Paris or New York. At that moment it seemed to me that I was standing in the artistic center of the universe.

When the reception was over, I walked up Fourteenth Street to Market to meet a friend, and I remember the streetlights seemed to be shimmering, glowing like jewels. Maybe it was only water particles in the air, but to me it was the magic of where I'd just been. It wasn't so much San Francisco that I fell in love with; it was the Mission, La Misión.

La Mission was rich in a forgotten history that ran like the underground creek that flows through this barrio. Costanoan Indians had prospered in its erratic climate, until a mission and a presidio were built in the 1760s. At one time or another La Mission was home to such disparate attractions as a racetrack on Army Street (now César Chávez Street); Woodward Gardens, a fabulous private park on Mission and Fourteenth Streets; and several blocks of Victorian mansions on what is now South Van Ness, including one of the biggest of its time, the Spreckels mansion. La Mission had been home to Bancroft's first library, where Saint Luke's Hospital now stands, and even to a minor league baseball team from the 1920s called the Mission Reds. It had also served as a neighborhood for all types of immigrants, from the Irish to the Central Americans.[2]

A few years later, a sociologist from U.C. Berkeley bitterly complained about La Mission, saying we were too high on art and poetry and this scene would soon play itself out. But sociologists have never understood art or history. The Mission District wasn't like Paris in the twenties; it was more like Mexico City in the forties—intense art and radical politics mixed with passionate love affairs.

Our lifestyle (I'm speaking of the poets I hung out with) helped rip apart all the holy restrictions society and the Catholic Church had strapped us with regarding our bodies and our sexuality. We were part of the sexual revolution, and for men (the hard-core *vatos*), it was a challenge to accept the new standards for relationships. Their openness for one: a lover might leave you for your best friend quick as changing socks, because women had the prerogative to do what they wanted. Or your friend might suddenly come into his or her own sexually and openly claim same-sex preference. But so what? That's how we imagined artists and writers lived their lives, and we were no different. Believe me, Frida Kahlo, Diego Rivera, and their crowd had nothing on us. We had no respect for traditional laws or morals. Why should we? We liked drugs; the establishment didn't. We liked music; they didn't. We loved art and literature; they hated it. We wanted life for our people, and they wanted death. Remember, this country was at war in Viet Nam, the United Farmworkers were at the height of their struggle, racism and corruption were rampant everywhere—so why should we respect the mores of the establishment? We believed we would create our own standards of love, just as we were creating our own standards of art and politics. For us it was open warfare between two diametrically opposite world-views. Our weapons were our art and our poetry, and we held nothing back.

• • •

La Mission wasn't one individual but a community, an unofficial group of artists who interacted, exchanged ideas, and helped each other in our projects. If there was an exhibit at the Galería, maybe Juan Fuentes showing some of his pen-and-ink drawings, everyone showed up to support the artist. If a big poetry reading was happening, Rupert García might do a silk-screen poster for the event. If there was a rally, we all marched and then afterward ate together and drank and talked and dreamed whatever the hell we wanted to dream. Or we'd meet in the little Nicaraguan bar on Mission Street, "El Tico Nica," to drink rum and talk about back home, and how back home seemed to be La Mission. In 1971, nothing beautiful had ever happened to Latinos in the United States, so we set out with our art to remake the world a beautiful place for ourselves. And we didn't ask anyone's permission to do it. Not knowing any better, we just went out and did it.

But if there was one individual who pushed all of us to get out there and do our thing, it was Roberto Vargas. At that time Roberto worked for the Neighborhood Arts Program, a city-funded project to promote arts in the "minority" communities. He was the Mission District organizer, and with him worked Rene Yáñez, who, along with Ralph Maradiaga, established La Galería de la Raza, the first gallery in the country devoted to Latino art. From Galería de la Raza would emerge the international cult of Frida Kahlo as well as the Día de los Muertos celebrations in the United States. Frida has her own connection to La Mission, having spent several weeks in Saint Luke's Hospital during 1940 being treated by her friend Dr. Leo Eloesser.

Roberto took the concept of organizer and expanded it to mean everything: organizer of poetry readings, writing workshops, film and theater projects, community dances, and eventually even political marches and rallies for Nicaragua. Whatever area Roberto didn't touch, Rene filled in by organizing art workshops, drawing and silk-screen classes, gallery receptions, murals, and everything else that was visual in nature.

But Roberto was the true dynamo of La Mission's arts scene. Without Roberto, La Mission would not be what it is now. He deserves a book about his life, or at least a plaque somewhere on Twenty-fourth Street. He arrived in San Francisco from Nicaragua at the age of five. By 1971, he'd already lived twenty-five years in La Mission, and he knew everyone in the barrio. He'd graduated from Mission High School and had experienced the Beat scene in North Beach and later the Haight-Ashbury Summer of Love. Like everyone else, he'd been radicalized by the sixties and had organized for the farmworkers movement led by César Chávez, had formed a Brown Beret chapter in La Mission, had fought the Tac Squad at the San Francisco State strike, and had organized around Los Siete de La Raza, seven young Latinos from La Mission who'd been charged with killing a cop on Twenty-second Street. In other words, he was what we called "high energy."

Roberto made an impression on a young man like me. He wore an earring, hippie beads, Indian bracelets, and a Viva La Raza button. When he didn't wear his brown beret, his hair puffed out in an Afro do. He sometimes drove a sports car, at other times a converted mail truck. He once totaled a 1954 Jaguar 120 XK roadster on the Bay Bridge and survived to tell me about it. He'd boxed at Newman's Gym, had been in the Marine Corps, had sailed to Viet Nam with the merchant marines, and he was the best poet I'd ever heard. He was the first I heard combine poetry with music, reading in his bebop Latin jazz style, accompanied by conga drums and sometimes *timbaleros*. His work was not just poetic, it was political, and excellent theater. He was such a standout that Jane Fonda picked him to go on tour with Donald Sutherland and her in their antiwar troupe called the FTA (Fuck The Army) Show. He also had the courage to turn down a publishing contract with Dell Books, considering publishing in New York to be selling out. Instead, he published with our own community-based press.

At a time when the entire body of Chicano literature consisted of three or four books, we formed our own publishing house: Editorial Pocho-Ché.[3] As short-lived as it was, Editorial Pocho-Ché published four books of poetry; the double-sided, upside-down editions featured Roberto Vargas, *Primeros cantos*, on one side and the flip side had Eliás Hruska-Cortés, *This Side and Other Things*. Rupert García did the cover and artwork, and Alejandro Stuart, who'd just returned from Chile, contributed photographs of Chilean murals. The following year the collective published *El sol y los de abajo*, the first book by José Montoya, a founder of the Royal Chicano Air Force of Sacramento, with etchings by Armando Cid. On the flip side was *Oración a la mano poderosa*, by yours truly, with photographs by the Puerto Rican Adál Maldonado. Pocho-Ché was a collective of poets intent on breaking the literary blockade that publishing houses had imposed, more through their own ignorance than anything else, on Chicano and Latino writers. We also came together with other San Francisco writers and artists and created Third World Communications, publisher of the first anthology of works by women of color, *Third World Women*.[4] This anthology featured some of the first published work of writers who would impact their generation: Ntozake Shange, Jessica Tarahata Hagedorn, Janet Campbell Hale, Elizabeth Martínez, Thulani Nkabinde, Nanying Stella Wong, and Janice Mirikitani, the current poet laureate of San Francisco. Later, the collective edited an anthology published by Glide Publications, *Time to Greez! Incantations from the Third World*.[5] The collective was loosely organized, sometimes with formal meetings and other times just as a collaboration among artists and writers.

Because we saw ourselves as cultural workers, and not just strictly poets, we organized readings, lots of readings. There was a good one with Fernando Alegría and Victor Hernández Cruz at the short-lived City Lights Theater on Mason Street, where the Mexican writer José Revueltas showed up. Another memorable reading was the one for Pablo Neruda and Chile, to protest the 1973 military coup that overthrew Salvador Allende. Rupert García did the poster, a dual portrait of Allende and Neruda, and Roberto and I posted it overnight on Mission Street. The night of the reading, October 4, 1973, Glide Memorial Church was packed with angry people. This event was a watershed poetry reading, ranging from works by Ishmael Reed to Janice Mirikitani to Michael McClure. Dr. Fernando Alegría, who'd been the Chilean cultural attaché in Washington and had escaped Chile dressed as a nun, brought the house down with his poem "Viva Chile M."

Another memorable reading occurred at the storefront occupied by Third World Communications at 1018 Valencia Street near Twenty-first. Pedro Pietri, a poet from New York, came into town, and David Henderson, who'd published a Latin issue of his Afro-American literary magazine *Umbra*, brought Pietri to La Mission. A reading was organized, and everyone was invited to read a poem: Jessica Hagedorn, Ntozake Shange, Victor Hernández Cruz—probably the only time when all these poets read on the same bill. And *coño*, Pedro Pietri was the featured reader. It was beautiful. That's the only way to describe it. There must've been 150 people jammed into the storefront, wine flowed, and the energy was intense. Pedro closed the show with his Rent-a-Coffin routine, delivered deadpan style in his mortician's outfit, with his black briefcase and his Rent-a-Coffin sign. The place just cracked up. One of the poems he read that night was "Puerto Rican Obituary," the great epic of the Neoricans.

Because we in the collective were reading all the Latin American poets, from Octavio Paz to Ernesto Cardenal, it was natural for me to develop an international perspective. And the whole Mission scene of poets and artists had this perspective, which was unique in the barrios, especially for the Southwest. Roberto, for instance, in *Primeros cantos*, published poems for Africa and for Angela Davis. We also made the international connection with other causes: South Africa, Viet Nam, Chile—we saw them all as one struggle.

In 1974, the Pocho-Ché collective published its own magazine, *Tin-Tan, Revista Cósmica*. In terms of the international perspective of the editorial staff, we were way ahead of our time. The premier issue featured two world-class artists doing the outside and inside covers. Michael Ríos did the outside covers, featuring a full-color, tropicalized Mission couple, with swaying palm trees in the background; the inside covers were powerful collages of South America and South Africa by Rupert García. Subsequent issues of *Tin-Tan* featured covers by the best artists in the Mission: Graciela Carillo, Juan Fuentes, and Rupert García again for issue No. 3, who did a beautiful dual portrait of Ché, in life and death. And the featured writers were a constellation not just of Aztlán but of all Latin America, which was the connection we wanted. We covered everything, from the FBI attack on the Oglala people on the Pine Ridge Reservation to the guerrilla war in Nicaragua; from Enrique Buenaventura and El Teatro Experimental de Cali to the death of Roque Dalton and the history of Salvadoran poetry. One of the founding editors of *Tin-Tan*, Daniel del Solar, recovered the lost text and photo of Frida Kahlo's painting *The Birth of Moses*, which was later cited by Hayden Herrera in her definitive biography of the artist. We also published Roberto Márquez, Víctor Manuel Valle, translations of Mayakovsky by Jack Hirschman, interviews with the Latino musicians Ray Barreto and Willie Colon, political analyses of Peru, El Salvador, and Nicaragua, as well as short fiction by Harry Gamboa Jr. and poetry by Lorna Dee Cervantes, among many, many others. And all of this was done during 1974–1976, when people in the barrios of the Southwest had not heard of these artists and writers, and when the typical Anglo American couldn't find Nicaragua or Colombia on a map, even if it bit them in the ass.

• • •

As poets, we also had our share of parties, some of which seemed to last for days, but sometimes they ended abruptly. Early one morning, after an all-night party celebrating the publication of my book, *Oración a la mano poderosa*, I drove up South Van Ness in a beat-up Triumph sports car with Roberto Vargas riding shotgun. Sunlight was already dressing Bernal Heights as I crossed Seventeenth Street. Suddenly, a cop car appeared out of nowhere. This was in the days of DWB (Driving While Brown), when cops pulled you over because of your skin color, or maybe the cops were just pissed off that two Latinos were enjoying life instead of going to work washing dishes.

It so happened I had no driver's license; my life was so transitory I didn't even carry a wallet. "Can you prove who you are?" the cop asked. In the backseat of the Triumph were some copies of my just-published book, and like a dummy, I told him I was the author. The cop was skeptical. I mean, two Latinos in a sports car at 6:00 A.M. in La Mission with a backseat full of poetry books? So, like a crazy poet, I recited one of the poems from memory while the cop read along, one foot on the running board. He just nodded his head and returned to the patrol car where his partner waited. Roberto and I placed bets as to which of us would be arrested. He insisted he'd be the one, for outstanding tickets.

While we were talking, the cop sneaked back to our car, and the next thing I knew, he shoved a .357 magnum up against my head. With each breath the cop took, I could feel the gun barrel trembling against my temple. He spoke through lips pursed as tight as a chicken butt: "You have a red warrant. One move and I'll blow your fucking head off."

I slanted my eyes at him and made like a ventriloquist, my lips barely moving, "Be cool. I'm not that bad a poet."

Poet or not, I was handcuffed and hauled off to the Mission police station, where I found out the warrant had to do with L.A. Some days later, I was chained to a seat in a sheriff's bus and taken south, where I spent time in the Glass House, the notorious city jail in downtown L.A. As soon as I could post bail, I jetted back to La Mission.

• • •

It was the summer of 1971. I was living on Twenty-sixth Street and working on the poems that would later get me arrested. One day I received a visit from a poet friend just returned from Honduras. I'd known Walter Martínez at Los Angeles City College, and when he came to San Francisco, we hooked up again. He showed up at my studio raving about a book he said was the greatest thing a Latin American had ever written. He threw a rather thick novel on the table, then, without pausing for breath, he recited the opening sentence: "Many years later, standing in front of the firing squad, Colonel Aureliano Buendía was to recall that distant day when his father first took him to see ice."

The author of this sentence, whom I'd never heard of, was Gabriel García Márquez, and the novel was *One Hundred Years of Solitude*. I don't think any book has ever made a bigger impression on me or so redefined who I was. As soon as I read it, I instantly transposed Macondo, the fictional pueblo in the novel, to the Mission District. I now saw La Mission as a little pueblo, an extension of Latin America. La Mission was so small I could stand on Twenty-fourth Street and look toward Potrero Hill and see only one sign hanging over the street—the yellow neon of Guadalajara de Noche. All the personalities that existed in the pueblos of Latin America could be found in La Mission: *los locos, los borrachos,* the poets, the political exiles, the women with their wide hips and *mercadera* mouths. And like any *pueblito,* everyone knew everyone, and you'd bump into friends at receptions, parties, street fairs, or just shopping for *pan dulce.* Or I'd walk down Twenty-fourth Street and hear the Spanish inflections of the entire continent—Nicoya slang, Chicano caló, rapid-fire *cubanismos,* the elegant phrasing of Chileans.

After reading *One Hundred Years of Solitude,* I took the paperback to Roberto Vargas and told him, "Man, you have to read this. Here's where it's at." Roberto read it, and he took it to Victor Hernández Cruz, the Puerto Rican poet. After Victor read it, we all got together and we knew— this was the book. Suddenly we reinterpreted our existence, we were no longer exiled in the cold north, in the pale United States. We transposed our Latino roots from Central America, land of volcanoes and revolutions; from the Caribbean, land of palm trees and salsa music; and from Aztlán, land of lowriders and *vatos locos,* and fused these tropicalized visions to our barrio and made the concrete sidewalks, the asphalt streets, and the sterile buildings sway to a Latin beat.

Victor Hernández Cruz was important to that beat. He was from New York, the Lower East Side, and was living in La Mission, on Oak and Eighteenth Street. Roberto had introduced us, and although Victor and I were the same age, he was already an established poet. He'd published his first book, *Snaps!* by Random House, when he was eighteen.[6] I can think of only three poets with a similar claim of greatness at such a young age—Jean Nicholas Rimbaud, Rubén Darío, and Pablo Neruda. Victor was softspoken and gave the impression of being shy, almost introverted—except when it came to music. One day the three of us went to Roberto's pad on Peralta Street, because Victor wanted us to hear an album he'd brought from New York. "Listen to this," Victor said. Then he put on Willie Colon and Hector La Voe doing "Vive tu vida contento," from the LP *Asalto navideño*. And there was that badass trombone of Willie's blending with Hector's high-pitched *jíbaro* voice, and it was just so good that you couldn't sit still. We started tapping our feet and keeping the beat with our fingers on a beer bottle, and Victor was doing this thing I'd never seen before—rubbing his hands together, making kind of a *güiro* sound. And it was like music I'd always loved, even when I had never heard anything like it before. This was what in Mexico was called "*música tropical*" but here it was called salsa, although we knew that was just a PR man's scheme to help the Fania label sell more albums. But it didn't matter; salsa became the music of La Mission, even replacing Santana, Malo, and all the West Coast bands. Soon all we were listening to was Willie Colon, Eddie Palmieri, Ray Barreto, Tito Puente, Celia Cruz, Johnny Pacheco, and all the rest. This was the beat that tropicalized La Mission.

So for months we walked around with our heads in the tropics, seeing everything through a tropical lens. We ate tropical food, *plátanos verdes con habichuelas,* or we had *nacatamales* or *pasteles* or ceviche. We dressed in guayaberas, Panama hats, and two-toned shoes. Naturally, we drank only rum or tequila. And our girlfriends dressed like Carmen Miranda, with big looped earrings, platform shoes, and gardenias in their hair. It seemed that the very air we breathed carried the scent of ripe papayas. The tropical motif soon appeared everywhere; the first two covers of *Tin-Tan* magazine, with their tropicalized figures and palms, spread the word. The artists picked up on our trip, and soon tropical villages started appearing in their murals that were now all over La Mission. The Mujeres Muralistas painted a mural, *Para el mercado,* at Twenty-fourth and Van Ness, that stretched for half a block and featured scenes from tropical America. Michael Ríos did a mural at the Twenty-fourth Street BART (Bay Area Rapid Transit) station showing workers in a tropical urban setting. Victor Hernández Cruz published the first book to incorporate the theme: *Tropicalization*.[7] The very concept of transposing the tropics to the United States was the title of the book. That's not to say that Victor hadn't previously written poems with a tropical motif; he had. What I'm saying is that this book, for me, had a definitive Mission *tropicalidad* stamp on it. And then that winter it rained for months at a time, day and night, till it seemed that we had willed the four-year flood from *One Hundred Years of Solitude* into our very own Macondo.

It was around this time that La Mission entered two new phases. One was the return to our indigenous roots, an idea that helped revive the concept of Aztlán, and the other was the expansion of our political involvement, which firmly established our link to Central America. The first occurred when Ysidro Macías, now studying at U.C. Irvine, invited us down to meet a friend of his named Andrés Segura. Ysidro claimed that Segura was a *brujo*, a bona fide practicing shaman in the style of Don Juan, the sorcerer who'd mentored Carlos Castañeda. So the three of us, Roberto, Victor, and myself, headed to Irvine, not knowing what to expect.

We met Andrés Segura at Ysidro's house, and yes, he had power and magic. Andrés was about 5'2", very Indian looking, with a glint of mischief in his eyes. We hit it off immediately. He knew everything about Indian culture and language, spoke Nahuatl fluently, was a *capitán* of the *danza*, and performed many rites and rituals of the ancient culture. He spoke to us for hours about our Mexica heritage, tracing for us the philosophy of our ancestors, the concepts of duality, and the lineage of our gods, in particular Quetzalcóatl, Coatlicue, and Tonantzín. His knowledge about the Mexicas was impressive; he spoke like a direct descendant, as if the thread of culture and history had never been cut.

At the end of the night, Andrés took us for a walk. Then suddenly and magically we were not on the campus anymore but in some other place. Andrés invited us to sit down, and he patted the grass saying, "Sit down here on your Mother, the Earth." Although the ground was moist with dew, it made no difference to us. We did as he told us, and I don't think any of us felt uncomfortable or even wet. He pulled out a Delicado, one of the Mexican cigarettes that he favored, warmed the length of it with a match, then lit up, and while the smoke swirled around him, he started talking to us about being *indios*. I am not making this up, but I swear he was glowing, as if a vibrant light had snapped on inside him. In the presence of Andrés, everything seemed sacred—the stars, the earth, my friends—and as I listened to him, I sensed release from everything that was evil and sour in this world, felt all the bad literally escaping from my body. That night I resolved to start living within the Mexica traditions: respecting the ancients and the earth, learning more about my indigenous culture, recovering our history of resistance, taking the time to appreciate nature.

When we returned to San Francisco, I think all of us were transformed. We realized the depth of our Indian roots—and like everyone else who knew Andrés, we called him Maestro from then on. That he was a master and a *brujo* was proven a few years later when Roberto suffered a collapsed lung. He was in Zion Medical Center, with a tube in his chest draining liquid. He'd been there a week, and it looked as though he might not make it. He called Andrés and asked him to come and give him a *limpieza*, a cleansing. Andrés flew up the same afternoon, and I helped sneak him in to Roberto's room after hours. Andrés pulled the curtains around the bed, and I stood guard near the door. Andrés performed a ritual that I cannot describe, and the next day, against his doctor's orders, Roberto pulled the tube from his chest and walked out of the hospital. Maybe that was craziness, maybe it was the healing power of Andrés, but whatever it was, Roberto got better, his collapsed lung healed, even the hole in his chest where the tube was inserted healed, and he never went back to see a doctor.

Because of Andrés, we now incorporated *indigenismo* into our lives. The house where Roberto and I lived we named Huehuetitlán, the House of the Drums, meaning the house of the poets. We read up on the Nahuatl poets and the Nahuatl scholars such as Angel María Garibay, Miguel León-Portilla, and the Mayan scholar Domingo Paredes. We started burning copal as Andrés taught us, we fasted during full moons, and we abstained from alcohol. We were also inspired to organize the biggest literary conference of that decade, the Festival of the Sexto Sol, in the spring of 1974.

Dr. Fernando Alegría, the well-known Chilean writer and a professor at Stanford, served as our guru in this matter. He had the contacts with all the big names, and he encouraged us to work with them. In this way, we expanded our circle to include such notable heavies as Joseph Sommers, the literary critic; Jean Franco, the author of *The Modern Culture of Latin America*;[8] Antonia Castañeda Shular; and Tomás Ybarra-Frausto—all of whom were at Stanford. Before the conference, we consulted with Andrés, and he guided us by phone on what rituals to follow. The key organizers, Roberto, Victor, Eliás Hruska-Cortés, Nina Serrano, and myself, fasted for three days and stayed up all night before the opening, taking baths, meditating, and basically getting our heads together.

The morning of the opening, all the participants gathered in the chapel at Stanford, where Jean Franco gave the opening remarks. After that, the Mission poets did a ritual burning of copal in the quad. Then the conference started. Some of the writers at the Sexto Sol were Miguel Algarín and

Miguel Piñero from the Neorican Café in the Lower East Side. Miguel Piñero's play *Short Eyes* was playing on Broadway, and he was a promising bigtime star. Carlos Monsiváis came from Mexico City, raúlrsalinas from Seattle, Ricardo Sánchez from Texas; Raymond Barrios, the author of *The Plum-Plum Pickers*, made an appearance, as did Alurista, the poet laureate of Aztlán, and many others. The conference was a four-day affair that opened at Stanford with a series of workshops, moved on to San Francisco State and the Palace of Fine Arts for readings, and closed in La Mission, at El Club Tropical, with an all-night *pachanga* that left everyone bleary-eyed but happy.

Our purpose with the Sexto Sol was to herald the new Sun, the era of peace and harmony that the ancients predicted would follow the Fifth Sun, the era of turmoil that we were living in. So part of our organizing consisted of telling people that the Sixth Sun was coming and that the Fifth Sun was dead. Right before the conference started, we got a call at Huehuetitlán from the Quinto Sol publishing house at Berkeley; they were complaining about us saying that the Fifth Sun, El Quinto Sol, was dead. "No, no," they said, "we're still publishing." We laughed because we didn't mean them; we were thinking of something bigger.

· · ·

Let me go back a bit now. There was another event that shaped us concurrently with the tropical and indigenous influences. What you have to understand is that we were usually doing three or four things at the same time, so it wasn't unusual for influences, committees, or events to overlap each other.

In 1972, Roberto had shown me a little chapbook by a Nicaraguan poet living on a small archipelago on Lake Nicaragua. The poet was Ernesto Cardenal, who was a priest and, according to Roberto, also a revolutionary. The book was *Gethsemani, Ky.* It was a series of small poems about Cardenal's stay in a monastery, under the tutelage of Thomas Merton, a Catholic writer-philosopher whom I had read in high school. This book was my introduction to Cardenal and to Nicaragua. Soon after, Roberto published a poem in the Latin issue of *Umbra* that connected the two realities, La Mission and Nicaragua. What follows are the opening lines:

> Carta/poema pa Ernesto Cardenal
>
> . . . y cuantas penas/hambres
> torturas no habras
> sufrido hermano . . . tu

en el sobaco de el
verdugo/titere de united
fruit co. y los e.e.u.u.
tacho tachito (como el
quien dice "ni mierda")
yo . . . nica/pocho
patarajada (en bota alta)
kneedeep in caca caca aca
en el mero josico de la
chancha de america u.s.a.
toda roja/blanca/azul
(come el quien dice . . .
"ni mierda") . . .⁹

Later that year, during the winter when it rained for months, a seminal event occurred in Nicaragua, although at that time no one was aware of the impact it would have on the history of our continent. On December 23, 1972, an earthquake destroyed Managua, leveling three-fourths of the capital and killing 10,000 people. Roberto, being Nicaraguan, rushed to the aid committee in San Francisco. But soon the word circulated among the exiled Nicaraguan community that Anastasio Somoza and his National Guard were stealing the aid, everything from money to canned goods. Somoza already owned everything in Nicaragua, from the biggest ranch to the Mercedes-Benz dealership, but his greed in the aftermath of the earthquake helped politicize the 50,000 Nicaraguans then living in La Mission.

Soon, blue-and-white leaflets (the colors of the Nicaraguan flag) started appearing in La Mission with Somoza's face and the words "Se Busca: Anastasio Somoza D., por masacre, extorción, torturas, violación, robo." (Wanted: Anastasio Somoza D., for massacre, extortion, torture, rape, theft). The leaflets were primitive looking in comparison to what we did, but they were intriguing. Roberto tracked them down till he found the person behind the leaflets; it turned out to be Casimiro Sotelo, a Nicaraguan architect living in Burlingame. Sotelo was one of a half-dozen brothers all named Casimiro Sotelo (his sister was Casimira Sotelo), just as names reappeared in the same family in the Márquez novel. One of the Casimiro Sotelos had been a member of a Frente Sandinista de Liberación Nacional (FSLN) cadre who had been tortured and killed by the National Guard. One day Roberto took me to meet what he said were the FSLN contacts in San Francisco. I expected Ché and Fidel, guerrillas in fatigues fresh from the mountains.

Casimiro Sotelo was not exactly the picture of the underground guerrilla

I had in mind. He dressed in suit and tie and was very middle class. I figured maybe he was just the front man for the real contact, so when he took us to a flat in La Mission to meet his partner, I went along thinking, "Now it's going to get good."

In a small rented room in the back of the flat on Valencia Street lived an elderly gentleman, white haired and friendly, who wore a dark suit like Casimiro's. Colonel Haslam, ex-member of the National Guard, was the uncle of Doris Reyes Tijerino, a key FSLN cadre member who at that time was incarcerated in Nicaragua. But this had no impact—who was Doris Tijerino to me? I was having a hard time believing that these two square guys could possibly have anything to do with a guerrilla movement. When Roberto asked Colonel Haslam about the FSLN, the old man's face lit up, "Yo soy del Frente" (I am of the Front). I just rolled my eyes.

But it wasn't until I understood that Nicaragua is connected through a network of clans, that everyone knows you by your relationship to this bigger clan-*familia* concept, that I understood the struggle of Nicaragua in intimate terms. The first thing a Nicaraguan does when meeting you is to relate you to your clan, "Oh, tú eres de los Bermúdez de Managua que viven frente el Mercado Oriental" (Oh, you're of the Bermúdezes of Managua who live across from the Eastern Market). Boom. Immediately you're identified and put in your historical place. That is a uniquely Nicaraguan trait. And so I came to understand Nicaragua through its network of clans, beginning with the one at the top, the Somozas, who for three generations going back to 1933 had dominated the country. And there were those who had opposed them, the Chamorros, the Fonsecas, and many more—such as Casimiro Sotelo and his brother of the same name who'd been assassinated, or Haroldo Solano, who lived in La Mission and had been captured with Daniel Ortega at Pancasán, site of an early guerrilla action. Haroldo knew every detail, it seemed, of Nicaraguan history and could recite the names of fallen martyrs, as well as the dates and places of combat, on request. Later, Colonel Juan Ferreti emerged from the Nicaraguan community and made the historical link between Augusto Sandino, the Nicaraguan hero after whom the Frente Sandinista was named, and ourselves. Juan Ferreti, "El Coronel," as we called him, was the uncle of Walter Ferreti, one of the first members of El Comité Cívico, formed as a support committee for the FSLN. Juan Ferreti was a veteran of the 1927–1932 war against the U.S. Marines in Nicaragua. "El Coronel" had been a member of Sandino's staff and had barely escaped being assassinated in 1933, when Sandino and many of his followers were wiped out by Somoza's henchmen. Juan Ferreti escaped to Costa Rica and eventually came to San Francisco, where he became a living connection to the original war of liberation. In so many ways, "El Coronel" was like Colonel Aureliano Buendía, the revolutionary who'd fought in thirty-two losing wars, another character out of *One Hundred Years of Solitude*.

Eventually I came to learn what it meant to be of the Frente. You knew everything about the FSLN and its founder, Carlos Fonseca, and the cofounders, Sylvio Mayorga and Tomás Borges. You read the political-military platform and studied it point by point. You knew the history of Nicaragua, how William Walker had invaded the country in 1855; the first war of liberation led by Benjamín Zeledón, in 1892; and you knew the story of the patriot Sandino, who had defied the mighty United States Marines, and the names of all the battles waged by his tiny "*ejército loco*": El Ocotal, El Chipote, and the rest. You knew all the battles of the Frente, from the days of the Río Coco and Pancasán to the Frente Sur Benjamín Zeledón. You knew the names of all the martyrs and the dates they'd fallen: Rigoberto López Pérez, Leonel Rugama, Arlen Siu, Julio Buitrago, and José Benito Escobar. And after knowing all this, and reading everything you could about Nicaragua, starting with Gregorio Selser's book on Sandino and ending with the latest communiqué from the Frente, you felt not only of the Frente: you felt *nicaragüense*.

You have to understand a few things. Being Xicano, with Mexica roots, I am connected to Central America through culture. In Mesoamerica, the Nahuatl culture spread as far south as Nicaragua, whose indigenous Nahuatl name, Nicarahuac, means "Hasta aquí llegó el Nahua" (The Nahuas came this far). So culturally I'm connected to Nicaragua, and therefore politically, it goes without saying. And historically, California and Nicaragua have been linked since 1849, when New Englanders headed for the goldfields would dock at Greytown on the Atlantic Coast of Nicaragua, sail up the Río San Juan to Rivas, then cross the fifteen-mile strip of land before boarding another ship on the Pacific to take them the rest of the way. One other point connects me historically to Nicaragua: when the Tennessee filibuster William Walker set out to invade Nicaragua in 1855, he sailed from San Francisco. During the years 1977–1979, when many of us flew out of San Francisco to help free Nicaragua, we would remember what William Walker had done, especially his burning of Granada, on the ruins of which he left this graffiti, so chillingly prophetic of North American involvement: Here Was Granada.

So for me it was natural to work for Nicaragua. I had long ago discarded the narrow nationalism of my youth and thus welcomed the struggle of this Central American country. A few months after our meeting with Sotelo and Haslam, Roberto came to my house early one morning before New Year's 1975. "We have to meet," he said. He had urgent news from Nicaragua. An

FSLN commando had taken over the house of Chema Castillo in Managua and had captured a slew of Somoza's lackeys. They wanted to exchange them for Frente prisoners, one million dollars, and passage out of the country. The Frente had issued a communiqué in Managua; our task was to translate it, print it, and distribute it here in San Francisco. I went to work immediately on the translation, while Roberto organized a march. That Saturday morning, with a thousand copies of the communiqué printed under the banner of *La Gaceta Sandinista*, we met with several dozen people at the Twenty-fourth Street BART Station. Casimiro and Roberto spoke at the rally; then we all marched down Mission Street. There were maybe thirty of us at that march. We carried these beautiful black-and-red posters of Sandino silk-screened by La Raza Silk Screen Center, and we waved them at passing traffic and stood outside El Tico-Nica bar exchanging insults with Somoza sympathizers. This was the first rally ever held for Nicaragua in the Mission District or in the United States.

Although it was a small start, word soon spread through the Nicaraguan community. The Frente sympathizers were organized around El Comité Cívico Latinoamericano Pro Nicaragua en los Estados Unidos (El Comité Cívico, for short), which published *La Gaceta Sandinista*, a newspaper that brought stories, reports, photographs, and Frente communiqués to an information-starved community of Nicaraguan exiles. The meetings of *La Gaceta* staff took place at a storefront on Twenty-second and Bartlett, and the first members were Walter Ferreti, Raúl Venerio, Lygia Venerio, Haroldo Solano, and Bérman Zúniga. All of them would later play an important role in the overthrow of Somoza.

I remember one meeting at which I heard that Somoza had 7,500 troops in the National Guard. I responded, "Then we're bound to win." Everyone looked at me as if I was crazy, since Frente at that time had about 30 guerrillas in the mountains. But to me it wasn't a question of numbers; from the very beginning I felt that Frente had the moral high ground in this battle, and because our fight was just and good, we were bound to win. You have to forgive my romanticism, but, remember, I had cut my teeth on Ché's legacy. Regardless, I always had faith that Frente would win.

Had you seen the first event *La Gaceta* put on you would surely have thought I was crazy—that we were all crazy, hopeless dreamers. It was a Sunday afternoon cultural event in the hall behind Saint Peter's Church on Twenty-fourth Street. We had typical Nicaraguan food, a slide show, and a cultural presentation featuring Walter Ferreti dressed in a guayabera doing a folkloric dance from Monimbó. I think seven people showed up. Three of them were Walter's relatives, who'd come to see him dance.

But we kept on organizing cultural events and printing the newspaper, and on the sly, we bought a couple of shotguns at a pawnshop on Mission Street. Later, the key contact of the Frente, Herty Levitez, who always stayed in the background and who was known by his pseudonym "Mauricio," was arrested crossing the border into Mexico in a car full of weapons: hunting rifles, shotguns, and pistols. He did six months in a federal penitentiary for that.

But other work was more successful. A solidarity committee popped up in L.A., another one in Washington, D.C. Roberto created a Non-Intervention in Nicaragua Committee (NIN), made up of North Americans, to pressure Congress to stop military aid to the Somoza regime. Eventually, NIN scored a two-day hearing on human rights in Nicaragua, Guatemala, and El Salvador before the Subcommittee on International Organizations of the House of Representatives in Washington, D.C. Several documents were submitted to the committee, including sworn statements by Pedro Joaquín Chamorro regarding human rights violations he had observed while being held a prisoner in Somoza's jails, and a letter from Monsignor Miguel Obando Bravo, archbishop of Nicaragua, regarding restrictions on religious expression. Father Fernando Cardenal, brother of Ernesto Cardenal and also a priest, testified at the hearings about the imprisonment, torture, and disappearance of campesinos in Nicaragua. The hearings also raised the contradictions in State Department policy in regard to Central America, in particular Nicaragua, since the United States was providing training to National Guard members in counterinsurgency, irregular warfare, jungle warfare, and advanced police and investigation tactics that were being used against workers, students, intellectuals, and other political opponents of the Somoza dictatorship. This support of the dictator was in direct violation of the Río Pact, a mutual-assistance document signed by the United States, which states "that the obligation of mutual assistance and common defense of the American Republics is essentially related to their democratic ideals." [10]

Just as the solidarity movement seemed to be gaining momentum, we were tripped by some bitter news. On November 8, 1976, Carlos Fonseca, the founder of the Frente, was killed in an ambush in the northern mountains of Nicaragua. A few days later, another key Frente leader, Eduardo Contreras, was killed in Managua. Contreras had been the idea behind the solidarity committees, the original Comandante Cero of the December 1974 raid, and perhaps the most charismatic of all the Frente leaders. It seemed that Somoza had effectively destroyed the leadership of the Frente and thereby set back the movement indefinitely.

La Gaceta continued publishing, but now internal divisions splintered the group. There was a period of about a year when La Gaceta didn't publish at all. That was when the first communiqués started circulating about the three factions that had emerged within the FSLN: the Terceristas, or Insurrectionists; the GPP, Guerra Popular Prolongada, or Prolonged People's War faction; and the Proletariat faction. It was during this period that Walter Ferreti disappeared from the group. A few months later, Raúl Venerio also vanished.

During this same year, 1976–1977, the Mission was infused with Nicaraguan language, culture, and politics. Nicaraguan slang became part of the Mission's patois, a vocabulary based on both the folklore and the politics of the time: *tüani*, exceptionally good; *comanche*, slang for *comandante*, or someone who is a leader; and *Patria Libre o Morir*—Free Country or Death. Roberto and I kept organizing on the cultural front, specifically working on the creation of a cultural center. We had our eyes on the Shaft's Furniture site, a four-story building that had been closed for years, half a block from Mission and Twenty-fourth Street. After months of organizing with community groups such as the Mission Arts Alliance, a Mission arts group coalition, and individuals such as Magaly Fernández, to name just a couple, the Mission Cultural Center became a reality in December 1976. Volunteers cleaned out the old furniture, rugs, and display racks. Community artists such as Gilberto Osorio, who also worked with *Tin-Tan* magazine, organized a gallery on the mezzanine and started preparing the walls for art exhibits. In March 1977, we held the first event, a poetry reading and mass said by the world-renowned poet Ernesto Cardenal, who flew in from Nicaragua. Cardenal celebrated the mass as he would have in Solentiname with the campesinos. For the communion, he tore pieces from a loaf of sourdough bread to use as the host, then he passed around a jug of table wine from which we all took a sip. How different this ritual was from my youth! About 250 people from La Mission celebrated mass that Sunday with Ernesto, and afterward, he baptized about 50 children and gave a poetry reading.

In October 1977, the Frente launched a series of surprise attacks on the National Guard barracks in Estelí, Masaya, and San Carlos. Although the Frente was unable to hold any of these cities, these incursions proved that the National Guard was not invincible. Two key participants in these attacks were the missing former members of *La Gaceta*, Walter Ferreti, now known by his nom-de-guerre, Chombo, and Raúl Venerio, known as Willy. Those of us who were in San Francisco were immeasurably proud of their valor and what they had done.

In February 1978 the situation in Nicaragua exploded again. A spontaneous uprising occurred in the Indian barrio of Monimbó, in Masaya. When the National Guard brutally put it down, people all over Nicaragua were outraged. The opposition against Somoza had never been stronger, and then, Pedro Joaquín Chamorro, a leading opponent of the dictator and publisher of *La Prensa*, the most widely read newspaper in the country, was gunned down in Managua. That was the kick that broke the monkey's balls. While the people of Nicaragua took to the streets in protest, we organized a nightly candlelight vigil at the Twenty-fourth and Mission BART station. Soon we were practically living at the BART station; besides the nightly vigils, every Saturday we held a rally demanding that Somoza step down, and soon everyone was calling the BART station Plaza Sandino. As part of our political actions we also stormed the Nicaraguan Consulate on Market Street, took over the office, and expelled the consul and his staff. We held the office for a whole day before finally agreeing to withdraw. We were, in a sense, preparing ourselves for the real battles that were to come.

It was now obvious to us that war was coming in Nicaragua. A new member now joined the revitalized *Gaceta*, Armando, a young Palestinian-Nicaraguan student at U.C. Santa Cruz who became the most dedicated member of the *Gaceta* collective. To harass Somoza's representatives in San Francisco we took over the Nicaraguan consulate on what seemed a monthly basis. Wearing red-and-black bandannas, we would storm the consulate, then usher out all the workers. Once inside, we'd phone the media—newspapers, TV, and radio—then we'd distribute communiqués denouncing Somoza. We might hold the consulate overnight before slipping out. To make it seem that we were more than the handful we actually were, we took turns wearing the bandannas and holding the consulate while others talked to the media. We also started going to a shooting range in Sharp Park, near Pacifica, to practice firing old M1 rifles and pistols. We would run early in the mornings, five laps around Bernal Heights counterclockwise, in other words, uphill. We trained in karate and wing-chun. We also read the Political-Military Platform of the Frente and *La Prensa* from Managua, so we were preparing ourselves not just militarily but politically as well.

During this time, Roberto was in daily phone contact with the Frente through Costa Rica and was also flying all over the country organizing fund-raisers and poetry readings. The support of North Americans was now critical, and several important poets and writers took the lead, including Miguel Algarín, Daniel Berrigan, Robert Cohen, Pedro Pietri, Allen Ginsberg, Muriel Rukeyser, and Ntozake Shange, who held a poetry reading benefit for Nicaragua in New York. Early in September 1978 the word came for everyone to prepare to come down to join the Front. At the last minute, perhaps because I was not Nicaraguan, I was ordered to stay behind and head *La Gaceta* and the solidarity committees. Roberto, Armando, and others left for Costa Rica in early August. Before I dropped them off at the airport, we all went to Mission Rock, a working-class café overlooking San Francisco Bay, and had one last beer together. On September 17, they formed part of the column that attacked the National Guard outpost at Peñas Blancas on the border between Nicaragua and Costa Rica. The assault squad was led by Toño "El Gringo" Zeledón, one of our comrades from *La Gaceta Sandinista*. This was one of the fiercest battles fought during the Insurrection of September, and Armando, a member of the assault squad, would be one of the casualties.

The following month, October 1978, the ubiquitous "Mauricio" organized an international conference in Panama in solidarity with Nicaragua. After the conference, I flew to Costa Rica and stayed in a safe house, where, late one night, a ragged-looking Daniel Ortega and Víctor Tirado López, the two *comandantes* of the Southern Front, appeared for a midnight press conference. As the cameras rolled, the two *comandantes* explained the tactics of the Terceristas, the strategy of popular insurrection in which the entire population would rise up to overthrow the dictatorship. After the conference, I introduced myself to Víctor Tirado López, who, though he was at the highest level of the FSLN, was of Mexican background and at one time had been a watchmaker in Puebla. Before leaving San José, I visited Armando in the hospital. During the attack on Peñas Blancas, a grenade had ripped his left foot to shreds, requiring the amputation of several toes. In spite of this wound, his morale was high. I left the hospital wondering what it would take to overthrow Somoza.

On my return to San Francisco, I left my position as director of the Mission Cultural Center to devote all my time to the Frente. Nicaragua was front-page news all over the world, and during a week of solidarity with the Frente, a who's who of the Bay Area literary scene appeared at a reading to raise funds for medical supplies: Victor Hernández Cruz, Diane di Prima, Jack Hirschman, Michael McClure, David Meltzer, Janice Mirikitani, Ishmael Reed, Max Schwartz, Ahimsa Sumchai, and Alma Luz Villanueva. When Armando returned from the Front, and then Roberto, my turn came to go. In June 1979 I left for Costa Rica with Armando, whose foot had healed, although he would always carry shrapnel buried in his flesh. From San José, we traveled to Liberia, and from Liberia we entered the Southern Front with a column of internationalists. A few weeks earlier, another group from Northern California had left for the Front. Included in this group were three Chicanos from Fresno, perhaps the first Chicano internationalists to participate in a guerrilla movement of Latin America. These experiences are recounted in an earlier book, *Southern Front*,[11] so I will not repeat them here.

After the overthrow of Somoza and the creation of a popular government, I returned to San Francisco. On the bus from the airport to the city, I stared out the windows watching the skyline, the buildings, the people, the bustle of the city. The lanky palms on Mission Street appeared a bit ragged and not all that tropical. I still wore a beard, what little of it that grew, and I was sunburned from the tropical sun; other than that, it was impossible to tell where I'd been and what I'd done.

After 1979, the solidarity movement took a new turn. North Americans took over the solidarity committees and made trips to Nicaragua; sometimes they worked picking coffee or in the cooperatives, sometimes they stayed and married Nicaraguans and had children. The Nicaraguans who'd lived in La Mission, for the most part, returned to savor the triumphs of the revolution, of living in their country without the Somozas. Colonel Ferreti, the old survivor of Sandino's army, went back and was feted by the Sandinistas as a living legend. Colonel Haslam went back too. Roberto Vargas was rightly named the Nicaraguan cultural attaché to the United States and moved to Washington, D.C., where he continued being a poet in the name of the revolution. Casimiro Sotelo was sent to Canada as ambassador and took his family to Toronto. Even now, twenty years later, when July 19 comes around, I think of those times when *La Gaceta Sandinista* started out with just a handful of people and how, by the time of the Final Offensive, thousands were marching down Mission Street shouting support for the Frente.

But in July 1979, it was too early to know what the outcome of the Nicaraguan Revolution would be. Nevertheless, a half-dozen of us from this barrio La Mission were now veterans of the struggle for our liberation that began when the first Indian threw the first rock at the first Spaniard.

• • •

During the decade of the 1970s, a man emerged from the Nicaraguan community in La Mission whom I consider the "Last American Hero." Modern-day heroes are hard to find, especially in Latin America. Those who aren't tainted by corruption seem to have been around for centuries, so it's difficult to associate one's personal life with these leaders, heroes or not. At a time when the Chicano movement had been stifled, and no one spoke about revolution or even social change, Walter Ferreti Fonseca became a true hero of Nicaragua and Latin America, when, against incredible odds, he took on the challenge of armed struggle. Because so much of Walter's political outlook and involvement was formed in the Mission District, I'd have to call him a hero of Aztlán too.

He came to San Francisco in 1970 from his native Nicaragua, a chubby twenty-year-old who wanted to study psychology and return to his native land. He never did study psychology, but he did return to Nicaragua—as a guerrilla. Walter was one of the first recruits of *La Gaceta* and soon revealed himself to be the most dedicated member of our group. He'd jump right into whatever had to be done, whether it was cleaning the storefront, printing *La Gaceta*, or organizing a rally. He was mostly autodidactic and a voracious reader of history, but he also enjoyed poetry, especially the work of Ernesto Cardenal, whom he greatly admired. In those years, Walter worked as a chef at the Mark Hopkins Hotel and was often dog-tired at the meetings, but he never let up; he always stepped forward.

Several traits in Walter's character were exemplary: self-abnegation, humility, courage. Coming from a working-class background in Managua, Walter had a deep affection for working people, in particular the dispossessed, those without the basic necessities of life, and in Nicaragua, that meant about 90 percent of the population. He was also completely dedicated to overthrowing Somoza. You have to understand how much some people hated this dictator. The Somoza family had been in power since 1933, and next to that of the Shah of Iran, theirs was the longest-running dictatorship on the planet. The family patriarch, Anastasio Somoza García, who had plotted the murder of Augusto Sandino in 1933, had been "*justiciado*," or brought to justice, by the poet Rigoberto López Pérez in 1956. After Somoza García's assassination, the oldest son, Luis, ruled the country until a heart attack brought him down. During the 1970s, the youngest son of the patriarch, Anastasio Somoza Debayle, held power, and many claimed he was the bloodiest of the lot. "Tacho," as he was called, was already grooming his son, a psychopathic killer called "El Chigüin," to follow in his footsteps.

Somoza Debayle was U.S. educated and ran the country according to his whim and U.S. interests. There was a joke at the time that because Somoza owned the foreign car dealership, Nicaragua had the only Mercedes-Benz garbage trucks in the world—a joke that, unfortunately, was true. Somoza took a cut of the top businesses, held the only export license for beef, and basically was your typical banana republic dictator. You didn't have to hate him for that—unless you knew the history of the FSLN, knew of heroes like Julio Buitrago, Sylvio Mayorga, Arlen Siu, and the poet Leonel Rugama, all of whom had died in unequal combat against Somoza's National Guard. If you were an apolitical Nicaraguan, you didn't know or care about these young men and women killed by Somoza. If you knew the story of the Frente militant David Tejada, how he'd been tortured and then his body flung into the Masaya volcano, it was hard to stay apolitical.

But no matter who you were or at what level in the economic standing you were, if you were Nicaraguan, you knew that Somoza had robbed the people blind after the earthquake of 1972. While the country was devastated, Somoza's National Guard sequestered the international aid that had poured in and then sold it to the people. And that act of greed made everyone hate him. After the murder of campesinos in the mountains during the period of 1973–1974, when you heard about the tortures and rapes as described by witnesses before the U.S. House of Representatives Subcommittee on Human Rights, then you hated Somoza as you had never hated anyone before.

Of all the members of *La Gaceta*, Walter was the first to join the guerrilla forces, returning clandestinely to Nicaragua in mid-1977. One day he just suddenly vanished from La Mission. By then, the organization was tightly compartmentalized, and we knew better than to ask questions. We suspected where Walter had gone, but we kept it real quiet.

Chombo soon became an outstanding member of the FSLN, working both in the urban resistance and in guerrilla columns that operated in the countryside. The stories associated with him were often humorous. Once, while Chombo was visiting an uncle in Managua, the National Guard came to arrest him and he escaped by jumping over a fence and running through the barrio. His pseudonym, "Chombo," was an affectionate way of saying he was chubby. He was also boyish and playful and would rather be kicking a soccer ball than handling a weapon.

In war, though, Chombo was implacable and unforgiving of the enemy. Soon his stature grew to legendary proportions. In February of 1978, we heard that he'd been killed in the Northern Front along the Honduran border. A few weeks later the word came that no, Chombo was not dead. He'd been taken out of the war zone strapped to a mule, with five bullet wounds in his body. They didn't know if he'd survive, but he did, and he came back even stronger.

On March 9, 1978, the Frente carried out an action that struck at the very heart of the Somoza military. The Chief of Staff of the National Guard (and a CIA collaborator), General Reynaldo Pérez, known as "Perro" Pérez, was brought to justice in a house in Managua. A few days later, a young woman named Nora Astorga de Jenkins wrote a communiqué from the Northern Front, claiming responsibility for the action. Her photo, in which she's wearing a beret and holding a rifle on her shoulder, captured the imagination of all of Latin America. What only a few knew was that Chombo was one of two guerrillas who'd hidden for days in a closet of Astorga's house waiting for Pérez to make an appearance. When Astorga finally lured Pérez into her house and into her bedroom, Chombo jumped out with a nine-inch serrated knife, the kind scuba divers use to kill sharks. The original plan was to kidnap Pérez and exchange him for FSLN members held by

Somoza. When Pérez resisted, Chombo had no choice. On their way out of the house, the guerrillas draped the FSLN flag over the dead Somocista general. That's the photo that was flashed all over Latin America: Somoza's most hated general dead, with his pants around his ankles, and the red-and-black FSLN flag draped over his body.

While the Frente and the people of Nicaragua prepared for the popular insurrection of 1978, a small Frente commando began a special training course in safe houses scattered around Managua. A key member of this top-secret operation was Chombo, who'd been assigned the code Number Three. Number Two was Dora María Tellez, Number One was Hugo Torres, and the head of the operation was Edén Pastora, who would gain fame as Comandante Cero. The mission they were planning was the most audacious ever carried out by the Frente and perhaps unequaled in all the liberation struggles of Latin America. Gabriel García Márquez, who chronicled the event in his essay "Los sandinistas se toman el Palacio Nacional de Managua," wrote this about the plan: "Parecía una locura demasiado simple" (It seemed an extremely simple crazy act). The commando would enter the National Palace in broad daylight disguised as National Guard members, and once inside, they would take captive the entire legislative body of Somoza's government and hold them till all the political prisoners were freed.[12]

On August 22, 1978, the FSLN commando "Rigoberto López Pérez," composed of twenty-five members, took over the National Palace, capturing nearly a thousand people, including several dozen legislators, among them José Antonio Mora, minister of the interior, and Luis Pallais Debayle, first cousin of Somoza and a key political figure of the dictatorship. When the first dramatic photos of the takeover were published in *La Prensa*, there was Chombo, unmistakable even beneath his gas mask and bulky uniform, holding a G3 to the neck of Luis Pallais Debayle while the latter talked to Somoza on the phone. According to García Márquez's account of the takeover, it was Chombo's squad, "Número Tres," that captured the Minister of the Interior José Antonio Mora, who was next in line for the presidency after Somoza. Mora was discovered hiding behind his desk in the ministry office, and he surrendered without asking questions, despite having a loaded Browning in his belt.[13]

This military action, so audacious and successful, confirmed the vulnerability of the dictatorship. Except for the top cadres, who were seasoned guerrillas, the rest of the FSLN commandos were kids, barely twenty years old, some as young as eighteen. They held the National Palace and the hostages for several days before Somoza gave in to the Frente and agreed to release the prisoners, air a Frente communiqué on the radio, and pay a ten-million-dollar ransom. When the Frente commando was driven in buses to the airport for their journey to freedom in Venezuela, the road was lined with people cheering them and shouting "¡Abajo con Somoza!" And there, once again, was Chombo in the *Newsweek* photograph, sitting in front, his eyes barely visible above the red-and-black bandanna that shielded his face.

But to overthrow a dictatorship that's held power for forty-five years and has the full support of the U.S. government is not that easy. The insurrection of September 1978, which raged from Estelí in the north to Peñas Blancas in the south, almost toppled Somoza, but not quite. During this period of heavy military engagements, Chombo was everywhere. One week he would appear in the Southern Front along the border with Costa Rica; the next week, he'd be in Managua organizing the urban resistance.

When the Final Offensive exploded in the spring of 1979, Chombo was the political-military commander of the column "Oscar Pérez Cassar," the shock troops in the battle of Managua. His assignment was to attack the National Guard wherever they penetrated the Frente's defense line. Thirty-six days he fought in the barrios of the capital where he'd grown up, street by street, house by house, brick by brick, and always supported by the people who fed his troops and gave them shelter.

By June 26, with their ammunition running low, the Frente was forced to evacuate the barrios of Managua and make a tactical retreat. When the order to leave Managua was given to Chombo, it is said that he replied, with tears in his eyes, "I'd rather die here than take one step back." But he followed orders and led his column from Managua to Masaya, some thirty kilometers, traveling on foot and by night to avoid the National Guard patrols, and bringing with them many civilian supporters of the offensive. Once the Frente regrouped in Masaya, Chombo led the attack on Jinotega, which he captured on July 17. From there he stormed the National Guard fortress in Granada known as "La Pólvora." As dawn broke on July 19, 1979, Chombo was in control of Granada and was one of the top military commanders of the FSLN. When he entered Managua at the head of his column, the barrios where he had fought gave him a tumultuous welcome, the people showering him with flowers and firing weapons into the air. He was treated like a conquering hero by the adoring masses, and he was barely twenty-nine years old.

• • •

Over the next nine years, as the fortunes of the Nicaraguan Revolution seesawed, I ran into Chombo several times. He never lost his enthusiasm and he took on each task with the same fervor as always. For a while, he was head of the Policía Sandinista, and later, at the height of the Contra War, he was head of the Special Forces for the Ministry of the Interior. He was still a soldier, but he never lost his boyish charm, and he stayed humble, very close to the people. I remember that his favorite drink, even when he was a high-ranking *comandante*, was *remolacha*, made from sugar beets—typically Nicaraguan, typically down-home working class, typically Chombo.

Chombo was untainted by personal ambition; his desire was always the good of the people. One of the reasons he went so aggressively against the Contra as head of Special Forces was because the Contra was destroying what he was trying to build—schools, medical clinics, campesino cooperatives. He fought the Contras just as hard as he'd fought the National Guard, and he bloodied their noses several times, including at a remote Indian community called Mulukukú, where he destroyed a large Contra staging area.

What he wanted more than anything was a Nicaragua that belonged to Nicaraguans, a Nicaragua that was Nicaraguan, not a cheap imitation of Miami. It is the same dream of sovereignty that Latin Americans have dreamed since the time of Simón Bolívar. And he held this dream close to his heart, pure as the *sacuanjoche* flower that blooms on the plains of Nicaragua. And it was this trait, this purity of intention, that I so admired and that the Frente would need as the elections of 1990 approached.

By 1986 Chombo was already expressing his artistic talents in songwriting. He'd written a song that was accepted in the annual Gaston Song Competition in Managua. And in 1988, he had another song accepted for the competition. On November 1, 1988, he arrived in Managua from his post as representative of the Ministry of the Interior in León to hear the rehearsals of his song "Para olvidarte." He stayed several hours, chatting with the musicians, excited about the upcoming competition, and then left about 11:00 P.M. for the return trip to León.

Twenty minutes outside of Managua the driver of his jeep ran over a bundle of branches placed on the road. Chombo, who was riding in front, stirred from his nap to tell the driver "Cuidado," then he closed his eyes again. Neither Chombo nor the driver imagined that a hundred meters ahead a flatbed truck loaded with cement had broken down on the road, and the branches they'd just run over were meant to be a warning. By the time Chombo's driver saw the truck, it was too late. The jeep made contact with the flatbed exactly in the spot where Chombo was riding. He died instantly.

The FSLN declared a day of mourning in Chombo's honor. He was buried with full military honors and was posthumously awarded the Order of Carlos Fonseca and the Medal of Valor Pedro Arauz. Of all the people I have known, Chombo was the best, in all ways, the best true heart of Latin America, the best example of my generation—on either side of the border. You can come up with lots of reasons why Chombo died—fate, luck—but I say he was killed by the U.S. embargo of Nicaragua, which was an important part of the Contra War that robbed the country of basic goods, including spare parts for trucks or even a simple flare for roadside emergencies. Both the International Court of Justice (World Court) in The Hague and the United Nations condemned the United States for waging a terrorist war against Nicaragua, the only time in history that any government in the world has been cited by international bodies for acts of terrorism. Chombo was just one of sixty thousand dead Nicaraguans, casualties of the Contra War.[14]

On December 11, we held a memorial for him in La Mission, on Valencia Street at New College. Evelyn Martínez sang the Nicaraguan national anthem. The last soldiers of the old solidarity movement—Jack Hirschman, Nina Serrano, and myself—read poetry. The Coro Hispano of San Francisco, led by Juan Pedro Gaffney, offered choral renditions of sixteenth-century music, "Dios Itla Tonantzine" by the Maestro Azteca Hernán Franco and the more contemporary "Semilla" from Ecuador, then ended with Violeta Parra's "Gracias a la Vida." It was a moving tribute, and many Nicaraguans and North Americans came to pay their final respects to this humble giant of a man who'd given so much for the liberation of his people.

The following year was the tenth anniversary of the Nicaraguan Revolution. I went to Managua to be decorated by the government for ten years of solidarity work, although in truth, others had given their life, and whatever I had done was nothing compared with their sacrifice. The mood of the people seemed somewhat subdued, but the Frente was unwilling to admit that the Contra War had drained the energy of the revolution. One night in Managua, I was sitting with Roberto Vargas, and we were talking about the July 19 celebration, and we both came to the conclusion that something in the celebration was missing, an intangible something, and we agreed that it was Chombo. His absence was palpable.

The following year, the Frente lost the presidential election, not because they hadn't delivered their promise of a free Nicaragua, but because the people were tired of the Contra War, of being bombed and of having their children killed. The United States had won after all; it had imposed on Nicaragua a new regime that would immediately begin dismantling what the revolution had created.

I talked to Roberto by phone the day of the election; he was as shocked as I was. His last words to me were, "This wouldn't have happened if Chombo was alive." I hung up the phone, bitter and disillusioned. I felt that by losing Nicaragua, all of Latin America had lost an opportunity to make a better society. And now who knows when we'll have another chance.

That was long ago, the Nicaraguan Revolution of 1979, and this historical memory is lost to the new generation of Chicanos and the current residents of La Mission. It was soon after the elections of 1990 that I put away all those albums of Carlos Mejía Godoy with the songs we used to sing at the rallies and when going into combat: "El Cristo de Palacagüina," "Vivirás Monimbó," "La Tumba del Guerrillero," "Nicaragua, Nicaragüita," and all the rest. The memories associated with those songs haven't healed yet; they're still open wounds in my flesh. After ten-plus years of a "democratic capitalist" government, and in spite of not having to fight a costly Contra War during those years, Nicaragua is now the poorest country of Latin America, and in the Western Hemisphere is second only to Haiti in lowest per capita income. This is the great benefit of the Contra War sponsored by the United States. This is the great benefit of "democratic capitalism" imposed on Nicaragua.

Since I'm Chicano, I stayed here in La Mission. Chicanos don't have embassies, so our poets don't have diplomatic postings abroad to sharpen their international perspective. I'm still here. If you are ever in La Mission and you go by Twenty-fourth and Mission Street, you will find the BART station where we used to hold our rallies every Saturday. You will see the plaza we named Plaza Sandino, and across from it you'll see that the mural by Michael Ríos is still bright, as if he painted it yesterday. You will see lots of people coming and going; you will also most likely see an evangelist or two shouting into hand-held megaphones, preaching about something or other, but no one will be listening. Me? I see the ghost of Chombo, Walter Ferreti, the Last American Hero, wearing his cocky beret and holding high the red-and-black flag of the Frente. And just thinking of Chombo, and July 19, and Managua—which now resembles the city of the Somoza regime, with snot-nosed kids selling Chiclets on the streets and fourteen-year-old girls prostituting themselves for food—my neck muscles get tight with anger.

PETROGLYPH OF MEMORY

No one knows for certain what the indigenous population of California numbered when the first missionaries, soldiers, and *pobladores* arrived in 1769. Estimates range from 300,000 people to perhaps a million, grouped into thousands of communities.[1] If these figures are even remotely accurate, California supported the highest concentration of indigenous population in North America outside of central Mexico. The Native Americans lived quite well here; they were healthy, robust, and they depended on little or no agriculture. Theirs was a hunter-gatherer society, more gatherer than hunter, a society so in tune with nature's cycles that its members survived off the plenty the land provided, without much need for hard labor. The climate was so temperate that they went most of the year with a minimum of clothes or without clothes, as if they lived in the fabled Terrestrial Paradise.

The exact number of Native Americans who flourished here might be a point of debate, but what is not debatable is that these communities and cultures were exterminated with the same passion, if not the thoroughness, the Nazis applied to the extermination of the Jews. By 1850, when the United States solidified its grip on California, the Native American population had declined to 100,000 or 50,000, depending on your source. By 1900, barely 15,000 Native Americans were left in California.[2]

Everyone who lives in this state owes a debt to the people who came before us—but it's a debt no one seems too anxious to repay. The Native Americans were the first to explore the landscape, name it, and live with it. They founded their villages on sites so appealing that modern California follows their pattern: the Spaniards and Mexicans established their first presidios, missions, and pueblos on the same sites, and later, the Anglos constructed towns and cities in the same locations. Native Americans suffered the brunt of successive waves of invaders: all of us who came afterward, whether Spaniard, Mexican, or Anglo, contributed to their slaughter—some more than others, but each of us had a hand in it.

We all know a story of the Native American holocaust: how the Yahi, a peaceful tribe in the Sierra foothills, were massacred and the tribe's only survivor, Ishi, lived alone for decades in the area of Deer Creek, avoiding all contact with white men, until he was finally captured and, like a specimen of an exotic species, exhibited as the "Last Wild Indian" of California. But before Ishi, there was a woman, another lone survivor of her clan, who lived eighteen years in solitude on San Nicolas Island, until in 1853 she was brought ashore to Santa Barbara. By then all of her tribe were dead, and we can't even name her, since her language was lost. That she lived only a few weeks after coming into contact with "civilization" is perhaps not to be pitied.[3] We "the civilized" are in many ways the pitiful ones, for we have lost an irreplaceable piece of our memory.

Obviously, every attack on a village, every massacre of a family, every death of a child is a story. Who could possibly tell all the stories of the Native American holocaust? Like stars in the sky, these stories are too numerous to count. But as a Mexica who knows his indigenous roots, I am conscious that a part of me was exterminated, bludgeoned with clubs, split apart with axes, riddled with bullets, and it does affect me. I cannot look at the California landscape without feeling a sense of loss, of sadness, and sometimes of anger at what human beings do to each other.

Unfortunately, the destruction of Native Americans in California is usually considered ancient history, as if it had happened in Roman times or even further back. But Ishi lived into the twentieth century, and the last full-scale military action against Native Americans in California occurred in 1873; this holocaust is closer to us than the Civil War or the Gold Rush. I do not consider 130 years ago ancient history; to me it is current events, so I see no point in closing my eyes and forgetting. The Native American Holocaust is barely twice the distance in time from the Jewish Holocaust of World War II, but our modern sensibilities are fogged with amnesia. And it is a holocaust ignored, glossed over, nearly erased from the slate of memory—a holocaust without a monument.

• • •

As a young man growing up in the San Fernando Valley, I was first introduced to arrowheads from the Borax Lake area by my friend and neighbor Dr. Mark Harrington. According to Harrington, Borax Lake is one of the oldest archaeological sites in California, dating to about 15,000 years before the present era. Many years later, when I was researching this book, I visited Borax Lake, where Harrington had excavated in the late 1930s and early 1940s. Actually, the area, which is about a two-hour drive from San Francisco, has a pair of lakes. One is Clear Lake, a popular recreation spot where people go camping on weekends, and the other is Borax Lake, a smaller version where no one goes at all. On the west side of Clear Lake, a still active volcano, Mount Konocti, rises 4,200 feet in an almost perfect cone barely eroded by the elements, though it was formed between 400,000 and 250,000 years ago.[4]

Both lakes are in dirt-poor Lake County, where nearly one-third of the population is on Supplemental Security Income (SSI), and everyone seems to live in a trailer. The residents are mostly Mexicans and African Americans, with a sprinkling of whites to add variety.

Harrington, in his study published by the Southwest Museum in 1948, had been quite precise as to the exact location he'd excavated in the dry bed of the lake.[5] I didn't know what I expected to find, but I was curious to see one of the oldest known sites of human habitation in California and the United States. Since my map didn't indicate any roads leading to Borax Lake, I more or less relied on intuition as to where the lake might be. Once I reached Clear Lake, I followed Arrowhead Road, an obvious reference to the abundance of arrowheads in the area, till I came over a hill; then, as I drove down a narrow road, I spotted a small body of grayish water cupped at the bottom of a little valley.

The town of Clear Lake has spread as far as this smaller, unused lake; on the south side of Borax Lake the mobile homes sit on the edge of the water. I stopped about fifty feet from the lake as two dogs ran out from their master's mobile home barking angrily at my car. I rolled up the windows and looked at the lake. Although I could make out a walnut grove on the opposite shore, a key landmark I was searching for, it was not quite like the pictures I had seen in Harrington's 1948 study. During Harrington's excavation, the lake was nearly dried up, covering only a small portion of the northeast end of the valley. But now nearly the whole ancient lake floor was flooded, and the trailer homes nearest the shore were sandbagged to stave off the rising waters. On the far side of Borax Lake, tractors were excavating and trucks were hauling dirt away. A woman emerged from the trailer and yelled at her dogs to shut up. After the dogs retreated, I left my car and asked her what was going on across the lake. She said they were building a winery. Her teeth had gone bad, and she spoke in the halting rhythm of someone suffering the aftermath of delirium tremens.

The water in the lake was murky, muddy, and unappealing. I couldn't even reach the water's edge without sloshing through several yards of black muck, and the entire shoreline was thick with cattails and thistles that thrived in the ooze. In front of the woman's trailer, several worn tires half stuck out of the mud, and an old plywood platform, perhaps once used for diving, appeared to be sinking into the water. It took a certain amount of imagination to picture this site attracting even the most hard-core wine-sipping tourist.

She spread her arm toward the lake. "Beautiful, isn't it?"

"Yes." I said. "Beautiful."

But we weren't looking at the same lake. I had no idea what she was referring to, and meanwhile, I was trying to imagine what it must have looked like during Harrington's visit, and even further back in time when Native Americans came here to chip arrowheads or to bathe in the healing thermal waters.

Across the lake I could see the walnut grove where Harrington had laid out the excavation trenches, but the water had now risen partly into the grove. I asked her about the water level in the lake. She was a native of Clear Lake, and she pointed out where the water level had been when she was a girl. It confirmed what the photos showed: in the past decades the lake had been one-fourth this size. I asked her when the water level had started rising and if she knew why.

According to her explanation, about ten years ago a construction company had sunk a shaft near the center of the lake, apparently to test if the lake bottom could support a floating structure, perhaps a hotel or a wine bar or something. Instead, the exploratory shaft had punctured the lake bottom and unexpectedly tapped into an underground water source that ever since had made the water level rise, year by year. She pointed to a spot in the lake about ten feet from the shoreline: "Just last year the water reached over there. Now look where it is."

I felt disappointed, thinking perhaps Harrington's excavation site was lost. I asked her if she'd ever found arrowheads, and she said no, but that others had. Then I looked at the ground and couldn't believe my eyes. Shiny black glasslike obsidian fragments covered the area I was standing on. I scooped up a handful for a closer look and saw that granite pebbles were mixed in with the black glass. Still, though I had expected to find some obsidian, its abundance was amazing. This got me excited again, and I told her what I was looking for—Harrington's old dig. I even showed her the book with his photos, and that seemed to spark something in her, and she nodded her head excitedly.

She pulled her stringy hair back and seemed to shake a little. "I knew it, I knew it," she said, her eyes shiny. "There's something special about this place."

Suddenly, as if embarrassed by her emotions, she confessed that she was an alcoholic and had been in detox for a month. Her boyfriend had left her alone while he went into Clear Lake for some groceries, but he should be back any minute. I asked her for directions to the walnut grove. I got a general idea of how to get there and then left quickly, not wanting to linger in her sad life.

On the other side of the lake, the mobile homes were not quite as run-down nor were they as close to the water. I parked my car and walked to the lake's edge. The mud oozed under my feet, and the pussy willows, thistles, and marsh grasses grew thick. The nose-curling scent of sulfur filled the air, and bubbles, rising from underground thermal sources, broke the lake's surface. To the side of the walnut grove I found what I believed was the alluvial fan, the small mound of earth Harrington had excavated. I got as close as I could to it, but the thick reeds and mud kept me from actually reaching the top of the mound. Instead, I stood at the base, now at the water's edge, and from this position, I faced northwest over Borax Lake, with the construction site of the winery to my right. A handful of western geese honked overhead, and a flock of pintail ducks swam in the lake. I tried not to see the old tires, the broken-up couches, or the busted television dumped in the mud; instead I imagined what the site had looked like 15,000 years ago, and only then could I see the beauty of the land. The hills surrounding the lake were beautiful, and the lake itself seemed alive in spite of the debris floating on it. I closed my eyes and tried to pick out the cacophony of sounds — geese, ducks, and redwing blackbirds that sounded like crying babies. The chorus went on and on; I must have stood there thirty minutes, and the living landscape was not silent for a second.

For thousands of years, this lake was the obsidian source for many Native Americans, precursors to the Miwok and Pomo, with different groups arriving each season to make arrowheads, hunt the water fowl, and take the thermal mineral waters of the lake. Indigenous people from all over California and the Southwest knew of this spot and camped here at different times of the year. Harrington also found pestles, metates, flake knives, choppers, and different types of rounded, pointed, keeled, and serrated scrapers. Among the cultures Harrington identified by the arrowheads and other artifacts he found there were the Folsom, Lake Mohave, and Pinto Basin; the Chiricahua stage of Cochise culture; and the Early Sacramento and Sandia cultures. This site had cradled the first human settlements in California, yet there wasn't even a simple marker to indicate any of that.

As the sun started to set, I made my way back to the car, but not before I picked up more pieces of obsidian, sharp as razors, several of them looking as if human hands had worked them. The pieces were beautiful, bright and shiny, and I wondered if the people living in the mobile homes understood their relation to this spot. World War II had disrupted Harrington's work, especially the gas rationing and other restrictions on civilian mobility. Harrington never came back to Borax Lake to discover what other treasures or insights this place might have revealed. Now, what we might have learned about California's first inhabitants will be lost with the rising level of the lake. Future generations might come here to sip wine, if they come at all, but they will not know the real treasure that we threw away like trash.

● ● ●

One hundred and fifty miles north of Borax Lake, Mount Shasta, a stunning, glacier-dressed volcano, peaks at 14,162 feet, dominating the landscape of Modoc land. If you scan east from Mount Shasta, you'll see a pattern of lakes: Lower Klamath Lake, Tule Lake, and, further east, Clear Lake (this is a different lake, not to be confused with the larger twin of Borax Lake), and Goose Lake. This Clear Lake is anything but clear, though it is the source of the Lost River. This river has no outlet to the sea: it rises out of Clear Lake in California, then swings through the Langell Valley in a northwesterly arc into Oregon, then through the Lost River Valley, sometimes seeming "lost" as it disappears beneath the earth, forming natural bridges, before finally spilling into Tule Lake. In this landscape, the wind is constant and untamed, pine forests grow thick, and ancient lava flows crosshatch the terrain. The Tule Lake area in general is pocked with evidence of volcanic activity. Seven thousand years ago the volcanic explosion of Mount Mazama, seventy miles away, covered the whole region with a cloud of fine gray ash. Even now, Mount Shasta smokes and trembles. Lava flows, fumaroles, flues, and ice caves are all distinct features of the landscape. It is easy to see why indigenous people incorporated nature into their world-view.

● ● ●

About a half mile from present-day Tule Lake, a rocky escarpment rises above the landscape. This escarpment was created some 270,000 years ago when magma, hot molten lava, burst through a fault, or crack, in the earth's crust and made contact with the water of Lake Modoc. The contrasting temperatures of the hot magma and the cold water caused an eruption that hurled fragments of suddenly cooled lava skyward, and when these fell back to earth, they piled up around the vent, forming a layer of volcanic material called tuff, which eventually became what is now called Petroglyph Point.

The Modoc have their own creation story of Petroglyph Point. Their creator god, Kumookumpts—or Kamookumchux, sometimes Kmu-kamtch—while resting on the shores of Tule Lake, looked around, saw nothing but water, and decided to make land. Kumookumpts, a dual god who was both male and female, scooped mud from the lake bottom and with this created the land and the mountains. The creator god also made everything in the world: rivers and streams, mountains and valleys, plants, animals, and humans. Kumookumpts made humans by throwing bones from a basket. He threw the Modoc last and said to them: "You will eat what I eat, you will keep my place when I am gone, you will be bravest of all. Though you may be few, even if many people come against you, you will kill them."[6]

When the creator god finished, Kumookumpts, tired from so much work, dug a hole under Tule Lake in which to sleep. And to mark the spot, Kumookumpts left the escarpment I'm referring to, which the Modoc consider the center of the earth.

For thousands of years after humans entered the Klamath–Tule Lake Basin, Petroglyph Point was an island in the middle of Tule Lake. The people were drawn to this island-rock under which Kumookumpts slept. They would paddle their canoes to the island's cliffs, and as they bobbed in the water, they would peck and drill designs on the soft rock. Perhaps these symbols are no more than youthful attempts by an Indian teenager to impress an Indian maiden, perhaps they are attempts to communicate with their gods, or perhaps they merely represent the age-old desire of humans to leave their mark, their tag on a wall.

• • •

Although not yet conclusively proven, evidence indicates that the Clear Lake watershed area ten miles east of Tule Lake might be the oldest continuously occupied area of western North America. Clovis points, distinctly chipped spearpoints used by the prehistoric Llano people to hunt mammoth, have been found in the Clear Lake–Lost River Circle. Clovis points predate Folsom points, which are usually found in association with Pleistocene-age bison. The Clovis points found in the Clear Lake watershed indicate that hunters were active here 12,000 to 15,000 years ago. (There's also evidence of atlatls, the arrow darts common throughout the Southwest and Mesoamerica that predate the bow and arrow.) Other artifacts found around Clear Lake and the shores of Lost River include the great quantity of bolas, hand-shaped stones that were hurled with a leather sling at the target, usually waterfowl or small game. Bolas predate the invention or introduction of bows and arrows in North America. They have been found as far south as Argentina, in association with the remains of the extinct sloth, the horse, and the camel, and are the precursors of the weapon the modern-day gauchos of the pampas still use.[7]

In the 1960s, on the banks of Sheepy Creek near Lower Klamath Lake, in the heart of Modoc country, Carrol Howe, an amateur archaeologist, discovered the earliest known settlements of indigenous communities in California. The Modoc called the site Shapasheni, the whites changed it to Sheepy Island, and Howe named it Night Fire Island, because of the evidence of many campfires. It seems likely, from the discovery of ancient pestles and mortars and other human artifacts at Night Fire Island, that the Llano culture of Clear Lake served as a cradle from which future genera- tions developed and eventually spread into the Tule Lake Basin about 11,500 years ago.[8]

If the Modoc are descendants of the Llano people, who roamed as far south as Central America, they are not an isolated community but are related to other clans of the continent. Their name derives from Modokus, the chief under whom they seceded from the Klamath Indians to form their own independent tribe in the early 1800s. The land occupied by the three Modoc clans was the area around Lost River and Tule Lake.

A brief catalogue of Modoc society follows: The people were of fine physique, rugged, with prominent cheekbones and thick, sensual lips. They oblongated the foreheads of their babies as a sign of beauty, as the Maya did. They had a predilection for tobacco, smoking it in intricately decorated clay or stone pipes. The women as well as the men tattooed their bodies, cutting their flesh with fish hooks or obsidian knives, then rubbing char- coal into the skin. The women often tattooed a design that resembled three vertical lines on their chins. They had a means of contraception, a decoc- tion of squaw carpet (*Cenaothus prostratus*) that, if taken for a long time in small doses, would reduce excessive menstruation and eventually prevent conception.[9]

The Modoc sense of government was based on community participation: major tribal decisions were taken in a community council, where every point of view was patiently listened to.[10] They cremated their dead, includ- ing those killed in wars against neighboring tribes, painting the bodies an ochre red and burning all the deceased's material goods along with the body.[11] They were pragmatists who tested their perceptions with practice, and if the theory worked, it was considered the right way.

They hunted the abundant game in the region of Tule Lake: bear, mule deer, bighorn sheep, and geese and ducks of all kinds. The Modoc also used the bolas to hunt waterfowl, trapping them with the cords. The lake pro- vided turtles, trout, and shellfish such as freshwater mussels, shrimp, and oysters; camas, onion-like bulbs, and ipo tubers; even seeds of edible water plants, like the wocus, or yellow waterlily. The pliable tule reed, which grew plentifully, provided material for construction of wickiups and rafts.

In the summer, the Modoc wore little clothing, a loincloth for men and grass skirts for women, while their kids ran naked. In winter, they wore fur coats or goose-feather blankets and built lodges for protection from temperatures that sometimes dipped below twenty degrees. They used sweat lodges for purification (like all California Indians) and for relaxation (like modern Californians). I think it is possible that sweat lodges originated in Modoc land, since the oldest remains of a sweat lodge, carbon-14 dated to 1,500 years ago, were uncovered at Night Fire Island.[12]

The truth is, without romanticizing their intertribal wars or primitive technology, the Modoc lived in about as good a world as could be hoped for. Really, you'd have to describe their life as a perpetual camping trip in one of the most beautiful, fecund, and awe-inspiring places in the world. The land, with its thermal springs, solidified lava flues, and vast pine forests; its rivers and lakes filled with fish and waterfowl; and dominated by the awesome sight of Mount Shasta, inspired in them a profound respect for their natural surroundings. As corny as it sounds to our modern sensibilities, the guiding tenet of their religion was to live in harmony with nature.

If you go to Petroglyph Point, you can still see the rock carvings. The U.S. Bureau of Land Reclamation has pumped Tule Lake nearly dry, so you don't have to paddle to the hill in a canoe as the Indians did. You merely drive to the site, park, and walk about thirty feet to where the barbed wire is wrapped around the point. Behind the barbed wire are the petroglyphs, geometric rock carvings done by human hands nearly 5,000 years ago. And interspersed with the ancient symbols you'll find modern ones, initials and hearts and whatnot that modern humans have carved. Sometimes these modern humans have destroyed the petroglyphs with hammers, as if they are hated reminders of another time and another people. And Tule Lake is a lake in name only; more properly it is a sump, a place where water is gathered for irrigation. The water goes to the barley and alfalfa farms around the lake, then is spilled into the Lower Klamath Refuge. Waterfowl of all kinds still gather along the water's edge, the basin having been turned into a nature preserve some time ago. The sandpipers, cranes, gulls, white pelicans, and, especially in the fall, the snow geese arrive by the thousands, too numerous to count. But already the lake is less than 2 percent of its original size, and it's not hard to see that within perhaps another decade there won't be any water left here; only the whitish alkali residue of evaporation will mark the onetime lake.

•   •   •

Obviously, no one had written of the Modoc in 1826, the year they came into contact with the whites. At this time some three thousand Modoc are living in their traditional homelands, the area of the Klamath–Tule Lake Basin and the Lost River, which they call "the Smile of God." The Modoc villages are spread over some 5,000 square miles of hunting range. The first Modoc-white encounter occurs when hunters and trappers of the Hudson Bay Company appear in the region, heavily armed and leading mule trains loaded with impressive material goods. Although the hunters and trappers of the Hudson Bay Company are not a threat to the Modoc, the Modoc way of life is definitively altered by contact with Europeans. Slowly, the new materialism (in modern terms: consumerism) introduced by the traders, the desire for goods never known before—rifles, mirrors, and in particular horses—changes the power base of Modoc society. The younger generation, intrigued by these Western ways and material goods, turn from their traditional life and leaders. The shamans lose influence, and the hereditary chiefs are challenged. As Keith A. Murray writes in *The Modocs and Their War*, "White miners crossed the Indian hunting ranges. Whites disturbed the streams. White traders changed their economic way of life. White settlers fenced the meadows along the lakes, white religious teachers upset the traditional Modoc system of ethical behavior."[13]

The initial contacts with whites augur a series of disasters for the Modoc. In less than fifty years the Modoc will be reduced to 153 prisoners confined to an Oklahoma reservation. A catalogue of their destruction must include the following: in 1830, a brutal winter during which their food stocks are lost weakens the tribe; in 1846, the Emigrant Road is cut through Modoc land, further disturbing and threatening the Modoc existence. Then in 1848 more settlers arrive, some searching for gold, others for land, and a smallpox epidemic ravages the native villages, wiping out whole bands of Modoc. By 1851, whatever gold there was in the Klamath–Tule Lake Basin had been found, and the new settlers trekked west, mostly to farm. Especially after the Civil War, thousands of young men, freed from the constraints of military service and hungry for a new beginning, start pouring into the area of the Oregon-California border.[14] The problem is that Modoc people are already living on that land.

For the next two decades a low-intensity war is fought between the Modoc and the settlers, which follows a recurring pattern: The settlers occupy Modoc land, and then the Modoc attempt to force them out by attacking their farms and emigrant trains. This causes the whites to retaliate by attacking Indian villages, leading the Modoc to strike back at settlers, and thus it goes, back and forth. The conflict flares up and dies, then flares up again. Since it is Modoc lands being invaded, I do not consider them the aggressors in this struggle.

One of the bloodiest incidents occurs in 1852 when a notorious Indian killer named Ben Wright leads the massacre of a Modoc village on the Lost River. Wright enters the village under a flag of truce but personally guns down the Modoc chief at point-blank range, which is the signal for the attack to begin. The Modoc are caught unprepared and are ruthlessly slaughtered. The son of the chief whom Wright guns down is a young man named Keintpoos, who favors peace and living with the whites. Keintpoos is not in the village that morning, but of the five Modoc who survive the Lost River massacre, one of them is John Skonches, who will later be a subchief to Keintpoos during the final armed hostilities with the whites.[15] Remember this truce business when we reach 1873.

There was no real reason why the white settlers didn't get along with the Modoc, except the settlers' paranoia, greed, and inbred hatred of Indians. Despite the antagonism between the two cultures, the Modoc were quite willing to adapt to Western ways. The men cut their hair short after the Western fashion; they also wore cowboy clothes, and the women, Western dresses; they used Western goods and often worked on Western farms. The Modoc didn't necessarily hate the white man; in fact, many of them often visited the Yreka mining district, where, like modern-day tourists, they marveled at the trappings of "big city life." In spite of his father's murder, Keintpoos himself, ironically enough, was a strong advocate of getting along with the whites and considered many of them his friends. So how he winds up as a leader of Indian resistance is a lesson in the failure of both diplomacy and human relations.

Regardless of the Modoc efforts to assimilate into the white world, the conflict between them and the settlers continued to simmer. By 1861, settlers had their eyes on the Lost River–Tule Lake area as ideal for farming and cattle raising, and they started pressuring the local military authorities for a solution to the Modoc "problem." They wanted the Modoc confined to reservations. Native Americans have long seen the reservation as nothing more than a concentration camp meant to destroy the body as well as the spirit of those restricted within its fences. That any Native Americans survived to tell of reservation life is a small miracle in itself. Some of the older Modoc leaders, like Old Skonches, brother of John Skonches, were willing to give up their freedom and accept the reservation life, but one clan was not.

• • •

The Modoc were in fact three different clans: the Gumbatwa, "people of the west," who lived in the area around Tule Lake; the Kokiwa, "people of the far-out country," who lived in the far reaches of Lost River, with many villages in the Langell Valley; and the Paskanwa, "river people," of the Lost River Valley.[16] Each clan was headed by a shaman (or religious leader), a military leader (for war), and, for want of a better term, a chief. The chief would be considered the political leader in regard to domestic affairs.[17] Keintpoos (whose father had been killed by Wright in 1852) was the nominal leader of the Modoc clan that rejected the reservation, and his clan lived in the area around Lost River, west of Tule Lake. As the Modoc came in contact with the white man, they were given English nicknames that somewhat replicated the sound of their native names. Keintpoos was nicknamed "Captain Jack" as a sort of joke, but I will use his Modoc name in the narrative that follows.[18] Keintpoos, in fact, knew no English, so how the name "Captain Jack" sounded to his ears is impossible to gauge.

Keintpoos is about thirty-seven years old when the final struggle for Modoc survival begins. This means that he lived his entire life within the span of the white man's arrival in Modoc country, and he therefore witnessed the decline of the Modoc from several thousand to the three hundred or so that left the reservation with him. For Keintpoos and the Modoc, the issue is simple: survival or extinction.

In the photograph of Keintpoos after his capture, he is wearing the striped collarless shirt of a prisoner—a prisoner of war, I might add. His hair is straight and falls just below his ear in a pageboy haircut, his eyes look sad, but his mouth shows no hatred, though I know he was angry with those who'd pushed him to war, like Ha-kar-jim, and then betrayed him to his enemies. But you do not see the anger in his face. He looks a lot like Ishi, with his dark skin, long eyelashes, and high cheekbones. He could be a model for a monument to Native Americans, to every Native American who fought for his homeland. I have the same skin, eyes, cheeks, hair, and buried rage. At times, while I was writing this chapter, I felt Keintpoos had taken possession of me, as if he was guiding me to those places where I could best understand his fight, which is why I visited the Lava Beds.

One night, about two in the morning, after a particularly hard struggle to write the story of the Modoc, when the words seemed to vanish from the screen, I shut down the computer and went to wash up. I left the bathroom light off I was so tired, and as I looked at myself in the dim light that leaked in from the streetlamp, a shadow seemed to pass over my reflection in the mirror. For an instant, I saw not myself but Keintpoos. I rubbed my eyes. When I looked again there was no one in the mirror but me. Of course, this was nothing more than a trick of my tired imagination, but I determined then to keep on with the story even when it seemed that to remember it would heal nothing.

There is another photo of Keintpoos, a sepia-toned dual portrait with John Skonches, taken soon after the two men were captured. Although Keintpoos is shackled at the ankle to Skonches, he stands with such beauty and utter grace he appears to be a ballet dancer, a breathtaking young Baryshnikov in chains. Skonches is older than Keintpoos, and he looks like a grizzled veteran, a hardened survivor of the white man's genocide. He is a thick-necked, bearlike man, with a turned-down mouth and a few white stubby whiskers on his chin, who will walk the gallows with Keintpoos. Two other Modoc will be hung with Keintpoos: his half brother, Te-te-tea-us (Black Jim), and a tall, splendidly built nineteen-year-old warrior named Bostin-Ah-gar.[19]

Other members of Keintpoos's Modoc clan include the shaman, Choocks, alias Woman Doctor–Medicine Man, known to the whites as Curly-Headed Doctor; and the half Modoc–half Pit River Indian Chik-chack-am (Scar Face Charley), whose right cheek was scarred from falling off a wagon as a boy. Other Modoc who fought in the Lava Beds can only be named by what the whites called them: Big Ike, Comstock Dave, Long Jim, Miller's Charley, Buckskin Doctor, Greasy Boots, Pit River Man, Curly-Haired Jack, Skukum Horse, Duffy, Sam, Mallie, Jerry.[20]

The Modoc women must also be mentioned. Some of the white settlers considered Keintpoos's sister, Ko-a-lak-a, Hard-Working Woman (Queen Mary), "the brains" behind the Modoc. She knew the ways of the whites, having lived with a white man in Yreka at one time. She was a trader, carrying out business in Yreka, and served as a liaison between the Modoc and whites—as a diplomat, in other words—and on one occasion, she is clearly the spokesperson.[21] Her story, along with those of women such as One-Eyed Dixie, Lizzie, Lauw-Lauw-Waush (Wild Gal), a half sister to Keintpoos, and others, needs to be further explored. In the photograph of three Modoc women and a girl captured after the battle in the Lava Beds, Hard-Working Woman, the other two Modoc females, and even the child, a daughter of Keintpoos, are all wearing Western-style dresses, showing just how much they had assimilated. But they also wear the straw basket hats, the traditional headdress of Modoc women, which shows that even in captivity they were resisting, asserting their identity as Modoc Indians.[22]

• • •

To reach the Lava Beds National Monument you must first pass some of the poorest towns in California. North of Redding on I-5, you take the turnoff toward Tule Lake at the town of Weed. You drive through Dorris, and later Newell, mirror images of Latin America, with houses from another century, tar-paper walls, corrugated tin roofs, barking dogs in every yard, and heaps of smoldering trash everywhere. My first impression was that I'd stepped into a time warp, but, no, this is merely the forgotten part of California, so far behind it will never catch up to the present.

• • •

In 1864 Keintpoos asked for and received a treaty from the Indian agent nominally in charge on the Oregon-California border, Judge Elisha Steele. The fundamental points of the treaty were that the Indians would quit raiding the white settlers and would obey the laws of the United States, including submission to punishment by the U.S. Army should they break the law. In return, they were allowed to be small businessmen, traders, and guides; to operate ferries for wages; and to stay at Lost River.[23] What more could a civilized society ask for?

Unfortunately, this was not enough to appease the white settlers and many of them demanded a more stringent control over the Modoc, whom they insisted were a threat and must be removed to a reservation. In particular, Keintpoos's clan had a reputation for living their own lives, in their own ways. At the same time, the white settlers refused to accept that Indians could live in "civilized ways." To complicate matters further, the Office of Indian Affairs ignored the treaty with Steele, hoping to arrange for a treaty of their own.[24] Succeeding agents after Steele were as incompetent as they were ignorant of Modoc ways.

At first, Keintpoos brought his clan to live on the Klamath Reservation with other Modoc and Shasta Indians, but this was not Modoc land, and issues soon arose. The Klamath were not friendly toward the Modoc, and the Shasta were old enemies. Keintpoos soon became discouraged with reservation life, and in April 1870, he chose to leave the reservation for his traditional home along the Lost River. This was their land, and they wanted desperately to continue living in the place they called "the Smile of God."

When Keintpoos's clan reached the Lost River, they found their land occupied by white settlers. The Modoc built two camps at the river's mouth, where it flows into Tule Lake, and challenged any white man, civilian or soldier, to disturb them. None did, and thus things stood for the next two years. Some of the younger braves often dropped in unannounced at settlers' cabins and sometimes badgered them for occupying Modoc land, but it was a relatively peaceful, if tense, relationship. During this time Keintpoos and other Modoc moved freely back and forth to Yreka, where Keintpoos was often seen and welcomed by white men who were his friends. He might have thought this situation could have lasted indefinitely, but if he did, he was mistaken.

• • •

One thing seems clear—the conflict is not a war, although it is always referred to as the Modoc War. Technically, for the conflict to be a war, the United States Congress would have had to declare hostilities between the two sides. But apart from the technicalities, the newspapers of the time, like television now, captured the public's attention with grand phrases like "the Modoc War." But even a cursory evaluation of the combatants deflates the term "war" and forces us to reconsider our language. On one side we have the United States, an industrial power with big cities, financial centers, a transcontinental railroad, a standing army, and a navy if needed; and on the other side, a handful of families whose main weapon is their courage and intimate knowledge of the terrain. This is not a war. We need to redefine the relationship between this powerful nation and this minuscule group of Modoc; we need to give the conflict its proper value—"a military aggression," perhaps, or "a forced relocation."

The military aggression against the Modoc that began in November 1872 had nothing to do with their fierceness, or their sometime occupation as raiders and slave traders, or their quarrelsomeness with neighboring tribes, or their description as savages, or any of the tags used by apologists to justify their forced relocation. The Modoc never said the white settlers couldn't live with them; it was the white settlers who didn't want the Modoc as their neighbors. This animosity, coupled with a series of muddled orders between the army and the Bureau of Indian Affairs, results in the attacks on the Modoc camps at Lost River.[25]

On November 29, 1872, two groups of Modoc, one headed by Keintpoos and one by Ha-kar-jim, were living along the Lost River when, without warning or a declaration of war, a combined force of soldiers and civilian volunteers attempts to arrest Keintpoos and other Modoc leaders. When Chik-chack-am resists, a gunfight breaks out between the two groups. The exact figure of how many Modoc were killed that morning is not really known. The Modoc claim that one Indian brave and several squaws were killed. Both sides agree that at least one Indian baby was torn apart by a blast from a sawed-off shotgun. But it gets worse. After the Modoc fled, the soldiers entered the camp and torched the wickiups, burning to death an old woman who had been left behind. Perhaps the death of the old woman was accidental, as some historians claim, although I'm sure "accidental" didn't mean much to the dead woman.

In the confusion that followed the early dawn attack, Keintpoos escaped, and in a freezing rain led the surviving Modoc across Tule Lake, a thirteen-mile journey, taking what they could carry on their rafts. They reached the Lava Beds, the place they called the Land of Burnt-Out Fires, a nearly impenetrable area of volcanic rocks and caves, and there, in desperate and depressing conditions, they regrouped.

While Keintpoos headed to the Lava Beds, another group of Modoc, led by Ha-kar-jim, John Skonches, and Cho-ocks, the shaman, circled the north side of Tule Lake, stopping only to take revenge on white settlers, killing all the males they could find—fourteen in all. But even these revenge-crazed Modoc left the white women and children unharmed. In contrast to Ha-kar-jim's group, Chik-chack-am (Scarface Charlie), one of the bravest

Modoc warriors, warned several white ranchers, including Pressly Dorris, a white man he considered a friend, to stay away from the region or they might be killed.

In the days that followed, a small band of Modoc from the Hot Creek area around Lower Klamath Lake, who were under the leadership of Shack-nasty Jim, sought advice from John Fairchild, a settler who farmed the area around Tule Lake and had good relations with the Modoc. Fairchild offered to escort them back to the Klamath Reservation, but rumors reached the Hot Creek Modoc that Oregon civilians were planning to hang them or burn them at the stake, and this makes them change their minds and decide, along with Ha-kar-jim's renegade group, to join Keintpoos at the Lava Beds. Thus all three Modoc clans are represented in the Lava Beds. But other non-Modoc Indians also joined them: Bogus Charley, an Umpqua Indian; warriors from the Columbia River; one from the Pit River; and some from the coast tribes.[26] The subsequent battle in the Lava Beds pits the Modoc and these other warriors against the settlers and the U.S. Army; the Indians' heavily outnumbered status makes this the most heroic stance in American history, overshadowing the Alamo and even the Battle of Chapultepec Castle in the War of 1846.

Throughout the winter of 1872–1873, the Modoc stayed in the Lava Beds, defying the army's efforts to drive them out. At the same time, they kept up a series of talks with a commission of military and Indian agents, trying to resolve the conflict. For the whites, the issue was simple: either the Modoc went to a reservation or they would be killed. By January 1873, the army had mustered 175 soldiers, 104 civilian volunteers, and 20 Klamath scouts, outfitted with howitzers, who were ready to attack about 55 Modoc warriors.[27]

The soldiers who fought against the Modoc that winter of 1872–1873 did so because they were getting paid $13 a month. It's as simple as that. I don't believe they had any particular vested interest in dying. A letter written by Major J. G. Trimble, often cited by historians, captured the mood of many soldiers as they bivouacked that winter in the field: "And for what? To drive a couple of hundred miserable aborigines from a desolate natural shelter in the wilderness, that a few thieving cattle-men might ranch their wild steers in a scope of isolated country, the dimensions of some several reasonable-sized counties."[28]

The Modoc fought because they had no choice. In theory, the Modoc could be at peace with the settlers and the U.S. government as long as their own space, laws, identity, and land went unchallenged. But once their space was violated, what were the rules of engagement? If we see the question through "Western eyes," then the rules are the white courts, laws, and theories of space, land, surveyors, and title maps—a bizarre concept to begin with. But seen through Modoc eyes, their fiercely independent spirit declared: I am a human being, not a dog, I will not live in captivity on a reservation. Talk to me with respect and I will listen, and then we can live together and share this land.

You don't need to be a wizard to divine that people will fight for their survival with all the will, energy, and cunning they possess, and if not for their survival, then for their children's survival.

• • •

The soldiers soon start calling the area of the Lava Beds that the Modoc occupy the Stronghold. In reality, the Stronghold is no more than a natural configuration of the volcanic landscape, made up of tunnels, caves, and glass-sharp rocks. For the most part it was the skill of the Modoc in using the terrain, the caves, and the passageways through the Lava Beds that gave them the upper hand defensively. In contrast, the army knew very little about this landscape. Nevertheless, the army, blindly overconfident, attacked the Modoc on January 16, 1873.

Before the army attacked, Cho-ocks, the shaman, led the Modoc in the Ghost Dance, an all-night mystical ritual enacted to help them destroy the white soldiers, return to their native lands, and resurrect the dead Modoc. The Ghost Dance, which would later spread to other indigenous communities desperate to stave of extinction, had been introduced by a Walker River Paiute. In many ways, it was the last hope for those Native Americans desiring to defeat the United States. Cho-ocks also built a circle of eight consecrated stakes around the Stronghold and linked them with red rope of braided tule fibers, promising that this magic would keep the soldiers out.[29] As their standard, the Modoc erected a medicine flag on a heap of stones: a mink's skin and the tail feathers of the Medicine Hawk with a white medicine ball tied to the end of a four-foot stick. Cho-ocks promised that no Modoc would die and that he would call down a tule fog to make them invisible to the soldiers' bullets.[30]

As the soldiers approached the Lava Beds, a heavy fog descended and they soon lost their way amidst the crevices and lava flows. The Modoc, who were in their natural surroundings, picked off the disoriented soldiers one by one. By late afternoon, the army was in full retreat, abandoning their dead and war materiel. No soldier had crossed Cho-ocks's red medicine rope, no Modoc had been killed, and the Indians had captured enough supplies to last them weeks, if not months, including government-issued Springfield rifles and a pair of field glasses. The Modoc did what every guerrilla army does—used the enemy to supply their needs. But John

Skonches, for one, didn't believe in Cho-ocks's power. He saw it was the bullets that stopped the soldiers dead.

After this debacle, the head of the army in the Pacific Northwest, General E. R. S. Canby, formally took command of the battlefield. While acting as the head of the military operations, Canby also served as a member of the so-called Peace Commission that was trying to negotiate a Modoc withdrawal from the Lava Beds and return them to the reservation. Keintpoos tried to negotiate a peaceful solution to the Modoc crisis. Among the Modoc in the Lava Beds, the warhawks Ha-kar-jim, Cho-ocks, and John Skonches wanted a war to the finish, while Keintpoos and Chik-chack-am advocated peace. Keintpoos's failure to achieve a consensus among the diverse opinions of his people, opinions that had to be listened to, is understandable, but it was also his tragedy. Only while under direct attack did the Modoc move as a unified body; the rest of the time they operated as different clans at odds with each other. Yet while Keintpoos offered different possible solutions to resolve the crisis, the so-called Peace Commission was fixed in its position: the Modoc who killed the settlers after the attack on Lost River would be tried for murder, and all the Modoc must be removed to Oklahoma. It was Canby's rigid stance vis-à-vis the Modoc that led to his assassination.

After the first battle of the Stronghold, a truce was established between the two sides, although Canby, while talking peace, followed a tactic of "gradual compression." He brought in more troops, ordered an increase in patrols, and moved observation posts nearer the Lava Beds. When a patrol of soldiers captured thirty-three Modoc ponies, Canby refused to return them—a blatant violation of the truce. On April 1, Canby moved his headquarters and a sizable contingent of troops to a bluff just three miles from the Modoc Stronghold.[31] Thus, it was obvious that during the truce Canby continued to take aggressive actions, which only proved to the Modoc that Canby was like Ben Wright: talk peace, but wage war. Canby, in fact, never wavered in his position that the Modoc must return to the reservation or they would be killed. It is not hard to see why the Modoc did not trust Canby, or his truce, which reminded them of the Ben Wright massacre at Lost River back in 1852.

What the Modoc wanted from the talks was a guarantee of their safety, some land of their own, and nominal justice. The penultimate meeting between the Modoc and the ironically named Peace Commission exposed the fundamental differences that divided them. In what was perhaps the most honest exchange between Native Americans and white men in California, Keintpoos, with the help of interpreters, reiterated the Modoc position to Indian Superintendent Colonel A. B. Meacham, whom Keintpoos had known since before the hostilities. They talked bluntly for seven hours.

Specifically, what Keintpoos asked was that the Modoc be given the Lava Beds as their permanent home, since no white man would want this pile of rocks to farm, and that if the whites were going to try the Modoc who killed the settlers, then the Modoc should try the whites who killed the Modoc baby at Lost River. If the Modoc couldn't try the whites, then the whites themselves should try them. By any standard, these were fair requests, but to the whites these were unreasonable conditions. As Meacham put it, "No. That's just not possible." Why it was not possible to share the land is the question no one has answered. If there was to be no justice, what was the point of talking at all? The meeting broke up, and the Modoc returned to their Stronghold.[32]

On April 11, 1873, the Modoc would meet one last time with the Peace Commission. A few nights before this meeting, the Modoc had gathered in Keintpoos's cave in the Lava Beds. Although Keintpoos wanted peace, the younger warriors, led by Ha-kar-jim, Cho-ocks, and John Skonches, those who would be tried for killing the settlers, demanded an all-out war against the army. In particular, what the warhawks planned was an ambush of the Peace Commission, believing that by killing the leaders the army would withdraw. Keintpoos and Chik-chack-am argued that it was ignoble for Modoc warriors to do such a thing. At a key moment in the council, while Keintpoos was speaking, the warhawks taunted him with a woman's shawl, calling him a coward. Losing his cool, Keintpoos screamed back: "I will do it. I will kill Canby, although I know it will cost me my life and all the lives of my people, I will do it. Still I know it is coward's work, I will do it."[33] But as someone who advocated peace with the whites, his acquiescing to the warhawks must have caused his heart great turmoil. And although he tried to the last minute to find a way out, in the end he was bound by his word at the council.

The following morning, before the peace talks got under way, Slolux and Brancho, two young braves, hid in the Lava Beds with a stash of weapons. Just after the talks started, the Modoc again requested that land be set aside for them. Canby insisted that the Modoc first surrender to him. At this point, Keintpoos excused himself from the group. When he returned, he pulled out a pistol, and from a distance of ten feet, fired at Canby, but the pistol jammed. Keintpoos recocked it and this time shot Canby below the left eye. Canby, no doubt in shock, jumped up and started running, only to stumble and fall a few yards away. Ellen's Man George then came up and, using a rifle stashed by Brancho, delivered the coup de grace. Ha-kar-jim, Bostin-Ah-gar, and Bogus Charley attacked the rest of the commissioners, killing one, the preacher D. D. Thomas, while two others escaped. Meacham, who was knocked unconscious by a bullet, was left for dead but lived to tell the story.[34]

Most writers express outrage at the killing of Canby, who was unarmed, and I understand their point of view. But I sympathize with the predicament of Keintpoos and the Modoc. They knew reservation life was humiliating and not much better than living in prison. They had no hope for justice. And Keintpoos couldn't possibly turn in the young braves of his clan so they could be hung. Remember Wright and the Lost River massacre in 1852? A precedent had been set—use peace talks to ambush the leaders. The Modoc played the best hand they had. In terms of tactics, a coup de roi makes perfect sense. Countless battles have been won by small forces against larger ones by striking and eliminating the leaders, the same tactic the army had bungled at Lost River less than six months before. (It was also, by the way, the same tactic that Cortés used on Moctezuma, and Pizarro on Atahualpa, the Inca ruler.) Canby, though personally unarmed, was determined to force the Modoc out, and although he talked peace, he prepared for war, drawing the circle tighter and tighter around the Modoc.

But if you are outraged at the murder of Canby, you must also be outraged at the murder of the Indian baby and the old woman at Lost River, and the slaughter of John Skonches's clan back in 1852 by Ben Wright, and ad infinitum. Forgive me if I ignore objectivity, but unless I defend the Modoc, I can only repeat the standard "objective" version that they were the bad guys. I'm not going to argue with myself; I'm going to tell this story from my subjective point of view. Western writers in general need to cross over and look at the world through indigenous eyes, otherwise they run the risk of always seeing us as either the stereotypical noble savage or the unfathomable wild Indian in their scope.

• • •

After the death of Canby, the army renewed its attack with added fury and motivation. Seven hundred troops as well as three batteries of artillery and seventy-two Warm Spring Indian scouts were hurled against the Modoc. (We might as well admit that part of the tragedy of the extermination of Native Americans—from the Aztecs to the Modoc and up to present-day indigenous peoples—is that there were always Indians who were willing to serve the whites. I'm sure the Jews had their quislings too.)

Every member of the Modoc clans joined the battle against the soldiers. Each brave handled two or three Springfields while the squaws reloaded the rifles. The children ran through the crevices carrying messages from one front to the other. The old people cooked and brought food to the front line. When the braves fell, squaws sometimes picked up the rifles, and at least one squaw killed a soldier. It was a people's army, the same as the Vietnamese or the Sandinistas against Somoza.

The Modoc fight captured the imagination of the world, and the *London Illustrated News* even sent an artist, Harry Simpson, to draw the battlefield for their readers. Some sympathizers ranked the Modoc with the great military minds of Europe, the Prussian von Clauswitz, for example, except that the Modoc hadn't read any Western military history; they invented their own tactics as they went along. This description of the Stronghold by a journalist who visited soon after the battle reveals the genius of the Modoc: "The ingenuity of the Modok [*sic*] has surpassed all understanding. Their engineering skill draws warm commendation from the best talent in the camps. Every picket-post is thoroughly protected from assaults by riflemen, and arranged to cover a retreat."[35]

Though the Modoc hold the soldiers off for another week—at one point, eight Modoc warriors pinned down an army column of four hundred soldiers—the army eventually cuts their access to Tule Lake and thus to their water supply. Remember, only about fifty of the Modoc in the Stronghold are warriors; the rest are women, young children—many under seven years old—and old people, some of whom are blind. As the situation grows desperate, heavily outnumbered, surrounded, with little food and less water and encumbered by their families, the Modoc pull off one of the great tactical retreats of all time. On the night of April 16, undetected, though right under the soldiers' noses, the Modoc slip out of the Lava Beds. The next morning, when the army finally takes possession of the caves, they find the Stronghold abandoned. In a scene that would be repeated many times a hundred years later in a place called Viet Nam, the soldiers stumble upon an old Indian couple too weak to have escaped. If you don't have a strong stomach, you'd better turn your head. The old man is shot dead and scalped—even his eyebrows are skinned and later claimed as trophies of war. The old woman raises her arms in surrender, pleading with the soldiers to spare her life. Instead, the officer asks who will rid them of the squaw, and a soldier steps forward, puts the muzzle of his rifle against her head, and pulls the trigger.[36]

When the army realizes that the Modoc are gone, they send the Warm Spring Indian scouts to find their trail; meanwhile, several army columns march out hoping to catch the fleeing Modoc. But it is the Modoc who trap an army column in a flat, open patch of sand about half a mile from the Stronghold. In history books, this is referred to as the Thomas-Wright massacre, named after the two West Point officers in charge of the column.

It is not quite a massacre, though it is a sound thrashing, administered with a bit of restraint. The Thomas-Wright column of sixty-six soldiers is routed at a place called Sand Covered Hill, about a mile from the Stronghold. The Indian warrior Chik-chack-am, barely twenty-one years old, leads the attack. He decimates the Thomas-Wright column, a force three times the size of his own small band of warriors, in perhaps the most well-planned and well-executed Indian victory in Western history.[37] The Modoc could easily have killed every single man in that column, but instead, Chik-chack-am allows some of the surrounded troops to live. It is said he yelled at the cowering soldiers, "All you fellows that ain't dead had better go home. We don't want to kill you all in one day."[38] The Modoc killed twenty-two soldiers, including all the officers of the column, graduates of West Point, and wounded nineteen. When the survivors return to the main army camp, they are so mauled that pure dread and near panic grips the soldiers. Had Chik-chack-am followed up the next day and attacked the main camp under the bluffs along Tule Lake, the Modoc, as far-fetched as it sounds, might have routed the U.S. Army from the Lava Beds. The army suffered as many casualties in this one day as it had in the entire six months at the Lava Beds. The Modoc lost one warrior and captured many rifles, munitions, and horses. But it would be their last victory.

The Modoc retreat into ice caves, where they are able to fill their water needs. But the ice was limited, and soon they have to keep moving. During this period, they ambush an army supply train at Scorpion Point, but besides capturing some whisky kegs, which they drink on the spot, they make off with little war booty. In the next encounter with the army, at Dry Lake, Ellen's Man George, a favorite of Ha-kar-jim and his clan, is killed. They carry his body with them when they retreat and cremate him that night in a ceremonial fire. Another loss at Dry Lake is the Modoc war supplies, which the army captures, along with most of their pack animals.

After this, the pressures of being on the run, short of supplies, and hunted like animals bring about a split within the Modoc ranks. One group, with Ha-kar-jim in the lead, deserts Keintpoos and goes off on its own. They enter the army camp riding on lame and skinny horses, the women dressed in rags, and the men in uniforms of soldiers they'd killed, their faces blackened with pitch as a sign of their defeat. Ha-kar-jim waited to see what would happen to these Modoc before rushing into the army camp and throwing himself at the feet of the military commander.[39] Eventually, Ha-kar-jim, Bogus Charley, Shacknasty Jim, and Steamboat Frank accept $100 a month to track down the remaining Modoc for the army. Had Keintpoos not been tracked down by his own people, he might have survived ten, twenty years in the mountains or, like the Yahi, maybe thirty years without coming into contact again with the whites.

By now, Keintpoos has about thirty-three men, and they are outnumbered ten to one. They have almost no water and little food, they are low on ammunition, and their clothes are torn to rags. Soon Keintpoos's clan falls apart, turning themselves in to the army one by one. His sister, Ko-a-lak-a (Hard-Working Woman), also turns herself in. Even Chik-chack-am eventually surrenders and joins in tracking down Keintpoos. John Skonches and twelve other men, along with their families, also give up the fight. The army stays on the trail of Keintpoos, which leads to the far eastern corner of what had been Modoc country. At a place called Willow Creek, five miles east of Clear Lake, the exhausted Modoc surrender. Keintpoos is the last to put down his rifle; with him is his family, two wives and his daughter, plus two half brothers who stayed with him till the end. After Keintpoos is brought to the military camp, to his great distress, he is shackled in leg irons, then his chains are fastened to those of John Skonches.

Many of the Modoc are photographed as prisoners, and you can see in their faces their bitterness over their crushing defeat and captivity. Curly-Headed Jack, who is chained to Weium and Buckskin Doctor, will commit suicide with a hidden pistol a few days later. Buckskin Doctor, a medicine man, still wearing his traditional Modoc hat, has the meanest, most miserable expression I have ever seen on a human being.

All the surviving Modoc are taken to Yreka. A few days later, four more Modoc with their families surrender to John Fairchild, one of the few white people with sympathy for the Modoc (although his sympathy did not stop him from renting horses and selling hay to the army, for which he earned $2,000).[40] As his brother, James Fairchild, is transporting the prisoners to a military camp, two white men stop the wagon, order Fairchild down at gunpoint, then shoot the Modoc men in cold blood.[41] A Modoc woman, though wounded in the fusillade, survived, and as usual, some writers claim it was an accident (her wounding, I mean—perhaps they meant to kill her too). As if whites never killed women and children, only unarmed prisoners.

There's not much left to tell of the story. The Modoc are moved to a military stockade at Fort Klamath, Oregon, where Keintpoos, John Skonches, Bostin-Ah-gar, Te-te-tea-us, Keintpoos's half brother (Black Jim), Slolux, and Brancho are tried by a military tribunal for the murder of General Canby and Thomas, the preacher of the so-called Peace Commission. So there will be no doubt as to the outcome, a gallows is erected before the trial starts on July 3, 1873. General William T. Sherman, head of the army, orders that Ha-kar-jim and the other traitors be spared punishment so as to encourage others to betray rebellious Indians. It was the old divide-and-conquer policy of Cortés brought home to California. The Modoc who betrayed and tracked down Keintpoos, including Ha-kar-jim, who led the massacre of the white settlers, are not tried or even placed in the stockade.

But, as usual, there must be the formalities, the pretense of justice, the spectacle of a trial. It makes no difference that the Modoc don't understand the proceedings, that Keintpoos, for instance, knows no English. It makes no difference that the Modoc have no counsel or defense, that they are shackled, that they don't know the concept of cross-examination, or that Slolux is so indifferent that he often falls asleep during the testimony. It makes no difference that the soldiers on the tribunal are the same ones who fought against the Modoc. The outcome is a forgone conclusion. Keintpoos offers this observation in his native tongue, "My heart is not strong; I cannot talk with the chains on my legs." But he tries anyway, and he delivers a sort of history of how he was badgered into killing Canby by the young braves. He blames Ha-kar-jim and Cho-ocks, the shaman, for the massacre of the settlers that made peace impossible. He ends angrily, "Now here I am. Killed one man, after I had been fooled by him many times and forced to do the act by my own warriors. The law says hang him. He is nothing but an Indian, anyhow. We can kill them any time for nothing, but this one had done something, so hang him. Why did not the white man's law say that about Ben Wright? So now I do quit talking. In a few days I will be no more. I now bid the world farewell."[42]

All six of the defendants are found guilty and sentenced to hang on October 3, 1873.

• • •

The day before the execution of the condemned Modoc, the military commander of Fort Klamath and a chaplain visited them in the stockade. In a half-hearted attempt to get their sentences commuted, Keintpoos and John Skonches ask to state their case to the president of the United States. Black Jim also seems repentant. Only Bostin-Ah-gar is unrepentant; tragic and wise, he tells the visitors: "You all knew me during the war. It seemed to me that I have two hearts, one Indian and the other white. I am only a boy and yet you all know what I have done; although a boy I feel like a man, and when I look on each side of me, I think of these other men as women. I do not fear death. I think I am the only man in the room. I fought in the front rank with Ha-kar-jim and the rest. I am altogether a man, and not half a woman. I killed Dr. Thomas, assisted by Bogus Charley . . . I would like to see all my people and bid them farewell. I would like to go to the stockade to see them. I see that if I were to incriminate others it would not amount to anything. I see that it is too late. I know that other chiefs were not at the bottom of that affair and they did not take so prominent a part in the massacre as the younger men. I know little, but when I see anything with my eyes, I know it."[43]

On Friday morning, October 3, the prisoners are taken in a wagon from the guardhouse to the gallows. It is quite an occasion for the whites of the region who hated the Modoc. Nearly every white man in Southern Oregon is present. Those Modoc who want to attend do so. All the soldiers are required to witness the hanging. The traitor Modoc are given front-row seats. At the last minute, by order of the War Department, Slolux's and Brancho's executions are stayed, and they are given life in prison on Alcatraz Island. At the foot of the gallows, Keintpoos is unshackled from John Skonches so he can climb the ladder to the platform. Then Old Skonches, the sell-out reservation Indian, as a final insult and humiliation, denounces his own brother, John Skonches. A priest garbles a prayer that doesn't mean much anyway, since, with the exception of Bostin-Ah-gar, the Modoc know only a few choice words of English, with which they'd taunted the soldiers in the Lava Beds, such as "Fuck you, dog-face soldier." Bostin-Ah-gar stands on the gallows casually chewing a plug of tobacco. He knew it was a war of survival, and he fought like a warrior, with everything he had. Bostin-Ah-gar dies a hero, a Modoc to the end.

The four Modoc bodies hang from the scaffold for half an hour before they are removed. The ropes are unraveled and the strands are hawked as souvenirs for $5 a piece. They say even strands of Keintpoos's hair were sold. Contrary to rumors, Keintpoos's body was not exhibited as a sideshow attraction for 10¢ a peek. Nor did it wind up at the Office of the Surgeon General, to be reduced to a skeleton and displayed as a model of Indian anatomy. Neither story is the truth, though the truth is no less humiliating. The heads of the four Modoc warriors are surgically removed from the bodies and shipped in a barrel to Washington, D.C., where the skulls are housed to this day in the Smithsonian Institution. Keintpoos's skull is specimen number 225070 and can be seen by appointment, along with the others, for scientific and scholarly use in the Department of Physical Anthropology.[44] The skulls of the defeated Modoc are the spoils of war, the final act of barbarity against a once proud clan, a Tzompantli, a skull rack of Manifest Destiny.

The rest of the Modoc, 153 men, women, and children, are put aboard an army train bound for Nebraska. From Nebraska they are shipped to Kansas, from Kansas to the Seneca Springs Reservation in Oklahoma. Almost a year to the day since the soldiers and civilians had attacked their camps on the Lost River, the Modoc are confined at the Quapaw Reservation in Oklahoma, their final destination. The fate they fought so hard to avoid was theirs in the end anyway.

By 1890, fifty of them had died on the reservation, including Ha-kar-jim. Others who died on the reservation are the shaman, Cho-ocks, and Chik-chack-am. But most of the dead are children.

In 1906, Ko-a-lak-a, the sister of Keintpoos, died at the Quapaw Reservation. In 1909, the U.S. government allowed those surviving Modoc who so wished the option of moving to the Yainax Reservation in Oregon.

A few returned.

• • •

I took a room in a motel in Tule Lake before visiting the Lava Beds. The sharp *tap-tap-tap* of water sprinklers could be heard all night, intermingled with the boisterous talk of some hunters who were staying in the next room. Hunting, by the way, is the main attraction out here. Hunters rent duck blinds, from which, safely ensconced with their shotguns and beers, they blast away at waterfowl without so much as getting their feet wet. In this part of the world, a nature preserve is the lure to bring hunters and boost the economy. In this part of the state, the concept of getting along with nature hasn't caught on, and perhaps never will. The motel operator asks me, "You come to hunt?" and then continues, "Best hunting in the world around Tule Lake, the last best place." Can you imagine what the relationship to the land must be like where there are no "nature preserves"?

The next morning, as the sun is rising, I drive south on Route 139 and stop at a place called the Stronghold. It's not really a town but a truck stop, with one coffeeshop called, you guessed it, Captain Jack's. Inside they sell Indian dolls and arrowheads. All around Tule Lake you can see the irrigation machines splashing water on the barley and alfalfa whose green fields clash with the brown tones of the Lava Beds. In the background, Mount Shasta rises majestic and snow capped, although it is the middle of summer. The landscape is vast, awesome, and inspiring—beautiful enough to fight for, even die for.

Outside Newell on Route 139 is the site of the Tule Lake Internment Camp, where 16,000 Japanese Americans were isolated during the first months of 1942. There's nothing left of the Internment Camp but the gate, one old brick building, and a stone marker, the latter a humble monument to the 110,000 Japanese citizens who spent most of the war behind barbed wire. I felt a chill standing at the ruined gates of the internment camp; perhaps it was the wind or the sight of another sort of camp across the street, a migrant camp freshly ringed with new barbed wire. But I think it's the feeling that this desolate, wind-swept landscape holds memories that slash like concertina wire.

The sun is barely above the horizon when I arrive at the Lava Beds. A lone marmot is standing guard on a rock, watching me as I approach. You have to see the Stronghold for yourself to believe that anyone could live here for six months, much less have the will to fight and keep at bay a much larger force. Lava is volcanic rock, as sharp and pointed as broken glass, and that's all there is here. In the heart of the Stronghold, there isn't a tree growing, nothing but bunchgrass and some wildflowers like flax and sagebrush buttercup. The caves where the Modoc lived would make you cry; they are barely small hollows in the ancient lava flow, and that's it. They are more like upside-down bowls than caves, and they offer little shelter from rain or other elements. And this is where they offered to live if they could live in peace.

I found the cave where Keintpoos had lived with his family: a natural amphitheater in the lava rocks that could seat maybe forty people, and at the bottom is the granite rock known as the rostrum, where the Modoc held their council. Actually, the cave is behind the rostrum, and has a depth of about thirty feet. I climbed down and stood at the rostrum, one hand on the chunk of granite, and I imagined myself a Modoc with his family, surrounded by the army, and what I would have done to save them. I wish I knew a Modoc song or prayer; instead, I burned some white sage in their honor and smoked a small pipe of tobacco.

Near the center of the Stronghold, you can still see the flattened, dusty area where the Modoc danced their Ghost Dance, led by Cho-ocks, the shaman, who tried with magic to hold back the soldiers. Not far from this site, on a small peak within the Lava Beds, someone has set up a medicine pole, a modern version of the one the Modoc erected during their war here. Sunglasses, plastic wrist name tags, scarves, a few coins thrown on the ground make up the medicine. What the medicine pole is supposed to ward off, though, is unclear—perhaps the sunburned tourists who rush through here anxious to get away from these godforsaken rocks.

• • •

At night in Tule Lake you can hear the sprinklers going, watering the barley and alfalfa fields. There's the pretense of life; the traffic on Route 139 contributes a background roar, the splayed headlights fading at last around 3:00 A.M. But when you walk through the land, through the Lava Beds, and see nothing but rocks and mountains for miles around, you realize how desolate Tule Lake is. If you drive, you won't meet a car on the road or see a cabin anywhere between the Stronghold coffeeshop on Route 139 and Medicine Lake thirty miles away. I saw not even a roadkill. It was the people, the stories, the songs that I wanted to hear, and those were gone. The Modoc, the clan that wanted to live in harmony with nature, the ones who most loved this land, where are they? I'm sure the land would look much different if they were here as caretakers. The lake would be ten times the size, the area would be home to a thousand times more birds, and everywhere there would be more life. But we never got to hear their lessons, their part of the story, or learn how it might have turned out.

This land is so vast I cannot comprehend why it could not have been shared. Why expel the first people here, perhaps the first people ever to live in this land we call California? The genocide of the Modoc creates a missing gap in the continuity of human history from 15,000 years ago to the present; the link is broken. It is as if we dropped a stone that left no ripple in the well of our memory. A million lifetimes ago a hand scratched a symbol on a rock in the middle of a lake, fabulous and magical. And from that time to the time of a small clan of Modoc who were brutally expelled from their native land is but an instant.

They say the surviving Modoc of Oregon and California are planning a reunion, a coming together of their clan to evolve a strategy for survival. If that is true, I want to be adopted. I will be a Modoc. I will live each day as if it were my last. I will respect and love nature. I want to go down fighting. When I die, paint my face red, wrap me in white buckskin, and cremate me with my pipe.

But tonight I ask the wind: Am I the only one that remembers this holocaust?

THE MARIN HEADLANDS

A Meditation on Place

It is a Sunday in the middle of July, and the hills above the Golden Gate strait are an explosion of wildflowers—blue lupines, red Indian paintbrushes, yellow monkey flowers—but the fog has rolled in from the Pacific, clamping its cold hand on my face. I am hiking through Fort Barry, the former U.S. Army base at the Marin Headlands, just across the Golden Gate Bridge from the city, and the trail gives me a spectacular view of San Francisco. It is a beautiful contradiction: the summer landscape, the frigid weather, and the abandoned army base now occupied by artists and writers.

I am headed for the Point Bonita Lighthouse. The trail curves past a crumbling concrete bunker, then clings precipitously to the cliff of Bonita Cove. Below me I can see the ruins of the old Coast Guard Life-Saving Station, just the rotten pilings of the pier left, like a whale carcass rotting on the beach.

The Point Bonita Lighthouse is one of the oldest on the Pacific Coast; its handcrafted Fresnel lens was made in Paris in the 1850s and shipped around Cape Horn.[1] The lighthouse sits on a rocky point at Land's End, staring out at the Pacific Ocean, and has served as a beacon to fog-bound San Francisco Bay for nearly 150 years. To reach the lighthouse, I go through a tunnel blasted out of solid rock, then cross a suspension bridge that spans a deep chasm. The bridge is so fragile only five people can cross at a time. On the other side of the bridge stands the lighthouse, its beacon flashing on and off. Three other visitors cross the bridge with me today, and the bridge sways in the wind like a toy. I keep my step light and my eyes straight ahead, not daring even one peek down to the jagged rocks below.

The early keepers of the lighthouse lived in harsh conditions—alone, cold, bored—but one error on the part of the lighthouse keeper could doom a ship trying to navigate the treacherous coast hidden by fog. Even with the lighthouse, hundreds of ships have wrecked off the Golden Gate strait, including the steamer *City of Rio de Janeiro* that went down in heavy fog in 1901, just off the Marin Headlands, taking with it 123 passengers and $50,000 in gold bullion.[2] On this Sunday, it's not the destruction of ships I'm interested in, but the creation of landscape.

The National Park Service volunteer at the lighthouse tells me that the wide chasm the bridge spans was carved barely forty years ago by the ocean pounding against the rocky cliffs that form Point Bonita. He shows me a picture to prove it. In the black-and-white, there is no bridge; the point is a solid landmass reaching all the way to the lighthouse, and it is easy to be awed by how quickly the landscape changes.

Point Bonita is made of basalt, a dark volcanic rock spewed out of the center of the earth as lava. Millions of years ago the lava poured out of fissures deep in the ocean, and as the molten lava made contact with the water, it hardened and pushed upward, eventually forming the landscape of Point Bonita. Oilmen weep if they have to drill through basalt, because the sharp rock wears out diamond bits, but the rock is no match for the powerful ocean waves and wind that batter it unmercifully, grinding it down, turning it to dust, and sweeping it back to sea.

The original site of the lighthouse was higher up on the cliffs, but fog frequently obstructed its beacon, so the location was moved to the tip of Point Bonita, literally Land's End. The move happened in 1877, and the lighthouse hasn't changed much since then. It is a beautiful structure, simple and classic in its design, the lantern room decorated with iron gargoyles, the original Fresnel lens still in service.

I stand at the railing of the polygon-shaped watch room and face west: straight ahead is the vast Pacific Ocean, beyond it, Asia and that whole other world. As I turn 360° counterclockwise, I can see the hazy finger of land that is Point San Pedro, then closer to me are Pacifica, Ocean Beach, and Point Lobos. I continue turning, and the mansions of Sea Cliff come into sight, then the majestic towers of the Golden Gate Bridge, and the hills of the East Bay, and way in the distance, the peak of Mount Diablo. As I continue my circle, I see the rocky south side of the Marin Headlands, and Hawk Hill, the best spot in the Bay Area to observe the migration of hawks during the autumn months. When I complete the circle, I have a front-row seat facing the jagged coastline of Point Reyes, which disappears in the distance as the coast stretches all the way to Alaska. The view from the lighthouse is awesome, one worth braving the swaying bridge.

The Point Bonita Lighthouse, perched at Land's End on a peak of rapidly disintegrating basalt, is a good place to contemplate the natural and human forces that created California. Geographically, Point Bonita is the very edge of the continental United States; historically, it is the culminating point of Manifest Destiny. And the Marin Headlands, as a whole, seems to hold the memory of all California—its geological creation, its past human history, its modern present, and what may or may not be its future.

•   •   •

The natural forces that created California are fairly clear to geologists. Anyone who's lived in California knows about earthquakes and faults and continental plates pushing against each other. What is not so obvious is the role of the ocean in this creation process. The ocean floor is not static at all, but in constant activity: volcanoes erupt underwater and push ocean sediment toward the continents, then, under great pressure, the sediment is crushed, creating new land and raising mountains. After millions of years, the mountains wear down into sand, which is washed back to the ocean, and all the while the ocean continues the process of forcing more sediment ashore, creating new land and new mountains. The planet is in a continuous process of creation and destruction, and nowhere is it more obvious than along this strip of California coast.

About 200 million years ago, there was no California at all; the edge of the North American continent was somewhere around present-day Utah, and where the Sierras now rise was a coastal plain. The edge of the North American continent hung like a lip over a deep trench. And very patiently, because geological time is in no hurry, because the memory of water and stone is as tireless as the memory of some people, the ocean filled in the trench with sediment, a thin layer at a time, perhaps no more than two or three inches thick. And this activity went on over millions and millions of years. At the same time, the ocean applied tremendous pressure to the sediment it was pushing toward the continent, forcing molten lava through it. When the lava finally broke through the earth's crust and poured out, volcanoes formed, erupted, died, and were eventually worn away by the snows, the rains, and the winds. What is left of those extinct volcanoes is the Sierra Nevada that Highway 80 crosses on the way to Tahoe.[3]

While the ocean floor was being crushed against the mass of the North American continent, smaller chunks of land welded themselves to the emerging landscape of California. Though the tectonic plates that meet along the San Andreas Fault move at the barely perceptible rate of a few centimeters a year, after millions of years, this movement has relocated a chunk of the southern Sierra Nevada the distance from Santa Barbara to

San Francisco. So while the North American plate, which forms the North American continent, is sliding one way, the ocean is crushing new sediment against it. These dual forces created the Coastal Range, the hills and mountains that run along the coast from Mendocino to Santa Barbara. The Coastal Range is a somewhat newer addition to California—newer in the sense that it's only 40 million years old, give or take a few million.[4]

Visible proof of the geological creation of California can be found at the Marin Headlands. The sediment the ocean used to fill in the North American trench is exposed by the road cuts; it looks like ribbons of reddish brown rock, each ribbon no more than a few inches thick, as delicate as a hundred-layer cake. How many millions of years did the ocean labor to build this landscape? How much pressure did the ocean exert to crush the sediment into rocks and hills? These very hills that the wind, the sand, and the ocean are now wearing away to take back to the sea.

It may seem to our human eyes that the earth is static, but if you could step back, even a mere twenty thousand years—which is nothing in geological time—the Marin Headlands would be unrecognizable. The beach where Sunday visitors now stroll was nothing but sand dunes stretching to the horizon; the ocean was twenty miles away at the Farallones. Even in the foreseeable future, with the climatic changes the planet is going through, the Headlands will not look like it does today in another forty or fifty years. When a new Ice Age comes, it will draw the ocean back to the Farallones; or the Green House Effect will flood the Headlands and the new coast will perhaps be the Oakland hills.

I like to take friends out along McCullough Road to show them the marvelous layers of Franciscan chert, sedimentary rock forty million years old that flakes and crumbles down the hills behind Fort Barry onto the road. Massive formations of it are revealed by the road cuts. They look like *S*'s crunched together, one row on top of the other, all the way up the hillside. What is our relation to a rock forty million years old? How do we measure our brief time on this planet to this age? I always tell my friends to touch the ribbons of chert, to place their hands on them. This sediment, made of the fossils of microscopic sea animals, is what the ocean used to create the land we stand on. For me, these chert formations are a vivid memory of our origins. It's a thrill to be able to see that far back, to reach out and literally touch this earth created by a living, active planet, to touch Mother Earth.

But creation is also mythical. The Coast Miwok, who lived for millennia around the Marin Headlands, have their own version of how the earth was created.

In the beginning, the earth was made by O'-ye, the Coyote-man, and it was covered with water. The only earth was the very top of Oon'-nah-pi's

(The Mount Where We Are From, present-day Sonoma Peak). The rest was all under water. Coyote-man had come from the west in a raft that was long and narrow and made of tules and split sticks. After Coyote-man landed on Oon'-nah-pi's, he threw his raft-mat over the water, and where the mat landed it created the land. The land was as narrow as his mat, the long part running north–south, and the narrow part running east–west.[5] (This myth explains the topography of the Bay Area: a narrow strip of land running lengthwise north–south. The great body of water that was San Francisco Bay was a sign for the Miwok that the waters that originally covered the earth had not fully receded yet.)

The Coast Miwok were the first people here. They were really one of three subgroups of the Miwok, and the original inhabitants of Marin County. They didn't live at the Headlands but used it seasonally. The two nearest Miwok villages were Liwanelowa, approximately where Sausalito is now, and Olema-loke, the site of present-day Olema. The actual Headlands was too cold for year-round living, so the Miwok came during particular seasons, to gather seeds, to fish, and to hunt. They harvested the seeds of four different types of grasses; they knew the medicinal properties of a variety of plants, such as wild cucumber, yarrow, coyote bush, monkey flower, nettle, and Douglas iris; and they used the roots and leaves to make poultices and teas. The children were given poison oak leaves to chew, making them immune to its poisonous qualities; the Miwok also used poison oak as a remedy against colds.[6] (It is possible that human saliva changes the chemical reaction of poison oak and releases other chemicals that may be beneficial. But don't rush out and try this.) The charcoal from poison oak was rubbed on the skin and then the skin was punctured to create tattoos. The Miwok harvested seaweed and kelp, which was dried, then cooked into cakes and stored for later eating. The sea was a plentiful source of food, providing long-necked clams, Washington clams, heart cockles, mussels, oysters, abalone, crabs, and lobsters. The Miwok feasted on these shellfish, and the remnants of their meals, the mounds of shells they left behind, are called middens and can still be found along the edges of Rodeo Lagoon. They also fished for eel, flounder, perch, trout, coho salmon, steelhead trout, bay shrimp, and octopus. They trapped all species of ducks and geese. They hunted the plentiful black-tailed deer, raccoon, gray squirrel, woodrat, and tule elk that roamed the hills. They lived a good life; they were natural people and excellent botanists, flowing with the rhythms of nature, and for everything they took, whether it was killing a deer or harvesting a plant, they offered a prayer or a gift as compensation to nature. And nature in return was good to them: it gave lots of trees and reeds for building shelter, and the food was plentiful and hardy. Although the Miwok had weapons, and surely had conflicts with other tribes, they were not a warlike people. From the first settlement along Point Reyes, dated about 1,500 B.C., the Miwok grew to over six hundred villages located as far north as Petaluma in Sonoma County. In the Marin area, 113 villages thrived at the time of the first encounters with Europeans in the sixteenth century.

In June 1579, the English pirate Francis Drake sailed along the California coast, eventually dropping anchor near the Marin Headlands to repair his ship, the *Golden Hind*. The chaplain of the expedition, Francis Fletcher, kept a detailed diary of the journey, and his description of the Miwok is unsurpassed. I offer here a brief quote, translated into modern English, from his published work, *The World Encompassed by Sir Francis Drake:*

> They are a people of a tractable, free, and loving nature, without guile or treachery . . . and yet are the men commonly so strong of body, that that which 2 or 3 of our men could hardly bear, one of them would take upon his back, and without grudging carry it easily away, up hill and down hill an English mile together: they are exceedingly swift in running, and of long continuance, the use whereof is so familiar with them, that they seldom go, but for the most part run. One thing we observed in them with admiration, that if at any time they chanced to see a fish so near the shore that they might reach the place without swimming, they would never, or very seldom never, miss to take it.[7]

There is cruel irony in the little we know of the Miwok culture today, yet it thrived less than two hundred years ago. By all accounts, they wove fine baskets decorated with feathers and shells, yet the only surviving example of Miwok basketry is in the Museum of Anthropology and Ethnography in St. Petersburg, Russia, collected in 1840–1841 by a young scientist, Ivan Gavrilovich Voznesenki, who was part of the Russian trading mission at Fort Ross. (The Miwok do not believe in keeping relics of their dead, and thus the baskets were buried with their owners or worn out in everyday use, which explains why so few baskets have survived. In fact, they have no desire to claim the baskets in St. Petersburg, because they believe these will have bad energy, but still, the now lost memory of their basket-weaving technique is also an example of the destruction of their culture.)

The encounter with the Europeans destroyed the world of the Miwok, altered their way of life, their harmony with nature, and we, the inheritors of that legacy, are now without their knowledge of plants, their respect for every living thing. In the holocaust of the indigenous world of California, the collective knowledge of the Miwok, handed down from generation to generation for over three thousand years, was irrevocably lost. Whenever the thread of tradition and culture is destroyed, it can never truly be recovered, and we are all poorer for it, less than the whole could have been.

About a thousand Coastal Miwok still survive into the modern era. They have petitioned the U.S. government to honor their claims to Tomales Bay, part of their ancestral lands, which the same government that summarily abolished the Miwok tribe in the 1950s had promised to return to them back in 1923. Not one of the surviving Miwok claims to be full-blooded. In December 2000, President Clinton finally restored federal recognition to this community. They had been selling fry bread and depending on donations to keep themselves going, but now, with their changed status, they'll be eligible for federal health, housing, and educational benefits. They now call themselves the Federated Indians of the Graton Ranchería. When the tribal chairman, Greg Sarris, a University of California at Los Angeles professor and established writer, heard the news on his car radio, he pulled off the road and cried.[8]

•   •   •

Other cultures have also left their mark along this strip of California coast. Point Bonita, the chunk of rock on which the lighthouse stands, is a Spanish name going back over two hundred years. *Bonita*, of course, means "pretty." But its original Spanish name was Punto de Bonetes, or Hat Point. The name first appears in Spanish diaries of 1776, around the time of the founding of San Francisco. Two centuries ago, the tip of the Headlands, as seen from a distance as a ship approached, appeared as three points above the water, resembling a tricornered hat worn by the Spanish clergy, hence the name *bonete*. The southernmost point was later cut down to give the lighthouse an unobstructed view.

Of the diaries concerning land discoveries, one of the best was written by Pedro Font, who traveled through California in 1776 as a chaplain in Anza's expeditions. It is in Font's diary that my family name first appears in association with California. The name Murguía is of Basque origin, heralding from the mountain village of Murguía in the Basque Pyrenees. Although the name is old in the Western Hemisphere, going back to Cuba in the 1500s, in California it first appears as the name of a point of land just beyond present-day Bodega Bay, twenty miles north of the Golden Gate strait. Why this topographical point was named after a Murguía, or even who named it, is unclear. It is possible that Font gives it the name, but why or for whom is his eternal secret. He writes in his diary for March 27, 1776: "a una legua al noroeste de la boca cae la punta de Murguía, por la qual sigue la costa" (one league northwest of the entrance [of Bodega Bay] lies Murguía Point, and from there the coast runs on).[9]

The early Spaniards and Mexicans left their names on much of the topography around the Headlands, and the Spanish names are now often mixed with English prefixes that give the area a certain bilingual flavor. Point Reyes, probably the most mentioned landmark in early diaries of discovery, was originally named Punta de Los Tres Reyes (Three Kings Point) by Sebastián Vizcaíno in 1603. Sausalito means "little willow," and the correct spelling should be Sauzalito. Tiburón, the pricey town across from Sausalito, means "shark." I cannot help but wonder what kind of shark it refers to. Alcatraz means "pelican," but the present island is misnamed; the name Alcatraz was first given to Yerba Buena Island because of the abundance of pelicans found there. Yerba Buena is "mint" and is used in brewing medicinal teas; it was so abundant in the region that San Francisco (obviously Spanish for Saint Francis) was originally called Yerba Buena, the Good Weed. Angel Island was named in August 1775, by Juan Manuel de Ayala, the first navigator to enter San Francisco Bay through the Golden Gate, and its full name is Nuestra Señora de Los Angeles (Our Lady of the Angels). And the Farallone Islands, twenty miles away, means "small rock rising from the sea" and was a common name given to similar landmarks by early Spanish navigators sailing off the coast of California.[10]

But the Spaniards and Mexicans left us more than just names. They were the first to change the landscape in a permanent manner when they introduced the mission system to the Marin area in 1817. San Rafael was the site of a mission founded in 1817, of which not a trace remains of the original building. The mission, named after San Rafael, Arcángel, the Healer, was built on the site of the Miwok village Nanaguanui. Originally a sub-mission called an *asistencia*, it was intended as a hospital for the neophytes who were dying off at Mission Dolores. Besides introducing cattle, grapevines, and the Catholic religion, the mission priests also brought annual grasses that soon displaced the bunch grasses that had covered the hills of the Headlands in a green mantle for thousands of years.[11]

In 1823, the *asistencia* was elevated to the status of Mission San Rafael, independent of Mission San Francisco de Asís. By then, Mission San Rafael owned the Headlands, where Mexican vaqueros, the precursors of the cowboy, tended herds of cattle and for sport hunted grizzly bears and elk on horseback with *riatas*. If these two forces, the missions and cattle raising, were destructive to the native inhabitants and landscape, the war with the United States in 1846 and the onslaught of the Gold Rush miners of 1849 were cataclysmic.

This is not to say that the Miwok and the Mexicans were always on friendly terms. They weren't. As the *asistencia* at San Rafael prospered and expanded, the Miwok population declined from the effects of semicaptivity, overwork, and disease. The Miwok who hadn't been incorporated into the mission system were often at war with the Mexican authorities. In 1824, Mission San Rafael survived a full-fledged attack by Miwok warriors. That same year, a young Miwok named Pomponio rose in armed rebellion from Marin to Santa Cruz, before he was captured in Cañada de Novato. He was jailed at the presidio and taken in chains to Monterey, where he was executed by firing squad. Marin was another Miwok leader feared by the Mexicans. After leading several raids, he turned ally of the Mexicans and subsequently became a master sailor on San Francisco Bay, ferrying boats from San Francisco across to Sausalito.[12]

In 1838, William A. Richardson, a naturalized Mexican citizen of English heritage, who was the first port captain of Yerba Buena (San Francisco) and built the first house there, acquired the Headlands as part of a 19,000-acre Mexican land grant named Rancho Sausalito. He took formal control in 1841 by taking a ceremonial ride around the perimeter of the ranch in the presence of a judicial officer and a witness.[13]

But the Mexican authorities were rather weak in comparison to the United States Army that invaded the region after 1846. Within a decade, the Miwok would practically be wiped out of the Marin area. Stephen Richardson, son of William Richardson, writes in his memoirs, "Days of the Dons," that "the killing of an Indian was regarded as a sportsmanlike pastime."[14] The Californios didn't fare much better in the path of the advancing U.S. military forces. Near Mission San Rafael, José Berreyesa, one of the most prominent Californios in the area, was shot in cold blood, along with his twin nephews, Francisco and Ramón de Haro, by Kit Carson, a scout for John C. Frémont, head of the U.S. military detachment. Besides being a rising Californio political star, Francisco de Haro was engaged to the daughter of William Richardson, Mariana Richardson, who would eventually inherit the debts of Rancho Sausalito.

Other Mexicanos who owned ranchos in the vicinity of the Headlands, like Antonio Osio, owner of Rancho Punta de los Tres Reyes, were forced to flee for their lives, leaving everything behind. Osio's other loss was Angel Island, which he held by a land grant from the king of Spain. In 1846, Osio grazed five hundred head of cattle on Isla de Nuestra Señora de Los Angeles, and no one in the Bay Area disputed his claim to the island. Unfortunately for him, when the U.S. Navy occupied the Bay Area in 1846, they didn't bother with formalities like ownership of land; the navy merely took over the island, slaughtered all of Osio's cattle to feed their crews, and never paid him a dime.[15]

After 1850, the policy of many white settlers pouring into California was to kill any Indians or Mexicans who might be around and grab their land.

The more subtle newcomers, whose names would go down in history books as pioneers, used the court system to steal the ranches. The new settlers also quickly wiped out the grizzly bears, wolves, mountain lions, condors, blue herons, and the huge herds of tule elk that roamed the Headlands.

Although William Richardson, the owner of Rancho Sausalito and the Headlands, had become a U.S. citizen and was the owner of several trading ships and ranches, a series of financial reverses in 1850 threatened to sink him. Then he was introduced to Samuel Throckmorton, a land speculator who offered to clear all debts on the Sausalito ranch in return for four-fifths of its land. Desperate to stay afloat, the old captain agreed. He died eight months later just as his creditors filed a massive lawsuit against him in San Francisco. Throckmorton quickly squeezed out the Richardson heirs, Mariana and Stephen, and paid them only a pittance for their share of the ranch. He then turned around and sold off or leased Rancho Sausalito in parcels and made himself a millionaire.[16]

By the 1880s, the U.S. Army had bought the southern portion of the Headlands, and Portuguese immigrants from the Azores who operated small dairy farms leased the rest of it. Although many Portuguese dairy farms prospered in Marin County, the Headlands was a tough place to raise milk cows: the work was hard, the hours long, and there wasn't much money in it. Nevertheless, three dairy farms were established, designated simply A, B, and C on the old maps. The Headlands was isolated from any real community, and the only time adults left the ranches might be to go to Mill Valley for Sunday mass or perhaps to attend one of the traditional festivals. On Pentecost, the Portuguese celebrated the Holy Ghost Festa, or Chama Rita, a religious feast that started with a cattle drive from Bolinas to downtown Sausalito. The cattle would be decorated with bells and flowers, and the cowboys then paraded them through the streets. There was a crowning of a queen and her court, offerings to the poor, and a huge traditional meal of soup, bread, and wine, followed by all-night dancing.[17]

• • •

As I start my way back from Point Bonita, I can't help but reflect on the Miwok, the rancheros, and the Portuguese dairy farmers, who represent a history that is hardly visible at the Headlands today. Time has erased it all, leaving only a few names and the changed landscape, the rattlesnake grass, the Harding grass, the new immigrants to the Headlands. The hills are now planted with nonnative Monterey pines, cypresses, and Australian blue-gum eucalyptus. The native oak trees are rarely found in the Headlands now. And the hilltops are strewed with the ruins of concrete gun emplacements that stare out at the Pacific, waiting for enemies that will never appear on the horizon.

Since the annexation of California by the United States, the Headlands has been considered important military turf. Back in 1866, the U.S. Army purchased its first portion of the Headlands from Samuel Throckmorton, 1,889 acres for $125,000. Although army engineers made several plans and started a few projects to build fortifications around the area of Point Bonita, nothing much ever came of it. By the time plans were drawn, money appropriated, and construction started, the fortifications and guns were obsolete. By 1904 the dairy farms were gone, and the army occupied an L-shaped area from Tennessee Valley to just beyond the Golden Gate Bridge. After World War I, they built a series of seacoast fortifications—huge concrete bunkers, with walls several feet thick to protect the impressive cannons— along the hills facing the Pacific. By World War II the old guns had been replaced by monster sixteen-inch guns that could shoot a 2,000-pound projectile thirty miles out to sea. The soldiers stationed here survived the cold, the loneliness, and the rigors of military life, but they never once fired their guns at enemy ships. It was a pointless occupation—San Francisco Bay has never been attacked. The last military encounter with the enemy was with the United States itself in 1846.

Then during the Cold War, the U.S. Army turned the Headlands into a missile site, with guided missiles hidden deep in the earth, set on launchers and armed with 20–40-kiloton warheads, ready to shoot down approaching enemy bombers as far away as forty to fifty miles out to sea.

As I walk back from the Point Bonita Lighthouse, headed for the Headlands Center for the Arts where I am staying, I pass the fenced-in site of the former U.S. Army Nike-Hercules Site, SF88L. During the Cold War, this was a high-security site, guarded by concertina wire, armed sentries, and specially trained dogs. Today, I enter casually through the gate and just inside I meet another park volunteer, retired U.S. Army Colonel Milton "Bud" Halsey, who carries his significant height with the bearing of George Patton and whose voice booms like John Wayne's. He is the head volunteer at the site, the one who coordinated over 37,000 hours of volunteer work to restore this base. His pride in the work he's done is obvious as he answers questions in the old control room and explains the workings of the missile base as if the Cold War was still on and this the first line of defense against Soviet bombers approaching from the Pacific.

After he's shown me the control room, Colonel Halsey offers a tour of the missile launching pads. I follow him down a flight of stairs, through the concrete tunnel, and into a room protected by a sliding steel door. Behind the steel door is the magazine room, known as "the pit," where the missiles were kept mounted on launchers, ready to be loaded, raised to the surface, and fired. Sitting on a launcher is a Nike missile—41 feet long and as sharp and pointed as a Renaissance dagger—totally restored down to the last detail. Colonel Halsey scavenged all over the United States to find parts to restore this Nike, the only one on display in this country. He describes the Nike's capabilities with obvious satisfaction: effective range 90 miles, maximum range 125 miles, altitude 150,000 feet (28 miles), speed Mach 3.65— and with a bit of grudging contempt in his voice, he mentions that these weapons are no longer available for use. The United States decommissioned them to comply with the Salt Treaties of the 1970s.

At the end of the tour, he offers me a ride up on the elevator where the Nike missile sits on its launching pad. The only thing missing from the Nike is the fuel and the warhead. Colonel Halsey's demonstration would be nostalgic, except that the decommissioned missile base attests to more than just a demonstration of the art of war—it is also a reminder of the art of annihilation. The Cold War rituals of my childhood come back to me like nightmares that won't go away: the Friday morning tests of the Early Warning System; the drills at school where we hid under a desk and faced away from the windows; the stockpiling of canned food in case we had to live in underground bunkers. What were we thinking of? That a school desk we carved our initials into would protect us from an atomic blast? We were going to survive a nuclear war with Spam and a battery-powered radio that would tell us when it was safe to come outside? How ridiculous it all seems to me now. As I ride the elevator-turned-launching-pad, I rest my hand on the Nike's pointed tip, where the warhead would have been mounted to shoot down the incoming ballistic missiles, and I feel the Nike's power of destruction, and it makes my gut wrench.

But perhaps the art of destruction can also be a prelude to the art of preservation. Five hundred yards from the missile base the Headlands Center for the Arts is restoring the former army quartermaster's building, now named the Three Sisters, into studio space for artists. The old army base is now a Center for the Arts, where artists from all over the world gather to study, create, and contemplate. And what better locale, I think to myself, as I leave the Nike missile site and its enclosed compound. Turning an army base over to artists and writers to create in, and also to scientists like those at the Marin Headlands Sea Mammal Rescue Center, may help heal the wounds of our presence on this coast.

As I walk to the mess hall for dinner, the brown pelicans, once nearly extinct, are flying in and out of Rodeo Lagoon. Along the banks of Rodeo

Lagoon, where the Miwok feasted on warm nights, I have found horsetail ferns whose ancestors on this planet go back 400 million years. The Pacific Ocean, which created the Headlands, is piling more sand along the lagoon's shore, sealing it off in summer. But each winter the pounding surf rises over the shore and the Pacific again claims the lagoon as its own. In the distance, I can see the Farallones, the same peaks that Pedro Font cited and drew in his diary of 1776. I recall that during the last Ice Age, about 20,000 years ago, the sand dunes of this area stretched all the way to the Farallones, some twenty miles away. With the sea at such a distance, life must have been very different along these hills. When the last Ice Age ended, the sea rose to its present level, flooding the valley where the Sacramento River had flowed and creating San Francisco Bay and tiny Rodeo Lagoon.

I'm not usually an enthusiastic hiker, but yesterday I decided to try one of the trails that wind through the Headlands. I climbed the Miwok Trail, and from the heights of Wolf Ridge I saw the spectacular view of the hills and the ocean the Miwok hunter-gatherers must have seen 3,500 years ago. The sun was a red dot blurred behind a tsunami-sized wave of fog that was sitting right at the ocean's edge, as if waiting until an appointed hour to move inland. I spread my arms out in homage to the Headlands, and a gust of wind responded with such power it nearly swept me off the hill.

I was on the trail in search of coyotes that are said to still populate the hills around the Headlands. I wanted to see one, to feel what the Miwok had felt when they christened Coyote-man their creator god. Though the trail was marked with coyote scat all the way up Hill 88, I saw no coyotes. But at the top of Hill 88, I found something else: the ruins of an old military observation station that, like the rest of the army base, had been long abandoned. The place was eerie in the misty sunset. The gates were unlocked; the sentry post house had been shredded by the winds, its paint peeling and the wood rotting. The great fortress of radar towers, communications antennas, and concrete fire stations had been gutted, even the doors had been hauled away, and now only the scrawled graffiti of younger generations and the empty parking spaces for the sergeants remained to keep watch atop Hill 88. Within sight of San Francisco but hidden by the fog banks of the Pacific, the rusting military installation stands like a modern Machu Picchu or Monte Albán, an undiscovered ruin holding the secrets of another civilization. I stayed up on Hill 88, in morose contemplation of these military ruins, till the cold and the approaching fog forced me down. As I headed back down the trail, my emotions were a trip wire of conflicts—I was awed and humbled by the beauty of the landscape, the hills and the ocean as seen from Wolf Ridge Trail, and at the same time,

I was terribly saddened by the rusted ruins of the military fire base atop Hill 88, guardian of our erroneous belief in salvation through weapons of destruction.

· · ·

That night, back in my studio, I contemplated the Marin Headlands as a microcosm of California: It seemed to me that all of California was embraced by this small block of land, the native as well as the non-native.

I asked myself these questions: What is the history of this place? What forces created it? Who was here before me? What is the future of this land known as the Headlands, and by extension, California? I believe that was when I had my first glimpse of this book. I took these questions with me as I went out today to see the lighthouse at Point Bonita.

As I pondered the Pacific Ocean from Point Bonita, I had an inkling that maybe the first Americans came from across this body of water and landed somewhere along the California coast, or maybe farther south in the Channel Islands, or perhaps on some beach in Central America. Don't ask me where this thought came from, and I have no proof of it, but something in my blood tells me this is so.

At the end of the day, I still didn't have the answers about the history of California; in fact, I had more questions, enough really to fill a lifetime and never be satisfied. But waiting to break bread in the former military mess hall were members of a community of artists from different countries and backgrounds: Bjarne Solberg from Denmark; Maya Khosla from India; Sheri Woods and Paul Mehas from North Carolina; Bob Young, the Chicano novelist from Ohio; Hisaya Kojima from Japan; Eduardo Morel from Puerto Rico; and Philip Ross, a young mycologist from the Bay Area, yet we all managed to communicate, to share work, ideas, hopes, and doubts about ourselves and what humanity is striving for in this world already embarked on a new millennium. We had arrived at the Headlands as strangers and had discovered we were a community that stretched around the world. I have to admit that before coming here I knew very little about the Marin Headlands. I suspect the other artists were in the same boat. But we all felt honored to share this space with each other, to share our knowledge and lack of knowledge with the remnants of the original landscape and with the landscape as it is now, even with the ruins of the gun emplacements—all of it filled with a brooding sense of California.

As I approached the lights of the mess hall, the moon was coming up over the hills of Fort Barry, bright as a Spanish doubloon. Carried by the wind rustling through the eucalyptus trees were the voices of my friends, and mixed with their voices were the sounds of coyotes baying up on

Hill 88. It felt good to know that not everything had been destroyed, that some indigenous life still survived in this landscape. I sensed that from the ruins of a military base, a new sensibility about ourselves and our environment was taking shape, a sensibility that declares we must guard our myths, our memory, our landscape, our present, and our future; and that from the ruins of our past, new things are created—must be created.

And I prayed the coyotes would multiply in the ruins of the old watchtowers of destruction.

THE HOMECOMING OF AN AZTECA-MEXICA CLAN

It's one of those freezing San Francisco summer days, typical July weather in the city. No doubt someone will get a flash of inspiration and think themselves quite original by quoting Mark Twain: "The coldest winter I ever spent was a summer in San Francisco." Twain never said that, but it's true, nonetheless. It seems that only La Mission is sunny and warm in the city.

As I write this, in the year 2001, there's a fierce struggle going on in La Mission between the families, artists, and working people who already live here and the affluent and arrogant who are moving into the area. La Mission is rapidly being converted into an extension of Silicon Valley—dot-com in the tropics. Only this new invasion is driving out all the tropical people. Illegal evictions by landlords are way up, and every empty warehouse, including the massive 250,000-square-foot National Guard Armory on Fourteenth and Mission, is up for conversion to dot-com office space. I'm sitting in the last little bar on Twenty-fourth Street that hasn't been overrun by this new invasion. Here, in the coolness that smells a little like Mexico, two guys are shooting pool, and the *cantinera* serves me a *bocadito* of dried shrimp with chile. El Mexicano Bar is so obscure it doesn't even have a sign outside. And I like it that way. It's a long way from the glory days of La Mission back in the seventies and eighties, and I'm one of the last *veteranos* of those decades still hanging on. From the way things look today, I'm feeling pessimistic and downright belligerent about what's been going on in this barrio.

What is happening to La Mission? Perhaps the last working-class community in San Francisco, a community of Central Americans but also of

Mexicanos and Latinos from all over the continent, is being destroyed. This was the pueblo that we dubbed "Little Macondo" in the seventies because it was so magical, tropical, and so ours. La Mission has always been working class, from its origins in the 1850s to the period of Woodward Gardens and later when American Can Company dominated the skyline around Florida and Eighteenth Street. The old Victorian houses in La Mission survived the earthquake of 1906 that destroyed a large part of the city, but who knows if they'll survive the dot-com earthquake.

•   •   •

Before leaving El Mexicano Bar, I call my friend Sal García, a longtime resident of La Mission and an all-around good guy. I buy his art pieces now and then when I can afford it. Carlos Santana buys his work regularly and pays thousands for it. I want to know what Sal's doing on such a bleak day. He tells me the sad story. He's being evicted, just like most everyone I know in La Mission. Rising rents, cold-hearted landlords, and economic pressures are the rule now. The influx of dot-commers has lowered the vacancy rate to one percent, and landlords are taking advantage of it to squeeze every last dollar out of tenants. Everywhere you go, someone has a horror story, each bloodier than the last: old grandmas being kicked out of houses they've lived in for forty years; nonprofit art organizations evicted in favor of offices.

Michael, a local artist, has a degenerative spine condition that keeps him from working. His landlord wants to evict him—supposedly so the landlord can move in himself. What's Michael supposed to do? He's lived here twenty years and he's supposed to go to the street? Is there no mercy? We're not talking about strangers or statistics here; we're talking about everyday people that I've known and worked with for years, or whose work I admire. Lourdes Portillo, an Academy Award nominee for her documentary on the Mothers of the Disappeared in Argentina, *Las Madres de la Plaza de Mayo*, was evicted from her studio on Bryant Street so an office development could go up. Now and then the artists win. Calixto, from Oaxaca, won his suit against the landlord. He got to stay in his apartment, paying the same rent. But mostly artists and poets are leaving the City and La Mission, and yet, the cultural milieu they created is what made San Francisco attractive in the first place.

And that's the thing. People move to San Francisco, and then they go into shock over the rents. San Francisco is the least affordable metropolitan area in the country. Eighteen hundred bananas for a one-bedroom apartment just big enough for you and your mattress. A two-bedroom apartment that rented for $1,275 per month in 1995 now fetches a whopping $2,514 in

2001.[1] So where are the working people going to live? And La Mission is the last place working people have in the city, though it may not last much longer. So when Sal tells me that he's packing and that these are the last great days of La Mission, I totally understand. He invites me to come over and have a drink while he packs. Sal is the only truly independent artist I know, so I go over to see him, depressed as all hell.

I drive down Harrison and turn left on Seventeenth, and the anger just wells up in me when I see the white-washed wall on the Lilly Ann Building. This blank fifty-foot wall is a prime example of what happens to a community when it is ruthlessly gentrified. The murals we'd painted, thinking they would last forever and show people our culture, are already being wiped out. Unless you've lived in La Mission and seen these murals, seen them being painted over the years by world-class artists like Chuy Campusano and all the rest, you may think I'm upset over nothing. But no—murals are a visual memory as important to us as any written text. Easier to read, too, and accessible to anyone walking by. I believe that for any art anywhere to be defaced is a crime. It doesn't matter if it's Diego Rivera's mural being smashed with sledgehammers at Radio City or Chuy Campusano's mural being painted over on the Lilly Ann Building. Art is art, and crime is crime.

What are these new entrepreneurs thinking about anyway? To them a buck is still a buck, and it doesn't matter how you make it, I guess. No one learned anything from the eighties when the savings and loans were sacked, and the pigs were left feeding at the trough. Couldn't they see the beauty of that mural? My anger is justified. At the site of the crime, instead of the eye-catching geometric designs five stories high, I find a blank white wall. I turned away in disgust. I know that many residents of the Mission District and the Bay Area, especially Latinos who participated in or remember the artistic movement of the 1970s, feel the destruction of Chuy's mural like a slap to the face.

Chuy Campusano was a soft-spoken, unpretentious man who never failed to offer a smile and a hug. Though small in stature, he was a giant among the Mission District community of artists and writers who flourished during the 1970s. He was respected as an artist and as a teacher, and he was a master at both silk screens and murals. He died young, at fifty-two, but he left behind a rich legacy of murals, some that were very political, but others were not, including the abstract masterpiece *Lilly Ann* that has now been painted over. The act of destroying this mural is not just an insult against the memory of a good man and a fine artist, but against a whole community.

Murals are public art, art that belongs to everyone, popularized in the twentieth century after the Mexican Revolution by the three Mexican giants of mural painting: Diego Rivera, David Alfaro Siqueiros, and José Clemente Orozco. Although these muralists had some of their works destroyed because of their political message, Chuy's mural was abstract, hardly a threat to the system: it was white-washed because of ignorance and greed.

Granted, there's major gentrification going on in the Mission District and the newcomers don't know who painted these murals that seem to line every block. But it was precisely the mural movement of the 1970s that gave the Mission District a sense of being permeated by art and that created the unique sensibility of living in a tropical bohemian pueblo—the very trait that has attracted newcomers like University Games, the occupants of the Lilly Ann Building who destroyed Chuy's mural. But Chuy's mural isn't the first to suffer this fate. Many other Mission District murals have been wiped out, destroyed by new owners or tenants who don't know or appreciate their value and history.

After leaving Chuy's white-washed mural, I made an inventory of other murals that have vanished. By the time I was finished counting up the lost murals, I felt that something must be done to save these artworks for future generations. Isn't that what consciousness is all about?

The colorful mural by Mujeres Muralistas, *Para el mercado*, on the corner of Twenty-fourth and South Van Ness, which was painted on a slat fence about eight feet high and some ninety feet long and featured scenes from tropical America, was destroyed several years ago and the wood carted off as scrap. My *comadre* salvaged a four-foot piece of it, the brown woman with a fishing net, and it now stands among the geraniums in her backyard. The developer who tore it down for an office/apartment building claimed he didn't know it was important. No one notified the women artists who painted the mural, nor any other community art group; not even the Art Commission knew about this act of vandalism. A half-dozen other murals have been destroyed, including the one by Gilbert Ramírez on the Lulac Building and the murals at the former Army Street (now César Chávez Street) projects that were recently torn down. Even the murals by the comic book artists Spain Rodríguez and R. Crumb, some of the first done in the early 1970s, have gone the way of dust. Spain Rodríguez's mural, a comic-strip panel of several Mission District views, was on the walls of Horizons Unlimited for nearly a decade, on the corner of Twenty-second Street and Folsom. R. Crumb's mural on South Van Ness near Eighteenth Street, the only one he ever painted, is now a roll-up garage door for a custom car stereo shop.

What happened to Chuy Campusano's mural is the cost of gentrification. And that's too bad. Not just because Chuy's mural brightened an otherwise drab industrial section of the city, but because corporations see a blank wall and want it to produce profits—which is the lame excuse that University Games spokesmen used as their rationale for destroying Chuy's mural: they wanted to put up a billboard.

Today when I went by the Lilly Ann Building the wall where Chuy's mural was painted is now covered with angry graffiti demanding the restoration of the mural. And the Bay View Building on Mission and Twenty-second that once housed several community organizations is now in the process of morphing into a dot-com office space. The last time I drove by the Bay View Building, some ingenious street artist had speckled the side of the wall with a paint gun. Vandalism or art? Maybe it is both. And I wondered what the soft-spoken Chuy Campusano would have thought of these tactics. But other groups are rising up: tenant organizations and community organizations that want to create a space for working families to grow and live in the city. Is that bad? I don't think so. It seems to be the same old fight we had thirty years ago. It's the same fight the Modoc had back in 1873; the protagonists might have changed, but the plea is the same: Let us live in peace in our communities.

•   •   •

I park on Sixteenth and Mission and head east toward Valencia Street. In the BART plaza, an evangelist is speaking into a tiny handheld megaphone that distorts his words so you can't tell what he's saying. But he doesn't care; he's deep into his sermon, his arms flaying and his voice hoarse. Fruitstands, bookstores, cafés, liquor stores, and hotels prevail up and down Sixteenth Street. A blonde woman dressed as a majorette, with a red and blue coat and wearing horizontal striped leggings, is waiting for the light or a cab. It's typical dress here. People do what they want. You want a junkie fix, you can get it. You want a building torched, leave the address. Half a block from where I park, on Hoff Alley, there's a new loft development going up— thirty-five new units at $450,000 each. Six months ago this was an empty warehouse and two small buildings that housed maybe thirty–forty people. The warehouse and the two little buildings burned down one night, and this is what rose up in their place. The Gartland Apartments used to be on the corner where the majorette is standing. When it was torched, twelve people died and thirteen were listed as missing. On the street, the word was that it was arson. Now a three-story apartment building with a doughnut shop on the street level fills the space. Around the corner on Valencia Street stands the burned-out hulk of the King Hotel. The fire just happened a few weeks ago, and already there's a Commercial Space for Lease sign on it. And someone has written over it: No Nos Vamos. I tell you there's a war going on here—you just have to discern the battleground.

Sal's place, a third-story apartment, is on Sixteenth Street above Doctor Bombay's, a popular bar. His doorbell doesn't work, so I stand outside and whistle. Sal's head pops out of a window, his hair tied back in a ponytail, and he says he'll be right down. He opens the door, and I go up the dark stairway. The hallway looks as though it hasn't been painted since the building was opened in about 1910. The rug is all torn up, and the wainscoting has peeled from the wall. His four-room flat looks out over the Sixteenth Street strip. The windows are cracked and taped together. There's an old, rusted kid's tricycle on the fire escape, along with a length of barbed wire.

But Sal is not packing today; instead he's working on a painting. He talks while he paints, spreading a blue glob of paint with a palette knife on the canvas. The figure he's working on is a guitarist, with cobalt blue the dominant color. It's a painting he's doing for Carlos Santana's father-in-law, and every now and then as he works, he steps back and looks at how it's going.

Sal actually has ten more days before he has to move.

"What's the deal?" I ask.

"Landlord wants to rent this unit for $2,200 a month."

I gasp. His place is no more than 450 square feet, even if it is four rooms. Except for the living room, which is about 10 ft. × 12 ft,, all the other rooms are about 6 ft. × 9 ft. But we both know that as soon as the For Rent sign goes up there'll be thirty people waiting in line to look at it, and the chances are excellent that it will rent the first day.

"So where you going, Sal?"

"I'm going to move in with my girlfriend, Laurie, over on the other side of town."

"You're leaving the Mission?"

"No choice, bro. I don't want to, but I have to."

"Is this what you mean by 'the last great days of La Mission'?"

"They're the last days of the Mission for me. I can't afford it any more."

"But the Mission will always be here."

"Yeah, it will always be here. But not for me."

"You know what I say? Wherever I stand is the Mission."

We drink a beer while he continues working on his painting, and we reminisce about people and places we used to know and how everything has changed, and not for the better—at least not in regard to Latinos. He pulls stuff out of everywhere that he's going to throw away, and as usual he has some very interesting things. He points to a wolf skin on the floor in one of the rooms. "A biology teacher gave that to me," he says. "What kind of biology do you teach with a dead wolf?" I can't answer that one.

My eye catches a magazine cover with a painting of a cavalry soldier. I thumb through it, and the 'zine turns out to be a twenty-year-old issue of *American History Illustrated*, and it just so happens that it has the fullest account of the Battle of San Pasqual that I have seen. I searched everywhere for just such an account, and here's where I find it, at Sal's place.

I linger at Sal's as long as I can 'cause I know I won't be coming back here anymore. After a final toast with a Dos XX, I say good-bye to him and wish him well in his new place. I'm going to miss dropping by and watching the scene on Sixteenth Street, but if there is one truism about life, it's that everything changes.

When I leave Sal's, there's a new cast of characters on the street: a drag queen is out early in front of Esta Noche and a leather-and-chains-clad man with tattoos on his skull and arms is walking down Sixteenth Street. In the window of Adobe Books, they're selling an autographed copy of Jack Micheline's *Sixty-seven Poems for Downtrodden Saints*. Too bad ol' Jack never got that much attention when he was alive. Half a block down there's a scatter of books on the sidewalk that someone has abandoned; next to them a man is wrapping himself in a blanket. I run into a young Filipino whom I know, and he's full of energy. He's on his way to catch a Poetry Slam. The young man is wearing a beanie and a green fatigue jacket and seems to have all the answers. "We have to organize," he says before hopping on the 22 Fillmore bus. His words echo in my head as I walk away. Where have I heard that phrase before?

•   •   •

As I wander aimlessly through La Mission this gray day, I'm thinking that everything is lost—until I hear drums coming from inside the Mission Cultural Center. There's a sign posted outside:

MAFEREFUN YEMAYÁ
Cumpleaños de Santo OCHA BIRTHDAY
Offered by Carlos B. Cordova
KI LAYE OMI
Celebration in Honor of Yemayá
And in Completion of his Year as IYAWO

Carlos and I go way back to the days when the Cultural Center first opened, so I go upstairs where the drums are pounding.

A group of some fifty people are celebrating the Tambor de Fundamento, a ceremony using sacred consecrated drums in which only the initiated priests of Santería are allowed to dance because a nonpriest could be possessed by an Orisha, a Santería deity. A Tambor is a particular ceremony of making Ocha, a Santo. This Tambor is in honor of Yemayá, Goddess of the Sea, but it also celebrates Carlos's first year as an Iyawo, an initiate to the priesthood. Carlos was initiated in a secret ceremony in Matanzas, Cuba, in July 1999. On the first day of that seven-day ceremony, his head was shaved. And then for a year he lived within the strict tenets of the Iyawo—a life of reflection, prayer, learning, and humility. During this time, he dressed all in white and used only white bedding, towels, and so on; he even drove a white vehicle. He couldn't use alcohol or drugs; he was restricted to a minimum of public life, no crowds, no concerts; and he was always supervised by the Padrinos and elder *santeros*. He was prohibited from touching people, not even a handshake, or having sexual relations, which must have been the hardest part of his initiation.

In one corner of the gallery where the Tambor is taking place, a beautiful altar is set up, with an intricate arrangement of flowers, coconuts, conch shells, arrows, machetes, watermelons, and candles—all offerings to Yemayá. The people—men, women, and children—are all dressed in white. The ceremony centers around three *bata* drummers who play these short drums from Cuba via West Africa held in their laps. The drums are decorated with sacred cloths, or *mantas*, representing the colors of Yemayá, Oshún, and Changó, and all the drummers are dressed in blue and white. The only exception to the white dress is the Oriaté, the head priest of the Tambor, who is dressed all in blue, also a color of Yemayá. The Oriaté, usually an elder, calls out to the congregation:

> Obatalá, orisha oooh!
> Aguanile, orisha oooh!

And the congregation responds:

> Obatalá, orisha oooh!
> Aguanile, orisha oooh!

A Tambor is a total experience: music, food, dancing, but above all, it is prayer and homage to Yemayá.

As the drums reach a high pitch of intensity, a member of the congregation is mounted by an Orisha and he suddenly starts behaving like a chicken, clucking and flapping his elbows as if they were wings. He scampers around, his head bobbing and pecking at imaginary grains of corn.

Sometimes he breaks into a dance, or he slams his shoulders into someone whom Yemayá wishes to greet. He seems under a spell, operating under a power that is beyond his control. Other members greet each other in spiritual crossings by throwing themselves on the floor and twisting one arm behind their back, in a sort of break-dance greeting. One exceptionally elegant-looking gentleman comes in wearing a white wimpled hat and a long white coat with tails and carrying a carved wooden cane in one hand. He prostrates himself before the altar and shakes a rattle. That's how humans greet a goddess, flat on your belly and face down.

The Santería religion is about twenty-five years old in La Mission. Among the first *santeros* here was a Cuban named Elpidio Alfonso Oba Tun, along with Papo de Jesús, Ricardo Montalvo, and Bobby Céspedes. But it was Oba Tun who brought in Petey de Jesús, who was the first to make his Santo, and therefore the only person in La Mission to have earned the right to hold a Tambor. Petey de Jesús is one of the elders now and is the Oriaté leading the congregation today, a position in Santería that takes years to achieve.

When Santería first came to La Mission, live goats and chickens were sacrificed. Men would offer gold watches at the altars. The woman would pull off solid gold bracelets and offer them to the Orishas. Now the offerings left on the altar are dollar bills. And sometimes the Oriaté has to stop the drummers and get people in the back to stop talking. He explains that this is prayer, and if you want to stay, you have to join in: "Is this how you pray to Yemayá? If you don't join in with more energy, we are going to pack our drums and go home. So you folks back there better shut up and join in right now!"

The Oriaté starts again, and you hear the ancient *santero* call reverberate through the Mission Cultural Center:

> Aguanile, ay, ay,
> Aguanile, ay, ay.

And the congregation responds. It goes back and forth like this, the Oriaté calling, the congregation responding, and the drummers pounding the *batas*.

All kinds of people are here: old, young, kids, black, Latino, white, even a few Asians. Everyone wants to belong, to feel a part of something. If you can't find it outside in the streets or the bar, you can find it here. This is good magic, good energy.

And I realize on this gray, bleak day that the cycles keep turning. Petey's daughter, Aisha, just made her Santo, the initiation into the Santería religion. And I can see that this is going to carry on down, generation after generation, right here in La Mission. Because what we are holding on to and creating is our roots, roots that can never be torn up, roots that go deep beneath the concrete surface that now surrounds us.

• • •

Now it's another day in La Mission, the sun is past its zenith and is heading into the arms of Twin Peaks, and I have come to the end of this journey. This is not the story I started out to write when I first told you of Francisco de Lugo landing off the coast of Mexico back in 1519, but this is the story as it evolved. I had originally meant to describe my sense of place and history in relation to California, my native land. I had wanted to explore the contradictions, knock down the sacred cows of California history. Instead, what happened was that I wound up confronting my own contradictions, attempting to reconcile all the people that I am, have been, and will be. The traditional approach to Xicano history is that we are victims. But the more I probed that idea, the less tangible it seemed, because my own family and my own sense of self tell me that we are not victims. History does not act upon us as we sway passively in our hammocks, but rather we participate in the creation of history every day. As I wrote these stories, I felt that the only way to make sense of my place in California was to insert myself into the history of California, and that's what I've tried to do—find my place in my native land.

I started at high noon, the middle of the day, but since the story is circular, the middle is really the beginning too. Any place in the circle is a good place to start. And this last story begins here. About a thousand years ago a Mesoamerican clan set out on a migration, not knowing or even guessing where they were headed. They wandered for many generations, and they never stayed long in any one place. Somewhere along their journey they were joined by other clans, perhaps more advanced or perhaps more primitive. But their coming together is confirmed by their use of the bow and arrow, the favored weapon of these nomads, and the atlatl, or dart thrower, a more primitive weapon.

But I'm digressing from the story. Several important things happen to this clan during their journey. Their priest, Huitzilopochtli (Hummingbird on the Left), who foresaw and encouraged the migration, ordered them to change their clan name from Azteca to Mexica to reflect their new home and environment. Also several divisions occurred within the original seven clans, or *calpullis*, that set out. At least three times the migration split or divided. The original place from where the migration started is called Aztlán, land of the cranes. And although Xicanos claim the entire Southwest as Aztlán, most likely it is somewhere along the Pacific Coast of Mexico, perhaps as far north as California. I'll give several reasons to support

California as the legendary Aztlán, all of them perhaps valid or invalid. The ancient codices show Aztlán as being surrounded by water, which would make Aztlán an island. In the past, California was believed to be an island (the long peninsula of Baja California), but also, California is filled with lakes and large bodies of water, like the Bay Area or the Klamath Lake area, for instance, that could have been the starting point for this migration. Also, if Aztlán means cranes, the waterways of California abound with cranes, even to this day. Although it is most likely futile to try to establish its definitive location, there is no doubt that Aztlán was somewhere to the north of the Valley of Mexico, where the Mexica finally established their clan. So I'll propose California as the starting point for the Azteca-Mexica migration southward and let others debate its merits and demerits.

What is important for our story is that the original migrating force split off into three branches. In about A.D. 1345, one of these groups reached the Valley of Mexico, where they established the grand city of Tenochtitlan, the city on the lake that would bedazzle the Spaniards, Francisco de Lugo, and all the rest. Another of the clans that split off rejoined the main migration soon after. But one branch of the Azteca-Mexicas is unaccounted for. Did they continue their wanderings? And if so, could they keep the historical memory of being Azteca-Mexicas? As far-fetched as it sounds, that's exactly what some Xicanos say when they claim Aztlán as their homeland. Our historical memory links us to the Mexica and, by extension, to all the Indian clans of the Southwest. This is the same belief that Maestro Andrés Segura taught us, that we are *indios*, that we are Mexicas. If Afro-Cubans and Afro-Boricuas can claim the gods of Africa as their own, why can't we claim the gods of the Mexica as our own?

Follow me now as I go to La Raza Park in the southeast corner of the Mission District. In the center of the park is a little valley, and next to the valley there's a small lake, not unlike a miniature Aztlán, as depicted in the codices. Whether this is by plan or accident I do not know. In the center of the park, a large circle has been marked out with red yarn. There's an altar in the center of the circle and one altar for each of the four directions. Several copal censers release pungent clouds of smoke skyward. Many people are gathered for a ceremony, some in *danzante* regalia, others in typical urban clothes. Some of the *vatos* who hang at the park have come to watch out of curiosity, and some have been invited.

I am here to witness the first Azteca-Mexica wedding ever performed in California or the United States. My godson, Ariel Vargas, is going to marry his high school sweetheart, María Xabela Sánchez, in the same ceremony a Mexica couple would have arranged five hundred years ago. A lot of people have been working on this ceremony for nearly a year. Some of the barrio folks here have never seen anything like this, so many *danzantes* together in one place, all in ceremonial regalia. Some of the families don't even know that their children are *danzantes;* this will be the first time they'll see them perform. And really, although the *danzante* movement has flourished since the time Andrés Segura first brought it to California in the 1970s, in the past five years or so, it has truly come into its own, especially among the youth. There is actually a whole subculture of *danzantes* and their rituals that hardly anyone knows about.

Twenty-six years ago, in a ceremony given to us by Andrés Segura, Roberto Vargas, Victor Hernández Cruz, Ricardo Carillo, Eliás Hruska-Cortés, and I formed a delegation of *brujos* and poets that took Ariel, then six months old, to the top of Bernal Heights, the hill that dominates La Mission. We had been fasting all day and all night, much as we had done to open the Sexto Sol, and as the sun rose, we offered little Ariel to the sun and blessed him with water gathered at a spring by Victor, Ntozake Shange, and me. Years later, Ariel would recount this event to his mother, only in his memory it would take place in a dream, but with every detail so precise it was as if he'd witnessed his own baptism, viewing it from above. Since he was baptized in a Mexica ceremony (later he was also baptized by Ernesto Cardenal and another time by Father Moriarty, in a traditional Catholic ceremony), he wanted to continue with the Mexica tradition for his wedding.

This is no simple wedding. The ritual is more complicated than anything in the Catholic religion. Soon after Ariel proposed to María at Chava's Restaurant on Eighteenth and Shotwell, they started thinking of a Mexica wedding. At first Ariel wasn't too particular about how he was married; a small ceremony was fine with him, perhaps just a few friends up on Bernal Heights, maybe with all of them naked. María had something else in mind. She definitely did not want a Catholic wedding. María wanted something that was natural to what they were doing. Since both of them had been *danzantes* for many years, they decided to be married within this tradition, something they could put their heart and energy into. An Azteca ceremony was the closest thing to them, and they could also bring all the elements of their clan, the *danzante* clan, into it.

María's family had wanted a traditional Catholic wedding, with the bride dressed in white silk and with the accompanying *damas* and *chambe-lains* (bridesmaids and groomsmen) and all that, but she wanted to have everything made by hand, not store-bought, so their ceremony would be stronger. She wanted to tell her friends when she gave out the gifts, "Here, we made this for you."

So María set up workshops to teach other women and men to make the gifts for the wedding guests and to work toward the ceremony. The gifts included miniature *copillis* (*danzante* headdresses), cornhusk dolls, *flores de papel* (paper flowers), sweet-grass wheels, and sashes containing tobacco, sage, cedar, and copal. The sweet-grass wheels, provided by Juanita Chávez, granddaughter of César Chávez, symbolized the great circle of their ceremony, the circle of life, with no beginning and no end. The circle was in fact the key motif, and at the park, the large yarn circle was created so that people would know they were entering a ceremony of life.

The workshops weren't just about the women and the men learning crafts, they were also about learning about themselves. Many of the women in the workshops became *comadres* and forged close links that are the heart of any clan. Thus, among the younger generation of Xicanos a new social relationship is being built around traditions hundreds of years old.

Ariel and María don't call themselves Azteca-Mexicas just because they are *danzantes* or belong to a *danza* group. Ariel doesn't belong to a group, he is more of a free-lance *danzante*, dancing when he feels the energy is right or the celebration-ritual is well organized. As he says, "My commitment is to the *danza*, not to any one group." But he does follow the Mexica ways as formulated by Dr. Miguel León-Portilla, the great investigator of ancient Nahuatl language and traditions. (But all across the Southwest, Xicanos are now tapping into their Indian roots, learning Nahuatl, offering ceremonies, performing rituals that recover our Native American heritage.) Ariel lives as much as possible as a Mexica, and considers himself and his *danzante* friends the new Mexicas of today. Several times during the year they gather for night-long ceremonies, such as the Xilonen ceremony to honor the tender corn. This ceremony appears all over Mesoamerica as far south as Nicaragua, where it is performed to this day. It represents the coming of age for young women, so on that day they honor the young girls, giving them advice, gifts, and responsibilities. The ceremony includes lots of Azteca dancing and singing and *ofrendas*. Another ceremony is for Mayahuel, the Goddess of Healing. This ceremony is for the sick people, to help them recover, to give them strength. It's not just dancing as a performance, it is prayer, and oftentimes the *danzantes* go on all night, from eight in the evening till dawn. And they are dancing not for an audience but for themselves, their community, their ancestors, and the cosmos.

When I question Ariel about his Azteca-Mexica identity, he tells me: "Why are people afraid to say we are Aztecas? When I began to learn about the Azteca view of identity, I found out that for them it was who you are and what you do. It had nothing to do with whether you were pure-blooded, or anything like that. Because, really, the concept of ethnicity comes from Europe; the Aztecas did not think like that. At one time they were Chichimecas—that's what they called themselves because they lived the life of dogs in the desert, in the sense that living was rough, the game smaller, and water scarce. But later on, when they came to Mexico-Tenochtitlan, they became Mexicas. They married into the Colhua-Mexica clan and also became Colhua-Mexicas. So it was a changing identity depending on where and how they were living. So why do I have to say that I'm simply *nicaragüense-mexicano* just because my parents were? If I can say I'm Xicano simply because I'm from here, why can't I also say I'm Azteca 'cause I'm in Aztlán?

"So I figured—*soy azteca*. Later on I thought, well, I'm a businessman too, I bring things to Mexico and from Mexico, so then I decided to call myself a *pochteca*, which is what they were called in Tenochtitlan. And these *pochtecas* were businessmen who spoke many languages and knew things that were going on socially and politically in the other lands they traveled. They were the ambassadors for their people. And that's what I am, that's what I do.

"I learned diplomacy since I was a kid, when my dad (Roberto Vargas) was in Washington. Just like the *pochtecas* did when they traveled around. So now I say I am a *pochteca* and I'm going to get married in a *pochteca* wedding with an Azteca ceremony. Some *danzantes* don't say 'I'm Azteca.' They say 'I'm El Salvadoran,' or 'Soy Xicano, soy Mexicano.' But for me, I say we're today's Mexicas. That's the way I see it. That's why I have to have this kind of ceremony."

He may not be right, in an anthropological sense, because anthropology is based on a European world-view that necessitates an unbending concept of race and heritage. But he speaks from the heart, so why not accept him as he sees himself?

The week before the ceremony, María and her *comadres* went to Humboldt County, where they rented cabins. The women rose early every morning and prayed, giving thanks to women everywhere. They also bathed María and gave her massages. They spoke about many things and were very truthful and forthcoming with each other, speaking *palabras del corazón*. Ariel went to sweats and prayed a lot. He focused on what he wanted and what he was doing, the changes in his life and what it meant for him. He asked his male *danzante* friends to dance hard at the ceremony, to send him good energy.

It's about four in the afternoon and the ceremony is about to begin; this is a communal affair, everyone has their own *manda*, or task, to do. Some brought food, others brought candles, copal, the *sahumador*. Everyone contributed a part of the whole. Ceremony is a communal event, with a communal vision. You do not come to watch, you come to participate, to give of yourself. Ariel and María specifically picked La Raza Park because it was in La Mission, but also because their friends could get there on the bus or by walking, as I did. They were of the community and saw no reason to go to Golden Gate Park or some other place for their ceremony. An unexpected windfall of the location was that many homeboys, whom both María and Ariel knew, were hanging in the park and just joined in, adding their energy to the ceremony.

The entrance to the ceremonial circle is a gate made of willow branches that faces east, the direction of the rising sun. A couple stands inside the gate and smokes you down with burning copal as you enter or leave the circle. The ceremony opens with the *danzantes*, the symbolic warriors, who secure the circle. They are in full regalia—bodies and faces painted, and wearing pheasant-feather headdresses—and they're pounding drums and singing. Then the four couples in charge of the altars of the four directions take their places. Next the families enter, along with Dr. Concha Saucedo, who will officiate at the ceremony. They form their own circle within the circle.

The wedding couple is the last to enter the circle. María wears a full-length white *huipil* and orchids in her hair, and Ariel, a *tilmatli*, or *tilma*, with a red bandanna. Both wear *ayayotle*-shell anklets. They look very Indian, very dark, and very beautiful. Their outfits are absolutely authentic, faithful reproductions from the codices depicting the wedding rites of the Aztecas. In reproducing the *trajes*, they had help from the well-known Chicana artist Carmen Lomas Garza, who is also a *danzante*. Carmen organized workshops and had them research the materials and designs so that both María and Ariel would be dressed in historically accurate clothing. She also taught them how to make their costumes and design the stencils and other decorations. It was Carmen's knowledge, gleaned from the codices, that helped them replicate the ceremony as accurately as they did. They even followed the traditional premarriage ritual of the groom being presented to María's family, as was the custom in Tenochtitlan. After the ceremony, their families will gather for a typical Mexica wedding meal of chicken in mole, three huge pots of frijoles, and about a thousand tortillas.

At the four altars are the *encargados*, couples picked to represent the symbolism of each particular altar. The men wear guayaberas, and the women are decked with orchids. The East altar represents fire, the male energy and wisdom. Irma and Miguel are the padrinos of this altar. They've been married for twenty-six years and they have wisdom, *sabiduría*. Plus, they lead a dance group named Xiucoatl, Fire Serpent, so they are appropriate representatives of the East. The West altar represents the women. The *madrinas* of this gate are also a couple, Estela and Roban, who've been together for twenty-five years. They're badass sisters, beautiful women, and a beautiful couple. For the elders' altar, the North, Ariel and María realized they didn't have much contact with elders, unless you think of someone who's fifty years old as an elder. So they selected a couple who'd gotten together late in life, when both of them were already in their late forties, Joana Uribe and Manuel Mena, social workers and musicians of "Crusin' Coyotes." And for the South, the altar of the youth, they picked a youth advocate community organizer, Ray Balberan, and his wife, Nancy, in some ways because Ray is the eternal youth. And the fifth altar, the one in the center, represents the cosmic force of the universe.

The ceremony begins with an introduction by Dr. Concha Saucedo: "We are here to focus on this couple, to support them . . ." Then Concha, Ariel, and María make offerings to the four directions, ending at the center altar. Then couples from the four altars come up and speak, giving counsel and advice. Then family members speak. My *comadre* speaks and says to Ariel: "Today I know it was worth it to take you away from the war for which you were drafted in Nicaragua." And it goes on like this; everyone who wants to say a few words or sing a song does so. Some of the *danzante* groups dance, furiously, impassioned as if they were going to war. A full-blooded Chumash Indian who has come up from Southern California for the ceremony offers a Chumash song. Then it is time for the vows. During the past year the bride and groom have been meeting with Concha, talking with her about their marriage and what they wanted and expected. Now here they are, getting married. Later on, some people at the ceremony would say they felt they were also getting married, to María and Ariel. They have each written their own vows, which they now repeat to each other. One of the things Ariel promises is not to throw away his family because of alcohol or drugs. Next Concha feeds them each a bit of blue cornmeal and the couple feed each other some blue cornmeal, which represents life; then Concha anoints their foreheads with it. They are kneeling before Concha, and she ties María's *huipil* and Ariel's *tilma* together in a knot, symbolizing their union together. Then the newly married couple offer a *danza*, the *danza* of the *paloma*. In this dance, the *danzantes* hook legs and spin around, representing two doves linked in midflight. Then the couple give away the gifts they had spent six months making by hand in the workshops. Being modern-day Mexicas (or urban Aztecas), there are also some store-bought gifts, especially for the kids, such as spotted backpacks with jaguar faces.

As the sun sinks into the arms of Twin Peaks (Los Pechos de la India) the ceremony concludes. It has lasted four hours, but everyone is smiling, happy. This day rich in ritual and ceremony is almost over, and my sense of what it means to be Xicano, to be Mexican, to be American, to be from

California is fulfilled. My *comadre*, Diana, the mother of Ariel, goes around hugging everyone, with big happy tears streaming down her face. The *encargados* of the altars start packing the artifacts—the traditional wedding dance and dinner is in a rented hall and everything still has to be set up there. A year from now, Ariel and María's first child, Joaquín Tonalli, will be born a few blocks away at County General Hospital, with Twenty-fourth Street, La Raza Park, and Bernal Heights all framed by the window of the delivery room. His birth will mark the beginning of a whole new cycle: he will be the first of many Xicanos who will be born with the historical memory of being Azteca-Mexica.

• • •

Though I don't know it yet, a year from now the dot-com heyday will be over, the high flyers will have crash-landed onto the refuse heaps of the dot-com economy. The newly built lofts will stand unrented, as empty as the hearts that built them. In April 2001, Ernesto Cardenal will return to La Mission and read poetry to a standing-room-only crowd at the Women's Building, and his reading will be a wake-up call, a resounding statement that we (La Raza) are not leaving La Mission.

Yes, La Mission has changed. We've lost some families to the forced evictions that cut a swath through our barrio, but we'll never stop coming, returning to our traditional lands, as it has always been. We'll never lose our heart here in La Mission, we'll always be *el corazón del corazón*. Our clan will grow again, just as the cactus does, and Tonalli and his generation will know that we belong here, that this land has always been ours.

I stay in the park talking to friends and enjoying the lingering energy of the ceremony. Many other people are staying too, as if we want to cling to this day a little longer. It feels exactly like home, as if we had never left. I know I have witnessed something unique, a reaffirmation of our culture, a reclaiming of our historical memory that will have repercussions for many generations to come. Everyone here today will remember this ritual; it's what we've been doing for hundreds of years. Only now we can do it in the open again, with no fear of persecution or of being Azteca-Mexicas. Already, other *danzante* couples are planning traditional Azteca-Mexica weddings. And everywhere the pure, good heart of our people is gaining strength.

Here's a story I've saved till the end, another version of how we became a mestizo people, but a version not cloaked in the angry rape of Anahuac. Of the two Spaniards shipwrecked on the coast of Yucatán in 1511, one of them, Jerónimo de Aguilar, will return to Cortés and reintegrate himself with the Spaniards and will be one of the two translators who interprets for

Cortés and Moctezuma. But the other Spaniard, Gonzalo Guerrero, will not return; instead he will stay with the Maya in Akumal, he will tattoo himself, and later he will lead the Maya in war against the Spaniards. He'll marry an Indian woman, Ixamal, and their children will be the first mestizos. So I refuse the concept that we are born of violence; instead, I see us as being born of love.

These are the wounds I've healed with the flowers of memory. They'll bloom here in the *corazón* of the Mexica clans that after a thousand years of wandering have at last returned to their ancestral home, a place named Aztlán by our grandfathers and our grandmothers, the land of cranes.

This is what my memory has brought me.

NOTES

PREFACE

1. A very limited and unofficial list of new Latino historians who are rethinking California history or whose work inspires my own includes Antonia I. Castañeda, Ramón A. Gutiérrez, Alberto Hurtado, Genaro Padilla, and Rosaura Sánchez.

2. For Bancroft's biases, see Rosaura Sánchez, *Telling Identities*, 16–32.

3. See Genaro M. Padilla, *My History, Not Yours*, 105.

4. Patricia Nelson Limerick, *Something in the Soil*, 36.

5. Néstor García Canclini, *Hybrid Cultures*, 172–173.

6. Mariano Vallejo, as quoted in Padilla, *My History, Not Yours*, 90.

7. Tomás Eloy Martínez, *Santa Evita*, 129.

8. Gore Vidal, "The Agreed-Upon Facts," 125–152.

9. The quote by Oscar Wilde is from Martínez, *Santa Evita*, 67.

PHANTOMS IN THE MIRROR

1. Arthur Dunning Spearman, S.J., *The Five Franciscan Churches of Mission Santa Clara*, 15.

2. For a list of founders of San José de Guadalupe, see Bancroft, *History of California*, 1: 312. For Los Angeles, see Thomas Workman Temple II, "Se fundaron un pueblo de espanoles [*sic*]," 69–149.

3. Nigel Davies, *The Aztecs: A History*, 238.

4. "The Chronicle of Fray Francisco de Aguilar," 137.

5. Bernal Díaz del Castillo, *The Conquest of New Spain*, 66.

6. Ibid., 72–73.

7. See Díaz, *Conquest of New Spain*, 172, and Alice del Pinal, "Malintzín: Mito e historia," 78–87.

8. Díaz, *Conquest of New Spain*, 178.

9. William H. Prescott, *The Conquest of Mexico*, 286–287.

10. Díaz, *Conquest of New Spain*, 214.

11. Ibid., 217.

12. For the role of women in pre-Cortesian era, see Arnoldo Carlos Vento, *Mestizo: The History, Culture, and Politics of the Mexican and the Chicano*, 78–79. For lineage through women, including Ilancueitl as the first ruler of Tenochtitlan, see Susan Dale Gillespie, "Aztec Prehistory as Postconquest Dialogue: A Structural Analysis of the Royal Dynasty of Tenochtitlan," 297–303.

13. Davies, *Aztecs*, 264–265.

14. Díaz, *Conquest of New Spain*, 227.

15. Ibid., 245–246.

16. Ibid., 297.

17. Miguel León-Portilla, *The Broken Spears*, 93.

18. Díaz, *Conquest of New Spain*, 236.

19. León-Portilla, *Broken Spears*, 110–112.

20. Ibid., 101.

21. Ibid., 109.

22. Díaz, *Conquest of New Spain*, 411.

23. See Francisco A. de Icaza, *Diccionario autobiográfico de los conquistadores y pobladores de Nueva España*.

24. Díaz, *Conquest of New Spain*, 224.

25. See José Vasconcelos, *The Cosmic Race: La raza cósmica*.

26. Ibid., 11–13.

27. See José Vasconcelos, *Breve historia de México*, 15–26.

28. See Michael E. Smith, *The Aztecs*, 44–49.

29. Octavio Paz, *The Labyrinth of Solitude: Life and Thought in Mexico*, 65–90.

30. Vento, *Mestizo*, 17–18.

31. Paz, *Labyrinth of Solitude*, 43.

32. For a chemical analysis of protein in tortillas and beans, see Smith, *Aztecs*, 68.

THE "GOOD OLD MISSION DAYS" NEVER EXISTED

1. Mrs. Fremont Older, *California Missions and Their Romances*, xxiii. "Spiritual conquest" is a term that appears in Spanish documents and other texts referring to Serra's expedition and related events, though Older herself does not use the term.

2. Maynard Geiger, O.F.M., *The Life and Times of Junípero Serra, O.F.M.: The Man Who Never Turned Back (1713–1784)*, 1: 146–147, 172–173.

3. Maynard Geiger, O.F.M., *Franciscan Missionaries in Hispanic California, 1769–1848: A Biographical Dictionary*, 162–164.

4. Zephyrin Engelhart, O.F.M. *The Missions and Missionaries of California*, 1: 304, 423.

5. Ibid., 339, 370.

6. Francisco Palóu, *Life and Apostolic Labors of the Venerable Father Junípero Serra*, 76.

7. Hubert Howe Bancroft, *History of California, 1542–1800*, 1: 138.

8. Palóu, *Life and Labors of Serra,* 179.

9. Bancroft, *History of California,* 1: 316.

10. Geiger, *Franciscan Missionaries,* 162–164.

11. Ibid., 163.

12. Arthur Dunning Spearman, S.J., *The Five Franciscan Churches of Mission Santa Clara 1777–1825,* 12.

13. Palóu, *Life and Labors of Serra,* 213.

14. See Spearman, *Five Franciscan Churches.*

15. Geiger, *Franciscan Missionaries,* 162–164.

16. Spearman, *Five Franciscan Churches,* 34–36.

17. Ibid., 38.

18. This figure is from a "spiritual table" adapted from Engelhart's *Missions and Missionaries of California,* published in *The California Missions: A Pictorial History,* ed. Dorothy Krell; Paul C. Johnson, original ed., 316.

19. Geiger, *Franciscan Missionaries,* 162–164.

20. Spearman, *Five Franciscan Churches,* 37.

21. George E. Tinker, *Missionary Conquest: The Gospel and Native American Genocide,* 18–20.

22. Susanna Bryant Dakin, *A Scotch Paisano: Hugo Reid's Life in California, 1832–1852, Derived from His Correspondence,* 269.

23. Daniel Fogel, *Junípero Serra, the Vatican, and Enslavement Theology,* 120.

24. Tinker, *Missionary Conquest,* 55–56.

25. Francis J. Weber, *Mission San Fernando,* 7–10.

26. Ibid., 16.

27. Tinker, *Missionary Conquest,* 51.

28. Fogel, *Junípero Serra,* 114.

29. Ibid., 131.

30. José del Carmen Lugo, "Vida de un ranchero," 227.

31. John Ogden Pohlmann, "California's Mission Myths," 157–158.

32. Ibid., 357.

33. Ibid., 351–353.

34. Ibid., 427.

35. Ibid., 335–339.

36. Robert H. Jackson and Edward Castillo offer a similar observation in their book *Indians, Franciscans, and Spanish Colonization: The Impact of the Mission System on California Indians,* 35.

37. Lawrence C. Jorgensen, *The San Fernando Valley, Past and Present,* 52–55.

38. Tinker, *Missionary Conquest,* 60–61.

39. Fogel, *Junípero Serra,* 138–140.

40. Mrs. Fremont Older, *California Missions and Their Romances,* 176.

41. Alberto Hurtado, *Indian Survival on the California Frontier,* 43.

42. Pohlmann, "California's Mission Myth," 212.

43. Fogel, *Junípero Serra,* 50, 122.

44. From author's notes taken on a visit to Mission San Fernando.

45. David J. Weber, *The Mexican Frontier 1821–1846: The American Southwest under Mexico*, 66–67.

46. Jorgensen, *San Fernando Valley*, 30–34.

47. Pohlmann, "California's Mission Myth," 287.

48. Ibid., 382–384.

49. For the complete history and analysis of the *Via Crucis* panels from Mission San Fernando, see Norman Neuerburg, "The Indian Via Crucis from Mission San Fernando: An Historical Exposition," 329–382.

50. See Octavio Paz's essay on Bustos, "I, a Painter, an Indian from This Village . . . ," 85–110.

51. H. N. Rust, "The Last San Fernando Indian," 110–112.

52. Marie Harrington, *On the Trail of Forgotten People.*

JOSEFA OF DOWNIEVILLE: THE OBSCURE LIFE AND NOTABLE DEATH OF A CHICANA IN GOLD RUSH CALIFORNIA

1. David D. Alt and Donald W. Hyndman, *Roadside Geology of Northern California*, 91.

2. Robert F. Heizer and Adan E. Treganza, *Mines and Quarries of the Indians of California*, 342.

3. Antonio Franco Coronel, "Cosas de California," 77–78.

4. S. J. Holliday, *Rush for Riches: Gold Fever and the Making of California*, 30.

5. John Bidwell, *In California before the Gold Rush*, 78–79.

6. Holliday, *Rush for Riches*, 124.

7. Robert F. Heizer, *The Destruction of California Indians*, 16.

8. Charles Howard Shinn, *Mining Camps: A Study in American Frontier Government*, 179–180.

9. Hubert Howe Bancroft, *Popular Tribunals*, 1: 587.

10. One of the worst retellings of Josefa's story can be found in Josiah Royce, *California: From the Conquest in 1846 to the Second Vigilance Committee in San Francisco*, 290–295.

11. Theressa Gay, in her definitive biography of Marshall, *James W. Marshall: The Discoverer of California Gold*, offers three different possibilities for the whereabouts of the first gold nugget found. Erwin G. Gudde, who edited *Bigler's Chronicle of the West*, the only eyewitness account of Marshall showing his find to the workers at the mill, states that he has found no evidence that the flake exhibited in the Smithsonian Institution has anything to do with "the first piece of gold ever discovered in the northern part of Upper California." I agree. (The flake loaned by the Smithsonian to the Oakland Museum was originally sent to Washington, D.C., by Capt. John Folsom, who supposedly acquired it from Sutter in August 1848, seven months after the original discovery. It was this detail—the time elapsed between the discovery and Folsom's acquisition of the nugget—that first led me to doubt the authenticity of the Smithsonian's claim.) Almost all stories of the Gold Rush are mired in myths and contradictions, including the exact date of Marshall's find, which was most likely *not* January 24, but sometime that week. History, then, is a very inexact profession.

12. The size of the nugget comes from the author's notes taken at the Oakland

Museum; other writers mention chunks of gold weighing as much as two hundred pounds. See John McPhee, *Assembling California*, 57.

13. Holliday, *Rush for Riches*, 152.

14. Bidwell, *In California before the Gold Rush*, 92.

15. Elliot H. Koeppel, *The California Gold Country: Highway 49 Revisited*, 119.

16. Oscar Zeta Acosta, *The Autobiography of a Brown Buffalo*, 108–111.

17. Roger Lescohier, *Gold Giants of Grass Valley: History of the Empire and North Star Mines, 1850–1956*, i.

18. The source for J. J. McCloskey is the *San Jose Pioneer*, November 12, 1881, as quoted by William Secrest. I have not seen the original, but I have no reason to doubt its authenticity. William B. Secrest, *Juanita: The Only Woman Lynched in the Gold Rush Days*, 29.

19. Coronel, "Cosas de California," 87.

20. Leonard Pitt, *The Decline of the Californios: A Social History of the Spanish-Speaking Californians, 1846–1890*, 60–64. For the miners' definition of "foreigner," see Winifred Storss Hill, *Tarnished Gold: Prejudice during the California Gold Rush*, 11–13.

21. Morefield, *Mexican Adaptation*, 9.

22. Koeppel, *California Gold Country*, 217.

23. Franklin A. Buck, *A Yankee Trader in the Gold Rush: The Letters of Franklin A. Buck*, 93. See also Erwin G. Gudde, *Gold Rush Mining Camps*, 100.

24. Ramón Gil Navarro, *The Gold Rush Diary of Ramón Gil Navarro*, 18.

25. Ibid., 94–95.

26. Ibid., 146.

27. Ibid., 218.

28. Ibid., 29.

29. Alt and Hyndman, *Roadside Geology of Northern California*, 130.

30. Lescohier, *Gold Giants of Grass Valley*, i.

31. The Empire Mine paragraph is from notes taken during a visit to the mine and from Lescohier, *Gold Giants of Grass Valley*, 15.

32. Secrest, *Juanita*, 7.

33. Koeppel, *California Gold Country*, 147.

34. Secrest, *Juanita*, 8–9.

35. Antonia I. Castañeda, "Gender, Race, and Culture: Spanish-Mexican Women in the Historiography of Frontier California," 8–20.

36. Ibid., 9–10.

37. Secrest, *Juanita*, 29.

38. The most complete account of Josefa's story appears in *The Steamer Pacific Star*, July 15, 1851.

39. Genaro M. Padilla, *My History, Not Yours: The Formation of Mexican American Autobiography*, 109–152.

40. Although Castañeda's essay is about Amerindian women, I think her observations can transfer to a dark Mexican woman such as Josefa. See Antonia I. Castañeda, "Sexual Violence in the Politics and Policies of the Conquest: Amerindian Women and the Spanish Conquest of Alta California," 15–33.

41. Padilla, *My History, Not Yours*, 128–129.

42. Koeppel, *California Gold Country*, 219.

43. Ibid., 219.

GATHERING THUNDER

1. Dave Ballard, "The Battle of San Pasqual," 4–48.

2. See José del Carmen Lugo, "Vida de un ranchero," 185–236.

3. Ibid., 236.

4. Ibid.

5. Ibid., 186.

6. "El Plan Espiritual de Aztlán," 402–406.

7. Carlos Muñoz Jr., *Youth, Identity, Power: The Chicano Movement*, 87.

8. Ibid., 87.

TROPI(LO)CALIDAD: MACONDO IN LA MISSION

1. Ysidro Ramón Macías, "The Evolution of the Mind," 13–21.

2. For a history of the Mission District, see *A Plan for the Inner Mission*, 7–14.

3. Editorial Pocho-Ché was an offshoot of the magazine *El Pocho-Ché*. It was basically a collective of poets from the Mission who published a series of poetry books and one magazine.

4. Third World Communications was a collective of collectives formed by the poets connected with Editorial Pocho-Ché and Asian American, Native American, and Afro-American writers. TWC produced and edited two anthologies, one of which was *Third World Women* (1973).

5. The second anthology by TWC was *Time to Greez! Incantations from the Third World*, with an introduction by Maya Angelou (1975).

6. Victor Hernández Cruz, *Snaps!*

7. Victor Hernández Cruz, *Tropicalization*.

8. Jean Franco, *The Modern Culture of Latin America*. This book exposed us to the political-artistic movements of Latin America and thus influenced our own perspectives on the politics of art and literature.

9. Roberto Vargas, "Carta/poema pa Ernesto Cardenal," *Umbra No. 5: Latin Soul* (San Francisco: Society of Umbra, n.d.), 62–63. Note: The slashes (/) indicate a compound noun and should be read as one word, as in "carta/poema," i.e., letter/poem. By combining the nouns, the meaning changes to be both a letter and a poem to Ernesto Cardenal. The same goes for other compound nouns, such as "nica/pocho" (meaning both *nicaragüense* and *pocho* (Chicano). A few other explanations: "tacho tachito," is the nickname and diminutive for Anastasio, the first name of Anastasio Somoza; "caca, caca, aca" is a play on *caca* (shit) and *acá* (here): here in the shit. "Patarajada" is a pejorative, meaning "without shoes," as in "indio patarajada" (shoeless Indian).

The poem is bilingual, but I offer here a translation of the poem fragment:

letter/poem for ernesto cardenal

. . . and how many pains/hungers
tortures haven't you

suffered brother . . . you
in the armpit of the
tyrant/puppet of United
Fruit Co. and the U.S.
tacho tachito (like he
who says "not worth shit")
I . . . nica/pocho
patarajada (in high laced boots)
knee-deep in shit shit (here)
in the very mouth of the
pig of america u.s.a.
all red/white/blue
(like he who says
"not worth shit") . . .

10. See U.S. Congress, House, *Human Rights in Nicaragua, Guatemala, and El Salvador: Implications for U.S. Policy*, 57–64, 228.

11. Alejandro Murguía, *Southern Front*, short stories (1990).

12. Gabriel García Márquez, "Los sandinistas se toman el Palacio Nacional de Managua," 7–21.

13. Ibid., 15.

14. For an analysis of the Contra War and the role of the United States, please refer to Noam Chomsky, *Turning the Tide: U.S. Intervention in Central America and the Struggle for Peace.*

PETROGLYPH OF MEMORY

1. Albert L. Hurtado, introduction to *The Destruction of California Indians*, v–ix.

2. Lawrence C. Jorgensen, ed., *The San Fernando Valley, Past and Present*, 34.

3. For the full story, see Theodora Kroeber, *Ishi in Two Worlds: A Biography of the Last Wild Indian in North America*; and Robert F. Heizer and Albert B. Elsasser, eds., *Original Accounts of the Lone Woman of San Nicolas Island.*

4. Mary Hill, *California Landscape: Origin and Evolution*, 47.

5. See Mark Raymond Harrington, *An Ancient Site at Borax Lake.*

6. Ibid., 175.

7. Carrol B. Howe, *Ancient Modocs of California and Oregon*, 19–34.

8. See Howe, *Ancient Modocs*, 19–35.

9. The name Modokus and the physical characteristics of the Modoc are from Stephen Powers, *Tribes of California*, 252–253. The item about contraception comes from Robert F. Heizer and Albert B. Elsasser, eds., *The Natural World of the California Indians*, 131.

10. Verne F. Ray, *Primitive Pragmatists: The Modoc Indians of Northern California*, 9–10.

11. See Howe, *Ancient Modocs.*

12. Ibid., 9 and 171.

13. Keith A. Murray, *The Modocs and Their War*, 8.

14. Ibid., 15–20.

15. Ibid., 27.

16. Ray, *Primitive Pragmatists*, 202–203.

17. Ibid., 3.

18. Murray, *Modocs and Their War*, 35.

19. The Modoc names are from Jeff C. Riddle, *The Indian History of the Modoc War, and the Causes That Led to It*.

20. For a full list, see Erwin N. Thompson, *Modoc War: Its Military History and Topography*, 168–170.

21. The description of her as "the brains" comes from William Thompson, *Reminiscences of a Pioneer*, 87; as a spokesperson, from Murray, *Modocs and Their War*, 154.

22. The photos of the Modocs appear in the books by Murray, Erwin N. Thompson, Dillon, and Riddle. The best were taken by Louis Heller; others by Eadweard Muybridge; see Richard Dillon, *Burnt-Out Fires*, 278. For a description of the process, see Arthur Quinn, *Hell with the Fire Out: A History of the Modoc War*, 171.

23. Murray, *Modocs and Their War*, 37.

24. Ibid., 37.

25. Ibid., 74–79.

26. See Murray, *Modocs and Their War*, 78–93. For non-Modoc Indians in the Lava Beds, see W. Thompson, *Reminiscences*, 85, and E. Thompson, *Modoc War*, 175.

27. E. Thompson, *Modoc War*, 43.

28. Major J. G. Trimble, "Reminiscences," from Brady's *Northwestern Fights and Fighters*, as it appears in Murray, *Modocs and Their War*, 110.

29. E. Thompson, *Modoc War*, 170.

30. Murray, *Modocs and Their War*, 118.

31. E. Thompson, *Modoc War*, 54–59.

32. Murray, *Modocs and Their War*, 169–170.

33. Riddle, *Indian History of the Modoc War*, 72.

34. Murray, *Modocs and Their War*, 188–192.

35. See Powers, *Tribes of California*, 253 and 261.

36. Dillon, *Burnt-Out Fires*, 260.

37. Ibid., 275.

38. A. B. Meacham, quoted in Murray, *Modocs and Their War*, 231.

39. Murray, *Modocs and Their War*, 261.

40. Ibid., 308.

41. Ibid., 277.

42. Riddle, *Indian History of the Modoc War*, 173.

43. Quinn, *Hell with the Fire Out*, 193.

44. Dillon, *Burnt-Out Fires*, 335.

THE MARIN HEADLANDS: A MEDITATION ON PLACE

1. Harold and Ann Lawrence Gilliam, *Marin Headlands: Portals of Time*, 13–14.

2. James Delgado and Stephen Haller, *Shipwrecks at the Golden Gate*, 76–79.

3. See David D. Alt and Donald W. Hyndman, *Roadside Geology of Northern California*, 1–35.

4. Ibid., 18–20.

5. Bonnie J. Peterson, ed., *Dawn of the World: Stories Told by the Coast Miwok Indians*, 13–14.

6. Glenn Keator, Linda Yamane, and Ann Lewis, *In Full View: Three Ways of Seeing California Plants*, 51.

7. Francis Fletcher, *The World Encompassed by Sir Francis Drake*, 131.

8. *San Francisco Chronicle*, December 30, 2000, sec. A, 17.

9. Frederick J. Teggart, ed., *The Anza Expedition of 1775–1776: Diary of Pedro Font*, 69.

10. Nellie Van de Grift Sanchez. *Spanish and Indian Place-Names of California: Their Meaning and Their Romance*, 134–174.

11. Older, *California Missions and Their Romances*, 275–289.

12. Ibid.

13. Barry Spitz, *Mill Valley: The Early Years*, 23.

14. Stephen Richardson, quoted in Jack Mason, *Point Reyes: The Solemn Land*, 13.

15. Antonio Osio, *The History of Alta California: A Memoir of Mexican California*, 9–10.

16. Barry Spitz, *Mill Valley*, 25–26.

17. Gilliam, *Marin Headlands*, 31.

THE HOMECOMING OF AN AZTECA-MEXICA CLAN

1. *San Francisco Bay Guardian*, May 30–June 5, 2001.

SELECTED BIBLIOGRAPHY

Books

Acosta, Oscar Zeta. *The Autobiography of a Brown Buffalo*. New York: Vintage, 1989.

Alt, David D., and Donald W. Hyndman. *Roadside Geology of Northern California*. 19th ed. Missoula, Mont.: Mountain Press, 1975.

Bancroft, Hubert Howe. *History of California, 1542–1800*. Vol. 1, facsimile. Santa Barbara, Calif.: Wallace Hebberd, 1963.

———. *Popular Tribunals*. Vol. 1. San Francisco: San Francisco History Company, 1887.

Bidwell, John. *In California before the Gold Rush*. Foreword by Lindley Bynum. Los Angeles: Ward Ritchie Press, 1948.

Broda, Johanna, David Carrasco, and Eduardo Matos Moctezuma. *The Great Temple of Tenochtitlan: Center and Periphery in the Aztec World*. Berkeley, Los Angeles, and London: University of California Press, 1987.

Buck, Franklin A. *A Yankee Trader in the Gold Rush: The Letters of Franklin A. Buck*. Comp. Katherine A. White. Boston: Houghton Mifflin, 1930.

Caughey, John W. *Gold Is the Cornerstone*. Berkeley and Los Angeles: University of California Press, 1948.

Chomsky, Noam. *Turning the Tide: U.S. Intervention in Central America and the Struggle for Peace*. Boston: South End Press, 1985.

Clappe, Louise A. *The Shirley Letters*. Santa Barbara, Calif.: Peregrine, 1970.

Collins, Maurice. *Cortés and Moctezuma*. London: Faber and Faber, 1963.

Costo, Rupert, and Jeannette Henry, eds. *The Missions of California: A Legacy of Genocide*. San Francisco: Indian Historian Press, 1987.

Dakin, Susanna Bryant. *A Scotch Paisano: Hugo Reid's Life in California, 1832–1852, Derived from His Correspondence*. Berkeley: University of California Press, 1939.

Davies, Nigel. *The Aztecs: A History*. Norman: University of Oklahoma Press, 1982.

Delgado, James, and Stephen Haller. *Shipwrecks at the Golden Gate*. N.p.: Lexikos, 1989.

Díaz del Castillo, Bernal. *The Bernal Díaz Chronicles: The True Story of the Conquest of Mexico.* Trans. and ed. Albert Idell. New York: Doubleday, 1957.

———. *The Conquest of New Spain.* Trans. J. M. Cohen. Middlesex, England: Penguin Classics, 1970.

Dillon, Richard. *Burnt-Out Fires.* Englewood Cliffs, N.J.: Prentice-Hall, 1973.

Engelhart, Zephyrin, O.F.M. *The Missions and Missionaries of California.* Vol. 1. Published in *The California Missions: A Pictorial History,* ed. Dorothy Krell; original ed., Paul C. Johnson. Menlo Park: Sunset Books, 1979.

Fletcher, Francis. *The World Encompassed by Sir Francis Drake.* Introduction by W. S. W. Vaux. 1854. Reprint, New York: Burt Franklin, n.d.

Fogel, Daniel. *Junípero Serra, the Vatican, and Enslavement Theology.* San Francisco: Ism Press, 1988.

Franco, Jean. *The Modern Culture of Latin America.* London: Penguin Books, 1972.

Fuentes, Carlos. *The Orange Tree.* Trans. Alfred Mac Adam. New York: Farrar, Straus and Giroux, 1994.

Fuentes, Patricia de, ed. and trans. *The Conquistadors: First-Person Accounts of the Conquest of Mexico.* Preface, Howard F. Cline. New York: Orion Press, 1963.

García Canclini, Néstor. *Hybrid Cultures: Strategies for Entering and Leaving Modernity.* Trans. Christopher L. Chiappari and Silvia L. López; forward by Renato Rosaldo. Minneapolis and London: University of Minnesota Press, 1995.

Gardiner, C. Harvey. *The Constant Captain: Gonzalo de Sandoval.* Carbondale, Ill.: Southern Illinois University Press, 1961.

———. *Martín López: Conquistador Citizen of Mexico.* Westport, Conn.: Greenwood Press, 1958.

Gay, Theressa. *James W. Marshall: The Discoverer of California Gold—A Biography.* Georgetown, Calif.: Talisman Press, 1967.

Geiger, Maynard, O.F.M. *Franciscan Missionaries in Hispanic California, 1769–1848: A Biographical Dictionary.* San Marino, Calif.: The Huntington Library, 1969.

———. *The Life and Times of Junípero Serra, O.F.M.: The Man Who Never Turned Back (1713–1784).* Vol. 1. Washington, D.C.: Academy of American Franciscan History, 1959.

Gilliam, Harold, and Ann Lawrence Gilliam. *Marin Headlands: Portals of Time.* N.p.: Golden Gate National Park Association, 1993.

Gudde, Elisabeth K., ed. *Gold Rush Mining Camps.* Berkeley, Los Angeles, and London: University of California Press, 1975.

Gudde, Erwin G. *Bigler's Chronicle of the West.* Berkeley and Los Angeles: University of California Press, 1962.

Gutiérrez, Ramón A., and Richard J. Orsi, eds. *Contested Eden: California before the Gold Rush.* Berkeley, Los Angeles, and London: University of California Press, 1998.

Harrington, Marie. *On the Trail of Forgotten People.* Reno, Nev.: Great Basin Press, n.d.

Harrington, Mark Raymond. *An Ancient Site at Borax Lake.* Southwest Museum Papers, No. 16. Highland Park, Calif.: Southwest Museum, 1948.

———. *Gypsum Cave, Nevada.* Southwest Museum Papers, No. 8. Los Angeles: Southwest Museum, 1933.

Heizer, Robert F. *The Destruction of California Indians.* Lincoln: University of Nebraska Press, Bison Books, 1974.

Heizer, Robert F., and Adan E. Treganza. *Mines and Quarries of the Indians of California.* Ramona, Calif.: Ballena Press, 1972.

Heizer, Robert F., and Albert B. Elsasser, eds. *The Natural World of the California Indians.* Berkeley, Los Angeles, and London: University of California Press, 1980.

———, eds. *Original Accounts of the Lone Woman of San Nicolas Island.* University of California Archaeological Survey, Report No. 55, 1961.

Hernández Cruz, Victor. *Snaps!* New York: Random House, 1969.

———. *Tropicalization.* Berkeley: Reed, Cannon, and Johnson, 1976.

Hill, Mary. *California Landscape: Origin and Evolution.* Berkeley, Los Angeles, and London: University of California Press, 1984.

Hill, Winifred Storss. *Tarnished Gold: Prejudice during the California Gold Rush.* Bethesda, Md.: International Scholars Publications, 1995.

Holliday, S. J. *Rush for Riches: Gold Fever and the Making of California.* Berkeley, Los Angeles, and London: Oakland Museum and University of California Press, 1999.

Howe, Carrol B. *Ancient Modocs of California and Oregon.* Portland, Oreg.: Binford and Mort, 1979.

Hurtado, Alberto. *Indian Survival on the California Frontier.* New Haven and London: Yale University Press, 1988.

Icaza, Francisco A. de. *Diccionario autobiográfico de los conquistadores y pobladores de Nueva España.* Vols. 1 and 2. Madrid: N.p., 1923.

Icazbalceta, Joaquín García. *Colección de documentos para la historia de México, Número 47.* Mexico City: Editorial Porrúa, 1980.

Jackson, Joseph H. *Anybody's Gold: The Story of California's Mining Towns.* New York: D. Appleton-Century, 1941.

Jackson, Robert H., and Edward Castillo. *Indians, Franciscans, and Spanish Colonization: The Impact of the Mission System on California Indians.* Albuquerque: University of New Mexico Press, 1995.

Johnson, Susan Lee. *Roaring Camp: The Social World of the California Gold Rush.* New York and London: W. W. Norton, 2000.

Jorgensen, Lawrence C., ed. *The San Fernando Valley Past and Present.* Los Angeles: Pacific Rim Research, 1982.

Keator, Glenn, Linda Yamane, and Ann Lewis. *In Full View: Three Ways of Seeing California Plants.* Berkeley, Calif.: Heyday Books, 1995.

Koeppel, Elliot H. *The California Gold Country: Highway 49 Revisited.* N.p. (Calif.): Malakoff, 1999.

Kroeber, Theodora. *Ishi in Two Worlds: A Biography of the Last Wild Indian in North America.* Berkeley, Los Angeles, and London: University of California Press, 1961.

Lapp, Rudolph M. *Blacks in Gold Rush California.* New Haven and London: Yale University Press, 1977.

Lee, Hector. *Heroes, Villains, and Ghosts: Folklore of Old California.* Santa Barbara, Calif.: Capra Press, 1984.

León-Portilla, Miguel. *De Teotihuacan a los aztecas: Fuentes e interpretaciones históricas.* Mexico City: Universidad Nacional Autónoma de México, 1972.

————. *Endangered Cultures.* Trans. Julie Goodson-Lawes. Dallas: Southern Methodist University Press, 1990.

————, ed. *The Broken Spears.* Trans. Lysander Kemp; foreword by J. Jorge Klor de Alva. Boston: Beacon Press, 1990.

Lescohier, Roger. *Gold Giants of Grass Valley: History of the Empire and North Star Mines, 1850–1956.* Grass Valley, Calif.: Empire Mine Park Association, 1995.

Limerick, Patricia Nelson. *Something in the Soil: Legacies and Reckonings in the New West.* New York and London: W. W. Norton, 2000.

Lopez, Barry. *Crossing Open Ground.* New York: Vintage, 1989.

Martínez, Tomás Eloy. *Santa Evita.* Trans. Helen Lane. New York: Knopf, 1996.

Martínez Paredes, Domingo. *El Popol Vuh tiene razón: Teoría sobre la cosmogonia pre-americana.* Mexico City: Editorial Orión, 1968.

Mason, Jack. *Point Reyes: The Solemn Land.* Inverness, Calif.: North Shore Books, 1970.

McPhee, John. *Assembling California.* New York: Farrar, Straus and Girous, 1993.

Mirikitani, Janice, Luís Syquia, Jr., Buriel Clay II, Janet Campbell Hale, Alejandro Murguía, and Roberto Vargas, eds. *Time to Greez! Incantations from the Third World.* Introduction by Maya Angelou. San Francisco: Glide Publications and Third World Communications, 1975.

Moctezuma, Eduardo Matos. *Treasures of the Great Temple.* La Jolla, Calif.: Alti Publishing, 1990.

Morefield, Richard. *The Mexican Adaptation in American California 1846–1875.* Berkeley: University of California, 1955. Reprint, San Francisco: R and E Research, 1971.

Muñoz, Carlos, Jr. *Youth, Identity, Power: The Chicano Movement.* London and New York: Verso, 1989.

Murguía, Alejandro. *Southern Front.* Tempe: Bilingual Review Press, 1990. Short stories.

Murray, Keith A. *The Modocs and Their War.* Norman and London: University of Oklahoma Press, 1959.

Navarro, Ramón Gil. *The Gold Rush Diary of Ramón Gil Navarro.* Ed. and trans. María del Carmen Ferreyra and David S. Reher. Lincoln and London: University of Nebraska Press, 2000.

Nieva López, María del Carmen. *Mexikayotl: Esencia del mexicano.* Mexico City: Editorial Orión, 1969.

Nunis, Doyce B., Jr., ed. *Mission San Fernando Rey de España 1791–1997: A Bicentennial Tribute.* Los Angeles: Historical Society of Southern California, 1997.

Older, Mrs. Fremont, *California Missions and Their Romances,* New York: Tudor Publishing, 1945.

Osio, Antonio. *The History of Alta California: A Memoir of Mexican California.* Translated, edited, and annotated by Rose Marie Beebe and Robert M. Senkewicz. Madison: University of Wisconsin Press, 1996.

Padilla, Genaro M. *My History, Not Yours: The Formation of Mexican American Autobiography*. Madison and London: University of Wisconsin Press, 1993.

Palóu, Francisco. *Life and Apostolic Labors of the Venerable Father Junípero Serra*. Trans. C. Scott Williams; introduction and notes by George Wharton James. Pasadena, Calif.: George Wharton James, 1913.

Paul, Rodman W. *The California Gold Discovery: Sources, Documents, Accounts, and Memoirs Relating to the Discovery of Gold at Sutter's Mill*. Georgetown, Calif.: Talisman Press, 1967.

Paz, Octavio. *Essays on Mexican Art*. Trans. Helen Lane. New York, San Diego, and London: Harcourt Brace, 1993.

———. *The Labyrinth of Solitude: Life and Thought in Mexico*. Trans. Lysander Kemp. New York and London: Grove Press, Evergreen Books, 1961.

Peterson, Bonnie J., ed. *Dawn of the World: Stories Told by the Coast Miwok Indians*. San Rafael, Calif.: Miwok Archaeological Preserve of Marin, 1995.

Pitt, Leonard. *The Decline of the Californios: A Social History of the Spanish-Speaking Californians, 1846–1890*. Berkeley and Los Angeles: University of California Press, 1970.

A Plan for the Inner Mission. San Francisco: Mission Housing Development Corporation, 1974.

Powers, Stephen. *Tribes of California*. 1877. Reprint, Berkeley, Los Angeles, and London: University of California Press, 1976.

Prescott, William H. *The Conquest of Mexico*. New York: Modern Library, 1957.

Quinn, Arthur. *Hell with the Fire Out: A History of the Modoc War*. Boston and London: Faber and Faber, 1997.

Ray, Verne F. *Primitive Pragmatists: The Modoc Indians of Northern California*. Seattle: University of Washington Press, 1963.

Riddle, Jeff C. *The Indian History of the Modoc War, and the Causes That Led to It*. 1914. Reprint, Medford, Oreg.: Pine Cone, 1973.

Rodríguez, Richard. *Days of Obligation: An Argument with My Mexican Father*. New York: Viking Penguin, 1992.

Royce, Josiah. *California: From the Conquest in 1846 to the Second Vigilance Committee in San Francisco*. New York: Alfred A. Knopf, 1948.

Sáenz de Santa María, Carmelo. *Historia de una historia: Bernal Díaz del Castillo*. Madrid: Consejo Superior de Investigaciones Científicas, 1984.

Sanchez, Nellie Van de Grift. *Spanish and Indian Place-names of California: Their Meaning and Their Romance*. San Francisco: A. M. Robertson, 1930.

Sánchez, Rosaura. *Telling Identities: The Californio Testimonies*. Minneapolis and London: University of Minnesota Press, 1995.

Secrest, William B. *Juanita: The Only Woman Lynched in the Gold Rush Days*. Fresno, Calif.: Saga West, 1967.

Shinn, Charles Howard. *Mining Camps: A Study in American Frontier Government*. Ed. Rodman W. Paul. New York: Harper and Row, 1965. Originally published by Charles Scribner's Sons, 1884.

Smith, Michael E. *The Aztecs.* Oxford and Cambridge: Blackwell, 1996.

Spearman, Arthur Dunning, S.J. *The Five Franciscan Churches of Mission Santa Clara 1777–1825.* Palo Alto, Calif.: National Press, 1963.

Spitz, Barry. *Mill Valley: The Early Years.* Mill Valley: Potrero Meadow Publishing, 1997.

Steiner, Stan, and Luis Valdez, eds. *Aztlán: An Anthology of Mexican American Literature.* New York: Vintage, 1972.

Teggart, Frederick J., ed. *The Anza Expedition of 1775–1776: Diary of Pedro Font.* Berkeley, Calif.: Academy of Pacific Coast History, 1913.

Thalman, Sylvia Baker. *The Coast Miwok Indians of the Point Reyes Area.* Point Reyes: National Seashore Association, 1993.

Third World Women. San Francisco: Third World Communications, 1972.

Thompson, Erwin N. *Modoc War: Its Military History and Topography.* Preface by Keith A. Murray. Sacramento, Calif.: Argus Books, 1971.

Thompson, William. *Reminiscences of a Pioneer.* San Francisco: N.p., 1912.

Tinker, George E. *Missionary Conquest: The Gospel and Native American Genocide.* Minneapolis: Fortress Press, 1993.

U.S. Congress. House. *Human Rights in Nicaragua, Guatemala, and El Salvador: Implications for U.S. Policy; Hearings before the Subcommittee on International Organizations of the Committee on International Relations,* 94th Cong., 2d sess., June 8 and 9, 1976. Washington, D.C.: U.S. Government Printing Office, 1976.

Vasconcelos, José. *Breve historia de México.* Mexico City: Compañía Editorial Continental, 1956.

———. *The Cosmic Race: La raza cósmica.* Trans. Didier T. Jaen; afterword by Joseba Gabilondo. Baltimore and London: Johns Hopkins University Press, 1997.

Vento, Arnoldo Carlos. *Mestizo: The History, Culture, and Politics of the Mexican and the Chicano.* New York and Oxford: University Press of America, 1998.

Weber, David J. *The Mexican Frontier 1821–1846: The American Southwest under Mexico.* Albuquerque: University of New Mexico Press, 1982.

Weber, Francis J. *Mission San Fernando.* Los Angeles: Westernlore Press, 1968.

DISSERTATIONS

Gillespie, Susan Dale. "Aztec Prehistory as Postconquest Dialogue: A Structural Analysis of the Royal Dynasty of Tenochtitlan." Ph.D. diss., University of Illinois at Urbana-Champaign. Ann Arbor, Mich.: University Microfilms International, 1987.

Pohlmann, John Ogden. "California's Mission Myths." Ph.D. diss, UCLA, 1974. Ann Arbor, Mich.: University Microfilms, 1990.

ESSAYS

Ballard, Dave. "The Battle of San Pasqual." *American History Illustrated* (Harrisburg, Pa.: National Historical Society) 12, no. 1 (1978): 4–48.

Castañeda, Antonia I. "Engendering the History of Alta California, 1789–1848: Gender, Sexuality, and Family." In *Contested Eden,* ed. Ramón A. Gutiérrez and Richard J. Orsi. Berkeley, Los Angeles, and London: University of California Press, 1998.

———. "Gender, Race, and Culture: Spanish-Mexican Women in the Historiography of Frontier California." *Frontier: A Journal of Women Studies* (University of Colorado, Boulder) 11, no. 1 (1990): 8–20.

———. "Sexual Violence in the Politics and Policies of Conquest: Amerindian Women and the Spanish Conquest of Alta California." In *Building with Our Hands: New Directions in Chicana Studies*, ed. Adela de la Torre and Beatríz M. Pesquera, 15–33. Berkeley, Los Angeles, and London: University of California Press, 1993.

"The Chronicle of Fray Francisco de Aguilar." In *The Conquistadors: First-Person Accounts of the Conquest of Mexico*, ed. Patricia Fuentes, 134–164. New York: Orion Press, 1963.

Coronel, Antonio Franco. "Cosas de California." In *The Mexican Adaptation in American California 1846–1876*, ed. Richard Morefield, 77–78. Thesis, University of California, 1955. Reprint, San Francisco: R and E Research Associates, 1971.

García Márquez, Gabriel. "Los sandinistas se toman el Palacio Nacional de Managua." In *La Batalla de Nicaragua*, by Ernesto Cardenal, Gabriel García Márquez, Gregorio Selser, and Daniel Waksman Shinca, 7–21. Mexico City: Bruguera Mexicana de Ediciones, 1978.

Hurtado, Albert L. Introduction to *The Destruction of California Indians*, by Robert F. Heizer. Lincoln and London: University of Nebraska Press, 1993.

Lugo, José del Carmen. "Vida de un ranchero." Trans. Helen Pruitt Beattie. *Historical Society of Southern California* 32, no. 3 (September 1950): 185–236.

Macías, Ysidro Ramón. "The Evolution of the Mind." *El Pocho-Ché* 1 (July 1969): 13–21.

McCloskey, J. J. Quoted in *Juanita: The Only Woman Lynched in the Gold Rush Days*, by William B. Secrest, 29. Fresno, Calif.: Saga-West, 1967.

Neuerburg, Norman. "The Indian Via Crucis from Mission San Fernando: An Historical Exposition." In *Mission San Fernando Rey de España 1791–1997: A Bicentennial Tribute*, ed. Doyce B. Nunis Jr., 329–382. Los Angeles: Historical Society of Southern California, 1997.

Paz, Octavio. "I, a Painter, an Indian from This Village . . ." In *Essays on Mexican Art*, trans. Helen Lane, 85–110. New York, San Diego, and London: Harcourt Brace, 1993.

Pinal, Alice del. "Malintzín: Mito e historia." *Canto* (San Francisco State University) 2, no. 2 (fall 1994–spring 1995): 78–87.

"El Plan Espiritual de Aztlán." Reprinted in *Aztlán, An Anthology of Mexican American Literature*, ed. Luis Valdez and Stan Steiner, 402–406. New York: Vintage, 1972.

Richardson, Stephen. "Days of the Dons." Quoted in Jack Mason, *Point Reyes, the Solemn Land*. Inverness, Calif.: North Shore Books, 1970.

Rust, H. N. "The Last San Fernando Indian." In *The San Fernando Valley: Past and Present*, ed. Lawrence C. Jorgensen, 110–112. Los Angeles: Pacific Rim Research, 1982.

Temple, Thomas Workman, II. "Se fundaron un pueblo de espanoles [*sic*]." *Historical Society of Southern California* (Los Angeles), 1931: 69–149.

Vidal, Gore. "The Agreed-Upon Facts." In *The Paths of Resistance: The Art and Craft of the Political Novel*, ed. William Zinsser, 125–152. Boston: Houghton Mifflin, 1989.

NEWSPAPERS AND PERIODICALS

Barricada, Thursday, November 3, 1988. Managua, Nicaragua.

Daily Alta California. San Francisco, California, July 9, 1851.

La Gaceta Sandinista 1: 1–4: 3 (1975–1979). San Francisco, Calif.: El Comité Cívico Latinoamericano Pro Nicaragua en los Estados Unidos and Editorial Pocho-Ché.

El Pocho-Ché 1–3 (1969–1972), Berkeley, Calif.

The Steamer Pacific Star. Sacramento, California, July 15, 1851.

Tin-Tan, Revista Cósmica 1, nos. 1–6 (1974–1976), San Francisco, Calif.: Editorial Pocho-Ché.

Umbra No. 5: Latin Soul. San Francisco, Society of Umbra, n.d.

INTERVIEWS

Lugo, Carmen. Interview by author, June 20, 2000. Sylmar, Calif. Tape recording.

Murguía, Enrique García. Interview by author, July 22, 2000. Mission Hills, Calif. Tape recording.

Vargas, Ariel, and María Xabela Vargas. Interview by author, June 12, 2000. San Francisco, Calif. Tape recording.

ACKNOWLEDGMENTS

This book is the result of the effort of many individuals, beginning with my own extended clan of the Lugos, the Olivas, and the Murguías of Mexico and Aztlán; my father, who kept telling me stories—*pues aquí están*; my *tía* Carmen, matriarch of the Lugos, and my cousin Selena López Yribe, who did the legwork in Los Angeles.

My *colegas* at San Francisco State University encouraged me to press on with this work: Dr. José Cuellar, Dr. Roberto Haro, Dr. Carlos Córdova, and Dr. Roberto Rivera. Other colleagues who offered moral support were Dr. Raquel Pinderhughes, Dr. James Quesada, Dr. Gustavo Calderón, Dr. Joely de la Torre, Carlos Baron, and Jan Gregory, and others too numerous to mention, including all the members of La Raza Faculty-Staff Association. My students, especially those who have gone on to their own successes, encouraged and inspired the work.

Dr. Roxanne Dunbar-Ortiz provided *consejos*; Dr. Abdiel Oñate, a review, as did David Syring and Dr. Nina Menéndez. Others who pushed include Elizabeth "Betita" Martínez, Walter Martínez at *Latin Style Magazine*, Keren Robertson, Víctor Manuel Valle, and Dr. Manuel de Jesús Hernández-G. I owe a heartfelt debt to Theresa J. May, who took on the risk of publication; to the editorial staff at the University of Texas Press; and to Nancy Bryan, David Cavazos, and Nancy Warrington, whose dedication to this manuscript made it a much better read.

Roberto Vargas and Anuar Murrar, fire starters, both participated in the struggle for the liberation of Nicaragua. Mary Ellen Churchill tracked down photos. Cris Carlsson shared the archives from the Shaping San Francisco Project. Ariel Vargas and María Xabela Sánchez recounted their memories of their marriage and the birth of their son, Tonalli. Francisco Domínguez and Eric Norberg lent their photos.

In La Misión, Sal García shared his thoughts and memories; Andrés Campusano provided the photo of his father's mural; and Alejandro Stuart contributed the photo of the first pro-Sandinista demonstration. Juan R. Fuentes shared with me the legendary archives of Misión Gráfica, where many groundbreaking graphic artists have worked; this historic collection of posters, kept well stored and organized, provided an important visual record, with each artist leaving a contribution à la Guadalupe Posada.

I first contemplated this book during a summer spent at the Marin Headlands Center for the Arts, whose staff encouraged me to think about location and also offered some warm meals and lasting friendships. I could not have started without release time from my teaching load, eased by two grants from San Francisco State University: Research and Development and a Presidential Award for Probationary Faculty. Here's the proof.

The helpful staffs at the McHenry Library at the University of California Santa Cruz, the Huntington Library Reader's Service, the California Historical Society, and the San Francisco Public Library History Section treated me graciously at all times.

From the first word to the last, I had the support of Magaly and Marisol; without them—nothing.

Muy agradecido to you all.

Thanking the above-named individuals and institutions is not meant to be a responsibility for them. The errors, though human, are all mine.

CPSIA information can be obtained
at www.ICGtesting.com
Printed in the USA
LVHW031344181121
703539LV00004B/25